ISBN 0-8373-0633-7

C-633   CAREER EXAMINATION SERIES

This is your PASSBOOK® for...

Public Health Sanitarian

Test Preparation Study Guide

Questions & Answers

NLC

NATIONAL LEARNING CORPORATION

Copyright © 2018 by

National Learning Corporation

212 Michael Drive, Syosset, New York 11791

All rights reserved, including the right of reproduction in whole or in part, in any form or by any means, electronic or mechanical, including photocopying, recording, or by any information storage and retrieval system, without permission in writing from the Publisher.

(516) 921-8888
(800) 632-8888
(800) 645-6337
FAX: (516) 921-8743
www.passbooks.com
info @ passbooks.com

PRINTED IN THE UNITED STATES OF AMERICA

PASSBOOK®
NOTICE

This book is SOLELY intended for, is sold ONLY to, and its use is RESTRICTED to *individual*, bona fide applicants or candidates who qualify by virtue of having seriously filed applications for appropriate license, certificate, professional and/or promotional advancement, higher school matriculation, scholarship, or other legitimate requirements of educational and/or governmental authorities.

This book is NOT intended for use, class instruction, tutoring, training, duplication, copying, reprinting, excerption, or adaptation, etc., by:

(1) Other publishers

(2) Proprietors and/or Instructors of "Coaching" and/or Preparatory Courses

(3) Personnel and/or Training Divisions of commercial, industrial, and governmental organizations

(4) Schools, colleges, or universities and/or their departments and staffs, including teachers and other personnel

(5) Testing Agencies or Bureaus

(6) Study groups which seek by the purchase of a single volume to copy and/or duplicate and/or adapt this material for use by the group as a whole without having purchased individual volumes for each of the members of the group

(7) Et al.

Such persons would be in violation of appropriate Federal and State statutes.

PROVISION OF LICENSING AGREEMENTS. — Recognized educational commercial, industrial, and governmental institutions and organizations, and others legitimately engaged in educational pursuits, including training, testing, and measurement activities, may address a request for a licensing agreement to the copyright owners, who will determine whether, and under what conditions, including fees and charges, the materials in this book may be used by them. In other words, a licensing facility exists for the legitimate use of the material in this book on other than an individual basis. However, it is asseverated and affirmed here that the material in this book *CANNOT* be used without the receipt of the express permission of such a licensing agreement from the Publishers.

NATIONAL LEARNING CORPORATION
212 Michael Drive
Syosset, New York 11791

Inquiries re licensing agreements should be addressed to:
 The President
 National Learning Corporation
 212 Michael Drive
 Syosset, New York 11791

PASSBOOK® SERIES

THE *PASSBOOK® SERIES* has been created to prepare applicants and candidates for the ultimate academic battlefield – the examination room.

At some time in our lives, each and every one of us may be required to take an examination – for validation, matriculation, admission, qualification, registration, certification, or licensure.

Based on the assumption that every applicant or candidate has met the basic formal educational standards, has taken the required number of courses, and read the necessary texts, the *PASSBOOK® SERIES* furnishes the one special preparation which may assure passing with confidence, instead of failing with insecurity. Examination questions – together with answers – are furnished as the basic vehicle for study so that the mysteries of the examination and its compounding difficulties may be eliminated or diminished by a sure method.

This book is meant to help you pass your examination provided that you qualify and are serious in your objective.

The entire field is reviewed through the huge store of content information which is succinctly presented through a provocative and challenging approach – the question-and-answer method.

A climate of success is established by furnishing the correct answers at the end of each test.

You soon learn to recognize types of questions, forms of questions, and patterns of questioning. You may even begin to anticipate expected outcomes.

You perceive that many questions are repeated or adapted so that you can gain acute insights, which may enable you to score many sure points.

You learn how to confront new questions, or types of questions, and to attack them confidently and work out the correct answers.

You note objectives and emphases, and recognize pitfalls and dangers, so that you may make positive educational adjustments.

Moreover, you are kept fully informed in relation to new concepts, methods, practices, and directions in the field.

You discover that you are actually taking the examination all the time: you are preparing for the examination by "taking" an examination, not by reading extraneous and/or supererogatory textbooks.

In short, this PASSBOOK®, used directedly, should be an important factor in helping you to pass your test.

SANITARIANS

NATURE OF THE WORK

Sanitarians, frequently called environmentalists, are specialists in environmental health. They perform a broad range of duties to protect the cleanliness and safety of the food people eat, the liquids they drink, and the air they breathe.

Sanitarians check the cleanliness and safety of food and beverages produced in dairies and processing plants, or served in restaurants, hospitals, and other institutions. They often examine the handling, processing, and serving of food for compliance with sanitation rules and regulations. Sanitarians also may develop and manage programs to prevent contamination, control insects and rodents, properly dispose of refuse, and insure adequate sanitary water supplies.

Sanitarians concerned with waste control oversee the treatment and disposal of sewage, refuse, and garbage. They examine places where pollution is a danger, perform tests to detect pollutants, and collect air or water samples for analysis. Sanitarians determine the nature and cause of the pollution, then initiate action to stop it.

Public health sanitarians work closely with doctors, nurses, and public health officers to prevent and investigate outbreaks of disease. They may conduct surveys to determine the adequacy of health regulations or perform sanitary inspections of schools, houses, swimming pools, and recreation facilities. They also plan for civil defense and emergency disaster aid. Sometimes sanitarians teach health education classes and lecture to student assemblies, civic groups, and other organizations.

Professional sanitarians work closely with a variety of other workers such as life and environmental scientists, waste water treatment plant operators, and environmental health technicians. Environmental health technicians may help them perform routine duties such as compliance inspections, collection of air and water samples, and testing for pollutants.

Sanitarians who have supervisory duties analyze reports of inspection and investigations, and occasionally give evidence in court cases involving violations of sanitation and health regulations. Sanitarians in top administrative positions plan and direct environmental health programs and coordinates them with the programs of other agencies. Other duties may include advising on difficult or unusual environmental health problems, and drafting health laws or regulations.

In large local and State health or agriculture departments, sanitarians may specialize in areas of work such as milk and dairy products, food sanitation, waste control, air pollution, institutional sanitation, and occupational health. In rural areas and small cities, they may be responsible for a wide range of environmental health activities.

Increasing numbers of sanitarians work in private industry to minimize contamination and pollution hazards and make sure that working conditions are healthy, safe, and clean. They frequently work closely with government sanitarians who enforce health, safety, and pollution laws and regulations.

PLACES OF EMPLOYMENT

More than 25,000 persons work as sanitarians. Three out of every four work for State and local governments. Most of the remainder work for producers and processors of food and dairy products. A small number are teachers in colleges and universities. A few are consultants. Others work in hospitals and for trade associations and other organizations. Most sanitarians work in populous areas.

TRAINING, OTHER QUALIFICATIONS, AND ADVANCEMENT

Laws in 35 States provided for the registration of sanitarians; in some States, registration is mandatory. Although requirements for registration vary considerably among States, the minimum educational requirement usually is a bachelor's degree. A bachelor's degree in environmental health is preferred for beginning sanitarian jobs, although a major in any environmental, life, or physical science generally is acceptable. Administrative, teaching, and research jobs usually require a graduate degree in some aspect of public health.

Fifty-eight colleges and universities offered undergraduate or graduate programs in environmental health. A typical curriculum leading to a bachelor of science degree in environmental health includes background courses in the humanities, social sciences, mathematics, chemistry, physics, and biology. Core courses include microbiology (bacteriology) biostatistics, epidemiology, environmental sciences administration, and field work.

Sanitarians usually begin at a trainee level and work under the supervision of experienced sanitarians for up to a year. They receive on-the-job training in environmental health practice, learn to evaluate health and sanitation hazards and recommend corrective action. After a few years of experience, they may be promoted to minor supervisory positions with more responsibilities. Specialization may begin after several years of experience, especially in large local health offices. Further advancement is possible to top supervisory and administrative positions.

To keep abreast of new developments and to supplement their academic training, many sanitarians take specialized short-term training courses in subjects such as occupational health, water supply and pollution control, air pollution, protection from dangers of radiation, milk and food inspection, metropolitan planning, and hospital sanitation.

Young people interested in becoming sanitarians should like working with detail and possess a mechanical aptitude, since sanitarians may operate various testing devices. An ability to communicate effectively, both orally and in writing, is necessary for writing detailed reports and tactfully dealing with persons concerning the correctionof unsanitary conditions.

EMPLOYMENT OUTLOOK

Employment opportunities for sanitarians who have a bachelor's degree in environmental health are expected to be very good through the 2010s, particularly in private industry. The outlook for those having degrees in life, physical, or environmental sciences is expected to be favorable.

Employment of sanitarians is expected to increase very rapidly through the next five years in response to anticipated expansion of public and private programs dealing with food sanitation, water and air pollution, and occupational health. Underlying the demand for sanitarians in the private sector will be industrial growth and an increasing recognition by industry of its responsibility for safe and sanitary products and healthful environment. Demand for sanitarians in the public sector will be generated by an expansion of the environmental health activities of State and local governments. Increasing public concern with health hazards, waste management, radiation danger, and pollution is expected to require the services of more sanitarians. Population growth, continued migration of people from rural to urban areas, and industrial growth will place a greater strain on food services, housing, and sewage disposal facilities of urban communities.

WORKING CONDITIONS

Sanitarians spend considerable time away from their desks. Some come in contact with unpleasant physical surroundings, such as sewage disposal facilities and slum housing. Transportation or gasoline allowance frequently is given, and some health departments provide an automobile.

SOURCES OF ADDITIONAL INFORMATION

Information about careers as sanitarians is available from the following associations:

American Public Health Association,
800 I Street, NW, Washington, D.C. 20001.

International Association for Food Protection
6200 Aurora Ave., Suite 200W, Des Moines, IA 50322.

National Environmental Health Association,
720 S. Colorado Blvd., Denver, CO 80246.

Information on stipends for graduate study is available from:

Bureau of Health Professions
U.S. Department of Health & Human Services
200 Independence Ave. SW, Washington, D.C., 20201

PUBLIC HEALTH SANITARIAN

DUTIES

Public Health Sanitarians, under the general direction of a senior sanitarian, conduct environmental health inspections in the health department's environmental health programs. They make on-site investigations of hospitals, nursing homes, food service establishments, x-ray units, temporary residences, labor camps, schools, state and local institutions, refuse disposal areas, swimming pools, bathing beaches, and realty subdivisions to insure that these facilities are operating in accordance with existing health laws and regulations. They also serve as public health inspectors in the following areas: vector control, housing hygiene, lead poisoning, on-site water supply and sewage disposal, and public water supply. They describe violations to facility operators and recommend appropriate remedial action; prepare reports of inspections made and conditions noted, with appropriate recommendations for corrective action or enforcement; make follow-up visits as required; assist in the training of local sanitary inspectors and help them with their inspection problems; investigate sanitation complaints; take samples and interpret laboratory reports; and make recommendations for correction of unsatisfactory conditions.

SCOPE OF THE EXAMINATION

The multiple-choice written test will cover knowledge, skills and/or abilities in such areas as:
1. Application of scientific principles and knowledge to public and environmental health protection;
2. Microbiology as related to disease prevention and control, sanitary chemistry, and toxic substances;
3. Inspection and interviewing techniques;
4. Reading comprehension; and
5. Preparing written material.

HOW TO PREPARE GUIDE FOR
PUBLIC HEALTH SANITARIAN/ENVIRONMENTALIST
WRITTEN EXAMINATION

I. THE JOB

Public Health Sanitarian/Environmentalist positions are with the Department of Public Health, Bureau of Environmental Services. The Bureau's goals and objectives are to enhance the quality of services and products of food, milk and lodging establishments and to enforce State Board of Health rules and policies relating to sewage disposal, vector control, indoor air quality, and lead assessment. Public Health Sanitarian/Environmentalist positions are located throughout the State.

Positions within this classification may be in a general or specific field of environmental health such as on-site sewage, food protection, lodging, solid waste, or vector control. Employees in this class are responsible for providing inspection services, collecting samples for laboratory analyses, and investigating complaints. Work is usually performed under the jurisdiction of a local health department and employees receive specific instructions about assignments.

II. THE EXAMINATION

The examination for this classification is a multiple-choice exam. This multiple-choice exam is designed to measure specific knowledges and abilities. The test is divided into six sections with each section measuring a different knowledge or ability. Applicants are presented with a test question and four possible responses to that question. Applicants then select the BEST possible response to the question.

During the exam, you will be required to respond to approximately 100 questions regarding six topics. These topics include prioritizing/organizing work, completing documentation, basic/intermediate math, following instructions, reading/comprehending, and English. You will have three (3) hours to respond to the items.

III. HOW THE WRITTEN EXAMINATION WAS DEVELOPED

A study of the Public Health Sanitarian/Environmentalist classification was conducted before developing the examination. Employees who work in this position and their supervisors participated in this study to determine what job duties are performed by Public Health Sanitarian/Environmentalists and what knowledges and abilities a Public Health Sanitarian/Environmentalist must possess in order to perform the job duties of the position.

The study showed that the following knowledges and abilities are associated with the job duties of the position. A Public Health Sanitarian/Environmentalist must possess the knowledges and abilities listed below on their first day of work before training:

- **Knowledge of basic math to include addition, subtraction, multiplication, and division as needed to calculate mileage, inspection scores, leave time, fee collection, monthly reports, and daily activity reports.**

- **Knowledge of intermediate math to include calculation of area, volume, flow rate, and calorimetry as needed to determine lot size, volume of septic tank, size of disposal field, and calculate head pressure on field lines and percent solution.**

- **Knowledge of basic English to include spelling, grammar, punctuation, sentence structure, and word usage as needed to coherently converse and communicate thoughts orally and in writing.**

- Ability to operate standard office equipment such as fax machine, calculator, telephone, copier, and computer as needed to prepare reports, communicate with medical personnel, communicate with the general public, and complete work assignments.

- Ability to communicate orally in one-on-one situations such as inspection reviews, complaint investigations, and technical assistance interviews as needed to obtain/provide information and ensure compliance.

- Ability to communicate orally in group situations such as meetings, conferences, training workshops, and seminars as needed to educate others and receive training.

- **Ability to follow instructions as needed to adhere to procedures and complete assignments.**

- **Ability to read/comprehend narrative information such as federal and state guidelines, legal documents, blueprints, grants, lab reports, and medical documents as needed to interpret/apply information, gain knowledge and understanding, and ensure compliance with rules/regulations.**

- Ability to interact effectively with individuals and individuals with socio-economic backgrounds such as law enforcement officials, county officials, judiciary officials, engineers, developers, government officials, contractors, attorneys, and the general public as needed to educate, ensure compliance, and request assistance.

- **Ability to prioritize/organize work to include records, assignments, travel, and work time as needed to create monthly reports, maximize efficiency of organization, and complete work in a timely manner.**

- Ability to deal with irate or upset people as needed to diffuse a volatile situation and provide information concerning the situation.

- Ability to adjust level of communication to individuals from a wide variety of backgrounds as needed to provide information to the public concerning technical topics.

- Ability to operate a personal computer to include word processing, spreadsheet application and databases as needed to document, access, store, and analyze information, process reports and evaluate program needs.

- Ability to establish and maintain effective working relationships to include co-workers, superiors, and the general public as needed to improve performance, communication, and achieve departmental goals.

- **Ability to complete documentation to include reports and forms as needed to document work, record information, and efficiently manage caseload.**

IV. HOW TO PREPARE USING THIS GUIDE

This Pretest Booklet can be used as a practice guide. The questions contained in the booklet are a representation of questions that will be on the actual examination. Familiarize yourself with the sample questions that follow. You would be well-advised to read the instructions and answer each question carefully. Like the examination questions (all of which are multiple choice), the sample items are presented in the following categories:

Section I: Ability to Prioritize/Organize
Section II: Ability to Complete Documentation
Section III: Knowledge of Basic/Intermediate Math
Section IV: Ability to Follow Instructions
Section V: Ability to Read/Comprehend
Section VI: Knowledge of Basic English

The sample items which follow are representative of the type of items that will appear on the exam. They are not necessarily based on the same information, diagrams, etc. as the actual exam. All questions will be multiple choice.

In addition, please review the General Instructions to Candidates Taking Written Examinations provided at the exam site on the day of the test.

V. SAMPLE TEST QUESTIONS

Section I: Ability to Plan/Organize

Question 1.

DIRECTIONS: Read the situation and then answer Question 1. Base your response on the situation only. Do not base your response on previous experience. Select the MOST appropriate choice.

Your supervisor will be out of the office today. You arrived at work at 7:55 A.M. You and your spouse have an appointment today at 11:00 A.M. with your family doctor who has advised you that the appointment should not be rescheduled. You need to leave by 10:30 A.M. and will be unable to return to the office later today. Sue Beck, a clerical aide and office receptionist, is the only other employee in the office today. However, she does not type. Your supervisor left a note listing the following tasks that must be done today.

- Type the Zicker report (2 hours to complete)
- Sort and distribute the mail (30 minutes to complete)
- Call Virginia Hall about the Zicker project (10 minutes to complete)
- Post new dividend rates by 12 Noon, today (20 minutes to complete)
- Set up the conference room for the next day's 8:00 A.M. meeting (30 minutes to complete)
- File dividend reports (2 hours to complete)

1. Which of the following tasks below would you be forced to perform yourself?   1.____
   A. File dividend reports
   B. Set up the conference room
   C. Type the Zicker report
   D. Sort and distribute the day's mail

Section II: Ability to Complete Documentation

DIRECTIONS: For Form 1 you are given a scenario. Review the form and read the scenario. Answer the questions, basing your answers solely on the information provided and not on any prior knowledge you may have of the subject.

Form 1

```
CLIENT SCHEDULE CHANGES

DATE:_____(A)_____

CLIENT NAME:_____(B)_____

CLIENT CHART NO.:_____(C)_____

ACTIVITY TO BE DROPPED:_____(D)_____

TIME/PERIOD:_____(E)_____

ACTIVITY TO BE ADDED:_____(F)_____

TIME/PERIOD:_____(G)_____

INSTRUCTOR FOR ADDED ACTIVITY:_____(H)_____


Signature of Employee Submitting Changes:_____(I)_____

(Send to clerical section by noon on Thursday.)
```

<u>Scenario</u>
Bobby White, a client of the Mental Health Rehabilitation Center, strained his ankle and could no longer participate in Mr. Pool's 3rd period swimming class.

On May 18, 2004, Kerry Short, an Activity Program Aide, was asked to pull Bobby's chart, #846, to drop the swimming class from Bobby's schedule and to include Mr. Gray's 3rd period pottery class.

2. According to the scenario, Section G of Form 1 should read
   A. pottery class
   B. swimming class
   C. 3rd period
   D. Mr. Pool

3. According to the scenario, Section I of Form 1 should read
   A. Mr. Pool
   B. Bobby White
   C. Mr. Clay
   D. Kerry Short

4. According to the scenario, what should the activity program aide type or write in Section F of Form 1?
   A. His signature
   B. 3rd period
   C. Pottery
   D. Swimming

Section III: Knowledge of Basic/Intermediate Math

5. Convert 28 grams into milligrams.
   A. 28000 milligrams
   B. 2.8 milligrams
   C. 280 milligrams
   D. .28 milligrams

6. Thirty-seven percent of 826 is equal to
   A. 275.60
   B. 280.75
   C. 295.50
   D. 305.62

7. In the fiscal year of 2004-2005, a total of 109,782 on-site sewage inspections were performed, 2/3 of which were for rural areas. The monthly average for rural areas was closest to
   A. 3659
   B. 6099
   C. 6100
   D. 9149

8. For the month of December, a local health unit reported that more restaurant inspections were performed than on-site sewage inspections. If the ratio of restaurant inspections to on-site sewage inspections is 9 to 7, and 270 restaurant inspections were performed during December, how many on-site sewage inspections were performed during the same period?
   A. 187
   B. 210
   C. 237
   D. 250

Section IV: Ability to Follow Instructions

DIRECTIONS: Assume you are employed with the Department of Health as a Public Health Sanitarian/Environmentalist. You have been given an office manual and written directions. Read them carefully and answer the questions that follow. You may refer to the directions as often as needed.

Reports
Each Public Health Sanitarian/Environmentalist is responsible for making and updating reports required by the Central and Area Offices. These reports are as follows:

1. Weekly itinerary including weekly work summary
2. Monthly Report
3. Travel Expense Report
4. Unsanitary Conditions Abatement Report

Original copies of the weekly itinerary including weekly work summary and monthly report will be sent directly to the Central Office with copies to the Area Office. The weekly itinerary, including the weekly work summary, should reach the State Office each Monday. The deadline for submitting information needed to compile the Monthly Report is the last working day of each month.

The Unsanitary Conditions Abatement Report will be due upon notification by the Central Office.

9. Which of the following is to be sent directly to the Central Office? 9.____
   A. Monthly Report
   B. All printouts
   C. Travel Expense Report
   D. Unsanitary Conditions Abatement Report

10. What is the deadline for submitting information needed to compile the Monthly Report? 10.____
    A. Upon notification by the Central Office
    B. The last working day of each month
    C. In time for it to reach the Central Office each Monday
    D. Weekly

Section V: Ability to Read/Comprehend

Questions 11-13.

DIRECTIONS: Questions 11 through 13 are to be answered on the basis of the following passage.

WHAT IS INFLUENZA?

It is an illness caused by influenza viruses. It generally affects people of all ages. Typically, people with influenza have fever, chills, headache, cough, and muscle soreness and may be sick for several days to a week or more. Most people recover fully. A small portion of cases are particularly severe, and patients may develop pneumonia or other complications. In some past epidemics, about one case out of every thousand was fatal. The risk of complications and death from influenza is highest for people with chronic health problems like diabetes, disease of the heart, lungs, or kidneys; severe anemia; or chronic illnesses (or medications) which lower the body's resistance to infection. It is also high for older persons generally – particularly those 65 years or older.

Influenza viruses frequently undergo changes in their chemical makeup. These changes make it possible to catch influenza even though immunity (antibodies) may have been developed against previous strains of influenza. Thus, having had influenza or influenza vaccine in past years may not prevent getting influenza again.

Although influenza epidemics are unpredictable, some influenza occurs each year. In very large epidemics, as much as 1/3 of the population has become sick as thousands have died.

11. Influenza is caused by a
    A. virus
    B. bacterium
    C. type of fungus
    D. protozoan

12. Why do people get influenza over and over again?
    A. The body develops no immunity against influenza.
    B. The influenza virus often mutates so that natural immunity is not effective.
    C. Both A and B
    D. None of the above

13. Influenza would be most dangerous to a
    A. seventy-three year old nursing home patient
    B. five-month-old infant
    C. six-year-old child in first grade
    D. forty-year-old man who works outdoors in all types of weather

Section VI: Knowledge of Basic English

Question 14.

DIRECTIONS: For Question 14, choose the answer that demonstrates the MOST appropriate English usage.

14. A. The supervisor and the aide, together with the rest of the office force, has unanimously agreed to send a representative.
    B. The supervisor, together with the aide and the rest of the office force, have unanimously agreed to send a representative.
    C. The entire office force, including the supervisor and the aide, have unanimously agreed to send a representative.
    D. The entire office force, including the supervisor and the aid, has unanimously agreed to send a representative.

Question 15.

DIRECTIONS: For Question 15, choose the phrase that BEST expresses the statement.

15. It is imperative that the owner _____ the changes now.
    A. effect   B. affect   C. effects   D. affects

KEY (CORRECT ANSWERS)

1.	C	6.	D	11.	A
2.	C	7.	B	12.	B
3.	D	8.	B	13.	A
4.	C	9.	A	14.	D
5.	A	10.	B	15.	A

HOW TO TAKE A TEST

I. YOU MUST PASS AN EXAMINATION

A. WHAT EVERY CANDIDATE SHOULD KNOW

Examination applicants often ask us for help in preparing for the written test. What can I study in advance? What kinds of questions will be asked? How will the test be given? How will the papers be graded?

As an applicant for a civil service examination, you may be wondering about some of these things. Our purpose here is to suggest effective methods of advance study and to describe civil service examinations.

Your chances for success on this examination can be increased if you know how to prepare. Those "pre-examination jitters" can be reduced if you know what to expect. You can even experience an adventure in good citizenship if you know why civil service exams are given.

B. WHY ARE CIVIL SERVICE EXAMINATIONS GIVEN?

Civil service examinations are important to you in two ways. As a citizen, you want public jobs filled by employees who know how to do their work. As a job seeker, you want a fair chance to compete for that job on an equal footing with other candidates. The best-known means of accomplishing this two-fold goal is the competitive examination.

Exams are widely publicized throughout the nation. They may be administered for jobs in federal, state, city, municipal, town or village governments or agencies.

Any citizen may apply, with some limitations, such as the age or residence of applicants. Your experience and education may be reviewed to see whether you meet the requirements for the particular examination. When these requirements exist, they are reasonable and applied consistently to all applicants. Thus, a competitive examination may cause you some uneasiness now, but it is your privilege and safeguard.

C. HOW ARE CIVIL SERVICE EXAMS DEVELOPED?

Examinations are carefully written by trained technicians who are specialists in the field known as "psychological measurement," in consultation with recognized authorities in the field of work that the test will cover. These experts recommend the subject matter areas or skills to be tested; only those knowledges or skills important to your success on the job are included. The most reliable books and source materials available are used as references. Together, the experts and technicians judge the difficulty level of the questions.

Test technicians know how to phrase questions so that the problem is clearly stated. Their ethics do not permit "trick" or "catch" questions. Questions may have been tried out on sample groups, or subjected to statistical analysis, to determine their usefulness.

Written tests are often used in combination with performance tests, ratings of training and experience, and oral interviews. All of these measures combine to form the best-known means of finding the right person for the right job.

II. HOW TO PASS THE WRITTEN TEST

A. NATURE OF THE EXAMINATION

To prepare intelligently for civil service examinations, you should know how they differ from school examinations you have taken. In school you were assigned certain definite pages to read or subjects to cover. The examination questions were quite detailed and usually emphasized memory. Civil service exams, on the other hand, try to discover your present ability to perform the duties of a position, plus your potentiality to learn these duties. In other words, a civil service exam attempts to predict how successful you will be. Questions cover such a broad area that they cannot be as minute and detailed as school exam questions.

In the public service similar kinds of work, or positions, are grouped together in one "class." This process is known as *position-classification*. All the positions in a class are paid according to the salary range for that class. One class title covers all of these positions, and they are all tested by the same examination.

B. FOUR BASIC STEPS

1) Study the announcement

How, then, can you know what subjects to study? Our best answer is: "Learn as much as possible about the class of positions for which you've applied." The exam will test the knowledge, skills and abilities needed to do the work.

Your most valuable source of information about the position you want is the official exam announcement. This announcement lists the training and experience qualifications. Check these standards and apply only if you come reasonably close to meeting them.

The brief description of the position in the examination announcement offers some clues to the subjects which will be tested. Think about the job itself. Review the duties in your mind. Can you perform them, or are there some in which you are rusty? Fill in the blank spots in your preparation.

Many jurisdictions preview the written test in the exam announcement by including a section called "Knowledge and Abilities Required," "Scope of the Examination," or some similar heading. Here you will find out specifically what fields will be tested.

2) Review your own background

Once you learn in general what the position is all about, and what you need to know to do the work, ask yourself which subjects you already know fairly well and which need improvement. You may wonder whether to concentrate on improving your strong areas or on building some background in your fields of weakness. When the announcement has specified "some knowledge" or "considerable knowledge," or has used adjectives like "beginning principles of…" or "advanced … methods," you can get a clue as to the number and difficulty of questions to be asked in any given field. More questions, and hence broader coverage, would be included for those subjects which are more important in the work. Now weigh your strengths and weaknesses against the job requirements and prepare accordingly.

3) Determine the level of the position

Another way to tell how intensively you should prepare is to understand the level of the job for which you are applying. Is it the entering level? In other words, is this the position in which beginners in a field of work are hired? Or is it an intermediate or advanced level? Sometimes this is indicated by such words as "Junior" or "Senior" in the class title. Other jurisdictions use Roman numerals to designate the level – Clerk I, Clerk II, for example. The word "Supervisor" sometimes appears in the title. If the level is not indicated by the title, check the description of duties. Will you be working under very close supervision, or will you have responsibility for independent decisions in this work?

4) Choose appropriate study materials

Now that you know the subjects to be examined and the relative amount of each subject to be covered, you can choose suitable study materials. For beginning level jobs, or even advanced ones, if you have a pronounced weakness in some aspect of your training, read a modern, standard textbook in that field. Be sure it is up to date and has general coverage. Such books are normally available at your library, and the librarian will be glad to help you locate one. For entry-level positions, questions of appropriate difficulty are chosen – neither highly advanced questions, nor those too simple. Such questions require careful thought but not advanced training.

If the position for which you are applying is technical or advanced, you will read more advanced, specialized material. If you are already familiar with the basic principles of your field, elementary textbooks would waste your time. Concentrate on advanced textbooks and technical periodicals. Think through the concepts and review difficult problems in your field.

These are all general sources. You can get more ideas on your own initiative, following these leads. For example, training manuals and publications of the government agency which employs workers in your field can be useful, particularly for technical and professional positions. A letter or visit to the government department involved may result in more specific study suggestions, and certainly will provide you with a more definite idea of the exact nature of the position you are seeking.

III. KINDS OF TESTS

Tests are used for purposes other than measuring knowledge and ability to perform specified duties. For some positions, it is equally important to test ability to make adjustments to new situations or to profit from training. In others, basic mental abilities not dependent on information are essential. Questions which test these things may not appear as pertinent to the duties of the position as those which test for knowledge and information. Yet they are often highly important parts of a fair examination. For very general questions, it is almost impossible to help you direct your study efforts. What we can do is to point out some of the more common of these general abilities needed in public service positions and describe some typical questions.

1) General information

Broad, general information has been found useful for predicting job success in some kinds of work. This is tested in a variety of ways, from vocabulary lists to questions about current events. Basic background in some field of work, such as sociology or economics, may be sampled in a group of questions. Often these are principles which have become familiar to most persons through exposure rather than through formal training. It is difficult to advise you how to study for these questions; being alert to the world around you is our best suggestion.

2) Verbal ability

An example of an ability needed in many positions is verbal or language ability. Verbal ability is, in brief, the ability to use and understand words. Vocabulary and grammar tests are typical measures of this ability. Reading comprehension or paragraph interpretation questions are common in many kinds of civil service tests. You are given a paragraph of written material and asked to find its central meaning.

3) Numerical ability

Number skills can be tested by the familiar arithmetic problem, by checking paired lists of numbers to see which are alike and which are different, or by interpreting charts and graphs. In the latter test, a graph may be printed in the test booklet which you are asked to use as the basis for answering questions.

4) Observation

A popular test for law-enforcement positions is the observation test. A picture is shown to you for several minutes, then taken away. Questions about the picture test your ability to observe both details and larger elements.

5) Following directions

In many positions in the public service, the employee must be able to carry out written instructions dependably and accurately. You may be given a chart with several columns, each column listing a variety of information. The questions require you to carry out directions involving the information given in the chart.

6) Skills and aptitudes

Performance tests effectively measure some manual skills and aptitudes. When the skill is one in which you are trained, such as typing or shorthand, you can practice. These tests are often very much like those given in business school or high school courses. For many of the other skills and aptitudes, however, no short-time preparation can be made. Skills and abilities natural to you or that you have developed throughout your lifetime are being tested.

Many of the general questions just described provide all the data needed to answer the questions and ask you to use your reasoning ability to find the answers. Your best preparation for these tests, as well as for tests of facts and ideas, is to be at your physical and mental best. You, no doubt, have your own methods of getting into an exam-taking mood and keeping "in shape." The next section lists some ideas on this subject.

IV. KINDS OF QUESTIONS

Only rarely is the "essay" question, which you answer in narrative form, used in civil service tests. Civil service tests are usually of the short-answer type. Full instructions for answering these questions will be given to you at the examination. But in case this is your first experience with short-answer questions and separate answer sheets, here is what you need to know:

1) Multiple-choice Questions

Most popular of the short-answer questions is the "multiple choice" or "best answer" question. It can be used, for example, to test for factual knowledge, ability to solve problems or judgment in meeting situations found at work.

A multiple-choice question is normally one of three types—
- It can begin with an incomplete statement followed by several possible endings. You are to find the one ending which *best* completes the statement, although some of the others may not be entirely wrong.
- It can also be a complete statement in the form of a question which is answered by choosing one of the statements listed.

- It can be in the form of a problem – again you select the best answer.

Here is an example of a multiple-choice question with a discussion which should give you some clues as to the method for choosing the right answer:

When an employee has a complaint about his assignment, the action which will *best* help him overcome his difficulty is to
   A. discuss his difficulty with his coworkers
   B. take the problem to the head of the organization
   C. take the problem to the person who gave him the assignment
   D. say nothing to anyone about his complaint

In answering this question, you should study each of the choices to find which is best. Consider choice "A" – Certainly an employee may discuss his complaint with fellow employees, but no change or improvement can result, and the complaint remains unresolved. Choice "B" is a poor choice since the head of the organization probably does not know what assignment you have been given, and taking your problem to him is known as "going over the head" of the supervisor. The supervisor, or person who made the assignment, is the person who can clarify it or correct any injustice. Choice "C" is, therefore, correct. To say nothing, as in choice "D," is unwise. Supervisors have and interest in knowing the problems employees are facing, and the employee is seeking a solution to his problem.

2) True/False Questions

The "true/false" or "right/wrong" form of question is sometimes used. Here a complete statement is given. Your job is to decide whether the statement is right or wrong.

SAMPLE: A roaming cell-phone call to a nearby city costs less than a non-roaming call to a distant city.

This statement is wrong, or false, since roaming calls are more expensive.

This is not a complete list of all possible question forms, although most of the others are variations of these common types. You will always get complete directions for answering questions. Be sure you understand *how* to mark your answers – ask questions until you do.

V. RECORDING YOUR ANSWERS

Computer terminals are used more and more today for many different kinds of exams.

For an examination with very few applicants, you may be told to record your answers in the test booklet itself. Separate answer sheets are much more common. If this separate answer sheet is to be scored by machine – and this is often the case – it is highly important that you mark your answers correctly in order to get credit.

An electronic scoring machine is often used in civil service offices because of the speed with which papers can be scored. Machine-scored answer sheets must be marked with a pencil, which will be given to you. This pencil has a high graphite content which responds to the electronic scoring machine. As a matter of fact, stray dots may register as answers, so do not let your pencil rest on the answer sheet while you are pondering the correct answer. Also, if your pencil lead breaks or is otherwise defective, ask for another.

Since the answer sheet will be dropped in a slot in the scoring machine, be careful not to bend the corners or get the paper crumpled.

The answer sheet normally has five vertical columns of numbers, with 30 numbers to a column. These numbers correspond to the question numbers in your test booklet. After each number, going across the page are four or five pairs of dotted lines. These short dotted lines have small letters or numbers above them. The first two pairs may also have a "T" or "F" above the letters. This indicates that the first two pairs only are to be used if the questions are of the true-false type. If the questions are multiple choice, disregard the "T" and "F" and pay attention only to the small letters or numbers.

Answer your questions in the manner of the sample that follows:

32. The largest city in the United States is
    A. Washington, D.C.
    B. New York City
    C. Chicago
    D. Detroit
    E. San Francisco

1) Choose the answer you think is best. (New York City is the largest, so "B" is correct.)
2) Find the row of dotted lines numbered the same as the question you are answering. (Find row number 32)
3) Find the pair of dotted lines corresponding to the answer. (Find the pair of lines under the mark "B.")
4) Make a solid black mark between the dotted lines.

VI. BEFORE THE TEST

Common sense will help you find procedures to follow to get ready for an examination. Too many of us, however, overlook these sensible measures. Indeed, nervousness and fatigue have been found to be the most serious reasons why applicants fail to do their best on civil service tests. Here is a list of reminders:

- Begin your preparation early – Don't wait until the last minute to go scurrying around for books and materials or to find out what the position is all about.
- Prepare continuously – An hour a night for a week is better than an all-night cram session. This has been definitely established. What is more, a night a week for a month will return better dividends than crowding your study into a shorter period of time.
- Locate the place of the exam – You have been sent a notice telling you when and where to report for the examination. If the location is in a different town or otherwise unfamiliar to you, it would be well to inquire the best route and learn something about the building.
- Relax the night before the test – Allow your mind to rest. Do not study at all that night. Plan some mild recreation or diversion; then go to bed early and get a good night's sleep.
- Get up early enough to make a leisurely trip to the place for the test – This way unforeseen events, traffic snarls, unfamiliar buildings, etc. will not upset you.
- Dress comfortably – A written test is not a fashion show. You will be known by number and not by name, so wear something comfortable.

- Leave excess paraphernalia at home – Shopping bags and odd bundles will get in your way. You need bring only the items mentioned in the official notice you received; usually everything you need is provided. Do not bring reference books to the exam. They will only confuse those last minutes and be taken away from you when in the test room.
- Arrive somewhat ahead of time – If because of transportation schedules you must get there very early, bring a newspaper or magazine to take your mind off yourself while waiting.
- Locate the examination room – When you have found the proper room, you will be directed to the seat or part of the room where you will sit. Sometimes you are given a sheet of instructions to read while you are waiting. Do not fill out any forms until you are told to do so; just read them and be prepared.
- Relax and prepare to listen to the instructions
- If you have any physical problem that may keep you from doing your best, be sure to tell the test administrator. If you are sick or in poor health, you really cannot do your best on the exam. You can come back and take the test some other time.

VII. AT THE TEST

The day of the test is here and you have the test booklet in your hand. The temptation to get going is very strong. Caution! There is more to success than knowing the right answers. You must know how to identify your papers and understand variations in the type of short-answer question used in this particular examination. Follow these suggestions for maximum results from your efforts:

1) Cooperate with the monitor

The test administrator has a duty to create a situation in which you can be as much at ease as possible. He will give instructions, tell you when to begin, check to see that you are marking your answer sheet correctly, and so on. He is not there to guard you, although he will see that your competitors do not take unfair advantage. He wants to help you do your best.

2) Listen to all instructions

Don't jump the gun! Wait until you understand all directions. In most civil service tests you get more time than you need to answer the questions. So don't be in a hurry. Read each word of instructions until you clearly understand the meaning. Study the examples, listen to all announcements and follow directions. Ask questions if you do not understand what to do.

3) Identify your papers

Civil service exams are usually identified by number only. You will be assigned a number; you must not put your name on your test papers. Be sure to copy your number correctly. Since more than one exam may be given, copy your exact examination title.

4) Plan your time

Unless you are told that a test is a "speed" or "rate of work" test, speed itself is usually not important. Time enough to answer all the questions will be provided, but this does not mean that you have all day. An overall time limit has been set. Divide the total time (in minutes) by the number of questions to determine the approximate time you have for each question.

5) Do not linger over difficult questions

If you come across a difficult question, mark it with a paper clip (useful to have along) and come back to it when you have been through the booklet. One caution if you do this – be sure to skip a number on your answer sheet as well. Check often to be sure that you have not lost your place and that you are marking in the row numbered the same as the question you are answering.

6) Read the questions

Be sure you know what the question asks! Many capable people are unsuccessful because they failed to *read* the questions correctly.

7) Answer all questions

Unless you have been instructed that a penalty will be deducted for incorrect answers, it is better to guess than to omit a question.

8) Speed tests

It is often better NOT to guess on speed tests. It has been found that on timed tests people are tempted to spend the last few seconds before time is called in marking answers at random – without even reading them – in the hope of picking up a few extra points. To discourage this practice, the instructions may warn you that your score will be "corrected" for guessing. That is, a penalty will be applied. The incorrect answers will be deducted from the correct ones, or some other penalty formula will be used.

9) Review your answers

If you finish before time is called, go back to the questions you guessed or omitted to give them further thought. Review other answers if you have time.

10) Return your test materials

If you are ready to leave before others have finished or time is called, take ALL your materials to the monitor and leave quietly. Never take any test material with you. The monitor can discover whose papers are not complete, and taking a test booklet may be grounds for disqualification.

VIII. EXAMINATION TECHNIQUES

1) Read the general instructions carefully. These are usually printed on the first page of the exam booklet. As a rule, these instructions refer to the timing of the examination; the fact that you should not start work until the signal and must stop work at a signal, etc. If there are any *special* instructions, such as a choice of questions to be answered, make sure that you note this instruction carefully.

2) When you are ready to start work on the examination, that is as soon as the signal has been given, read the instructions to each question booklet, underline any key words or phrases, such as *least, best, outline, describe* and the like. In this way you will tend to answer as requested rather than discover on reviewing your paper that you *listed without describing*, that you selected the *worst* choice rather than the *best* choice, etc.

3) If the examination is of the objective or multiple-choice type – that is, each question will also give a series of possible answers: A, B, C or D, and you are called upon to select the best answer and write the letter next to that answer on your answer paper – it is advisable to start answering each question in turn. There may be anywhere from 50 to 100 such questions in the three or four hours allotted and you can see how much time would be taken if you read through all the questions before beginning to answer any. Furthermore, if you come across a question or group of questions which you know would be difficult to answer, it would undoubtedly affect your handling of all the other questions.

4) If the examination is of the essay type and contains but a few questions, it is a moot point as to whether you should read all the questions before starting to answer any one. Of course, if you are given a choice – say five out of seven and the like – then it is essential to read all the questions so you can eliminate the two that are most difficult. If, however, you are asked to answer all the questions, there may be danger in trying to answer the easiest one first because you may find that you will spend too much time on it. The best technique is to answer the first question, then proceed to the second, etc.

5) Time your answers. Before the exam begins, write down the time it started, then add the time allowed for the examination and write down the time it must be completed, then divide the time available somewhat as follows:
   - If 3-1/2 hours are allowed, that would be 210 minutes. If you have 80 objective-type questions, that would be an average of 2-1/2 minutes per question. Allow yourself no more than 2 minutes per question, or a total of 160 minutes, which will permit about 50 minutes to review.
   - If for the time allotment of 210 minutes there are 7 essay questions to answer, that would average about 30 minutes a question. Give yourself only 25 minutes per question so that you have about 35 minutes to review.

6) The most important instruction is to *read each question* and make sure you know what is wanted. The second most important instruction is to *time yourself properly* so that you answer every question. The third most important instruction is to *answer every question.* Guess if you have to but include something for each question. Remember that you will receive no credit for a blank and will probably receive some credit if you write something in answer to an essay question. If you guess a letter – say "B" for a multiple-choice question – you may have guessed right. If you leave a blank as an answer to a multiple-choice question, the examiners may respect your feelings but it will not add a point to your score. Some exams may penalize you for wrong answers, so in such cases *only*, you may not want to guess unless you have some basis for your answer.

7) Suggestions
   a. Objective-type questions
      1. Examine the question booklet for proper sequence of pages and questions
      2. Read all instructions carefully
      3. Skip any question which seems too difficult; return to it after all other questions have been answered
      4. Apportion your time properly; do not spend too much time on any single question or group of questions

5. Note and underline key words – *all, most, fewest, least, best, worst, same, opposite*, etc.
6. Pay particular attention to negatives
7. Note unusual option, e.g., unduly long, short, complex, different or similar in content to the body of the question
8. Observe the use of "hedging" words – *probably, may, most likely*, etc.
9. Make sure that your answer is put next to the same number as the question
10. Do not second-guess unless you have good reason to believe the second answer is definitely more correct
11. Cross out original answer if you decide another answer is more accurate; do not erase until you are ready to hand your paper in
12. Answer all questions; guess unless instructed otherwise
13. Leave time for review

  b. Essay questions
    1. Read each question carefully
    2. Determine exactly what is wanted. Underline key words or phrases.
    3. Decide on outline or paragraph answer
    4. Include many different points and elements unless asked to develop any one or two points or elements
    5. Show impartiality by giving pros and cons unless directed to select one side only
    6. Make and write down any assumptions you find necessary to answer the questions
    7. Watch your English, grammar, punctuation and choice of words
    8. Time your answers; don't crowd material

8) Answering the essay question

Most essay questions can be answered by framing the specific response around several key words or ideas. Here are a few such key words or ideas:

M's: manpower, materials, methods, money, management
P's: purpose, program, policy, plan, procedure, practice, problems, pitfalls, personnel, public relations

  a. Six basic steps in handling problems:
    1. Preliminary plan and background development
    2. Collect information, data and facts
    3. Analyze and interpret information, data and facts
    4. Analyze and develop solutions as well as make recommendations
    5. Prepare report and sell recommendations
    6. Install recommendations and follow up effectiveness

  b. Pitfalls to avoid
    1. *Taking things for granted* – A statement of the situation does not necessarily imply that each of the elements is necessarily true; for example, a complaint may be invalid and biased so that all that can be taken for granted is that a complaint has been registered

2. *Considering only one side of a situation* – Wherever possible, indicate several alternatives and then point out the reasons you selected the best one
3. *Failing to indicate follow up* – Whenever your answer indicates action on your part, make certain that you will take proper follow-up action to see how successful your recommendations, procedures or actions turn out to be
4. *Taking too long in answering any single question* – Remember to time your answers properly

IX. AFTER THE TEST

Scoring procedures differ in detail among civil service jurisdictions although the general principles are the same. Whether the papers are hand-scored or graded by machine we have described, they are nearly always graded by number. That is, the person who marks the paper knows only the number – never the name – of the applicant. Not until all the papers have been graded will they be matched with names. If other tests, such as training and experience or oral interview ratings have been given, scores will be combined. Different parts of the examination usually have different weights. For example, the written test might count 60 percent of the final grade, and a rating of training and experience 40 percent. In many jurisdictions, veterans will have a certain number of points added to their grades.

After the final grade has been determined, the names are placed in grade order and an eligible list is established. There are various methods for resolving ties between those who get the same final grade – probably the most common is to place first the name of the person whose application was received first. Job offers are made from the eligible list in the order the names appear on it. You will be notified of your grade and your rank as soon as all these computations have been made. This will be done as rapidly as possible.

People who are found to meet the requirements in the announcement are called "eligibles." Their names are put on a list of eligible candidates. An eligible's chances of getting a job depend on how high he stands on this list and how fast agencies are filling jobs from the list.

When a job is to be filled from a list of eligibles, the agency asks for the names of people on the list of eligibles for that job. When the civil service commission receives this request, it sends to the agency the names of the three people highest on this list. Or, if the job to be filled has specialized requirements, the office sends the agency the names of the top three persons who meet these requirements from the general list.

The appointing officer makes a choice from among the three people whose names were sent to him. If the selected person accepts the appointment, the names of the others are put back on the list to be considered for future openings.

That is the rule in hiring from all kinds of eligible lists, whether they are for typist, carpenter, chemist, or something else. For every vacancy, the appointing officer has his choice of any one of the top three eligibles on the list. This explains why the person whose name is on top of the list sometimes does not get an appointment when some of the persons lower on the list do. If the appointing officer chooses the second or third eligible, the No. 1 eligible does not get a job at once, but stays on the list until he is appointed or the list is terminated.

X. HOW TO PASS THE INTERVIEW TEST

The examination for which you applied requires an oral interview test. You have already taken the written test and you are now being called for the interview test – the final part of the formal examination.

You may think that it is not possible to prepare for an interview test and that there are no procedures to follow during an interview. Our purpose is to point out some things you can do in advance that will help you and some good rules to follow and pitfalls to avoid while you are being interviewed.

What is an interview supposed to test?

The written examination is designed to test the technical knowledge and competence of the candidate; the oral is designed to evaluate intangible qualities, not readily measured otherwise, and to establish a list showing the relative fitness of each candidate – as measured against his competitors – for the position sought. Scoring is not on the basis of "right" and "wrong," but on a sliding scale of values ranging from "not passable" to "outstanding." As a matter of fact, it is possible to achieve a relatively low score without a single "incorrect" answer because of evident weakness in the qualities being measured.

Occasionally, an examination may consist entirely of an oral test – either an individual or a group oral. In such cases, information is sought concerning the technical knowledges and abilities of the candidate, since there has been no written examination for this purpose. More commonly, however, an oral test is used to supplement a written examination.

Who conducts interviews?

The composition of oral boards varies among different jurisdictions. In nearly all, a representative of the personnel department serves as chairman. One of the members of the board may be a representative of the department in which the candidate would work. In some cases, "outside experts" are used, and, frequently, a businessman or some other representative of the general public is asked to serve. Labor and management or other special groups may be represented. The aim is to secure the services of experts in the appropriate field.

However the board is composed, it is a good idea (and not at all improper or unethical) to ascertain in advance of the interview who the members are and what groups they represent. When you are introduced to them, you will have some idea of their backgrounds and interests, and at least you will not stutter and stammer over their names.

What should be done before the interview?

While knowledge about the board members is useful and takes some of the surprise element out of the interview, there is other preparation which is more substantive. It *is* possible to prepare for an oral interview – in several ways:

1) Keep a copy of your application and review it carefully before the interview

This may be the only document before the oral board, and the starting point of the interview. Know what education and experience you have listed there, and the sequence and dates of all of it. Sometimes the board will ask you to review the highlights of your experience for them; you should not have to hem and haw doing it.

2) Study the class specification and the examination announcement

Usually, the oral board has one or both of these to guide them. The qualities, characteristics or knowledges required by the position sought are stated in these documents. They offer valuable clues as to the nature of the oral interview. For example, if the job involves supervisory responsibilities, the announcement will usually indicate that knowledge of modern supervisory methods and the qualifications of the candidate as a supervisor will be tested. If so, you can expect such questions, frequently in the form of a hypothetical situation which you are expected to solve. NEVER go into an oral without knowledge of the duties and responsibilities of the job you seek.

3) Think through each qualification required

Try to visualize the kind of questions you would ask if you were a board member. How well could you answer them? Try especially to appraise your own knowledge and background in each area, *measured against the job sought*, and identify any areas in which you are weak. Be critical and realistic – do not flatter yourself.

4) Do some general reading in areas in which you feel you may be weak

For example, if the job involves supervision and your past experience has NOT, some general reading in supervisory methods and practices, particularly in the field of human relations, might be useful. Do NOT study agency procedures or detailed manuals. The oral board will be testing your understanding and capacity, not your memory.

5) Get a good night's sleep and watch your general health and mental attitude

You will want a clear head at the interview. Take care of a cold or any other minor ailment, and of course, no hangovers.

What should be done on the day of the interview?

Now comes the day of the interview itself. Give yourself plenty of time to get there. Plan to arrive somewhat ahead of the scheduled time, particularly if your appointment is in the fore part of the day. If a previous candidate fails to appear, the board might be ready for you a bit early. By early afternoon an oral board is almost invariably behind schedule if there are many candidates, and you may have to wait. Take along a book or magazine to read, or your application to review, but leave any extraneous material in the waiting room when you go in for your interview. In any event, relax and compose yourself.

The matter of dress is important. The board is forming impressions about you – from your experience, your manners, your attitude, and your appearance. Give your personal appearance careful attention. Dress your best, but not your flashiest. Choose conservative, appropriate clothing, and be sure it is immaculate. This is a business interview, and your appearance should indicate that you regard it as such. Besides, being well groomed and properly dressed will help boost your confidence.

Sooner or later, someone will call your name and escort you into the interview room. *This is it.* From here on you are on your own. It is too late for any more preparation. But remember, you asked for this opportunity to prove your fitness, and you are here because your request was granted.

What happens when you go in?

The usual sequence of events will be as follows: The clerk (who is often the board stenographer) will introduce you to the chairman of the oral board, who will introduce you to the other members of the board. Acknowledge the introductions before you sit down. Do not be surprised if you find a microphone facing you or a stenotypist sitting by. Oral interviews are usually recorded in the event of an appeal or other review.

Usually the chairman of the board will open the interview by reviewing the highlights of your education and work experience from your application – primarily for the benefit of the other members of the board, as well as to get the material into the record. Do not interrupt or comment unless there is an error or significant misinterpretation; if that is the case, do not hesitate. But do not quibble about insignificant matters. Also, he will usually ask you some question about your education, experience or your present job – partly to get you to start talking and to establish the interviewing "rapport." He may start the actual questioning, or turn it over to one of the other members. Frequently, each member undertakes the questioning on a particular area, one in which he is perhaps most competent, so you can expect each member to participate in the examination. Because time is limited, you may also expect some rather abrupt switches in the direction the questioning takes, so do not be upset by it. Normally, a board member will not pursue a single line of questioning unless he discovers a particular strength or weakness.

After each member has participated, the chairman will usually ask whether any member has any further questions, then will ask you if you have anything you wish to add. Unless you are expecting this question, it may floor you. Worse, it may start you off on an extended, extemporaneous speech. The board is not usually seeking more information. The question is principally to offer you a last opportunity to present further qualifications or to indicate that you have nothing to add. So, if you feel that a significant qualification or characteristic has been overlooked, it is proper to point it out in a sentence or so. Do not compliment the board on the thoroughness of their examination – they have been sketchy, and you know it. If you wish, merely say, "No thank you, I have nothing further to add." This is a point where you can "talk yourself out" of a good impression or fail to present an important bit of information. Remember, *you close the interview yourself.*

The chairman will then say, "That is all, Mr. _____, thank you." Do not be startled; the interview is over, and quicker than you think. Thank him, gather your belongings and take your leave. Save your sigh of relief for the other side of the door.

How to put your best foot forward

Throughout this entire process, you may feel that the board individually and collectively is trying to pierce your defenses, seek out your hidden weaknesses and embarrass and confuse you. Actually, this is not true. They are obliged to make an appraisal of your qualifications for the job you are seeking, and they want to see you in your best light. Remember, they must interview all candidates and a non-cooperative candidate may become a failure in spite of their best efforts to bring out his qualifications. Here are 15 suggestions that will help you:

1) Be natural – Keep your attitude confident, not cocky

If you are not confident that you can do the job, do not expect the board to be. Do not apologize for your weaknesses, try to bring out your strong points. The board is interested in a positive, not negative, presentation. Cockiness will antagonize any board member and make him wonder if you are covering up a weakness by a false show of strength.

2) Get comfortable, but don't lounge or sprawl

Sit erectly but not stiffly. A careless posture may lead the board to conclude that you are careless in other things, or at least that you are not impressed by the importance of the occasion. Either conclusion is natural, even if incorrect. Do not fuss with your clothing, a pencil or an ashtray. Your hands may occasionally be useful to emphasize a point; do not let them become a point of distraction.

3) Do not wisecrack or make small talk

This is a serious situation, and your attitude should show that you consider it as such. Further, the time of the board is limited – they do not want to waste it, and neither should you.

4) Do not exaggerate your experience or abilities

In the first place, from information in the application or other interviews and sources, the board may know more about you than you think. Secondly, you probably will not get away with it. An experienced board is rather adept at spotting such a situation, so do not take the chance.

5) If you know a board member, do not make a point of it, yet do not hide it

Certainly you are not fooling him, and probably not the other members of the board. Do not try to take advantage of your acquaintanceship – it will probably do you little good.

6) Do not dominate the interview

Let the board do that. They will give you the clues – do not assume that you have to do all the talking. Realize that the board has a number of questions to ask you, and do not try to take up all the interview time by showing off your extensive knowledge of the answer to the first one.

7) Be attentive

You only have 20 minutes or so, and you should keep your attention at its sharpest throughout. When a member is addressing a problem or question to you, give him your undivided attention. Address your reply principally to him, but do not exclude the other board members.

8) Do not interrupt

A board member may be stating a problem for you to analyze. He will ask you a question when the time comes. Let him state the problem, and wait for the question.

9) Make sure you understand the question

Do not try to answer until you are sure what the question is. If it is not clear, restate it in your own words or ask the board member to clarify it for you. However, do not haggle about minor elements.

10) Reply promptly but not hastily

A common entry on oral board rating sheets is "candidate responded readily," or "candidate hesitated in replies." Respond as promptly and quickly as you can, but do not jump to a hasty, ill-considered answer.

11) Do not be peremptory in your answers

A brief answer is proper – but do not fire your answer back. That is a losing game from your point of view. The board member can probably ask questions much faster than you can answer them.

12) Do not try to create the answer you think the board member wants

He is interested in what kind of mind you have and how it works – not in playing games. Furthermore, he can usually spot this practice and will actually grade you down on it.

13) Do not switch sides in your reply merely to agree with a board member

Frequently, a member will take a contrary position merely to draw you out and to see if you are willing and able to defend your point of view. Do not start a debate, yet do not surrender a good position. If a position is worth taking, it is worth defending.

14) Do not be afraid to admit an error in judgment if you are shown to be wrong

The board knows that you are forced to reply without any opportunity for careful consideration. Your answer may be demonstrably wrong. If so, admit it and get on with the interview.

15) Do not dwell at length on your present job

The opening question may relate to your present assignment. Answer the question but do not go into an extended discussion. You are being examined for a *new* job, not your present one. As a matter of fact, try to phrase ALL your answers in terms of the job for which you are being examined.

Basis of Rating

Probably you will forget most of these "do's" and "don'ts" when you walk into the oral interview room. Even remembering them all will not ensure you a passing grade. Perhaps you did not have the qualifications in the first place. But remembering them will help you to put your best foot forward, without treading on the toes of the board members.

Rumor and popular opinion to the contrary notwithstanding, an oral board wants you to make the best appearance possible. They know you are under pressure – but they also want to see how you respond to it as a guide to what your reaction would be under the pressures of the job you seek. They will be influenced by the degree of poise you display, the personal traits you show and the manner in which you respond.

ABOUT THIS BOOK

This book contains tests divided into Examination Sections. Go through each test, answering every question in the margin. We have also attached a sample answer sheet at the back of the book that can be removed and used. At the end of each test look at the answer key and check your answers. On the ones you got wrong, look at the right answer choice and learn. Do not fill in the answers first. Do not memorize the questions and answers, but understand the answer and principles involved. On your test, the questions will likely be different from the samples. Questions are changed and new ones added. If you understand these past questions you should have success with any changes that arise. Tests may consist of several types of questions. We have additional books on each subject should more study be advisable or necessary for you. Finally, the more you study, the better prepared you will be. This book is intended to be the last thing you study before you walk into the examination room. Prior study of relevant texts is also recommended. NLC publishes some of these in our Fundamental Series. Knowledge and good sense are important factors in passing your exam. Good luck also helps. So now study this Passbook, absorb the material contained within and take that knowledge into the examination. Then do your best to pass that exam.

EXAMINATION SECTION

EXAMINATION SECTION
TEST 1

DIRECTIONS: Each question or incomplete statement is followed by several suggested answers or completions. Select the one that BEST answers the question or completes the statement. *PRINT THE LETTER OF THE CORRECT ANSWER IN THE SPACE AT THE RIGHT.*

1. In the course of his inspection of a plant, a sanitarian obtains information about a process which he thinks would be useful to a friend engaged in a similar business.
   Of the following, the MOST advisable course of action for him to take is to

   A. consider such information confidential and not disclose it
   B. consider such information not confidential and, therefore, disclose it to his friend
   C. give his friend the information, but not disclose its source
   D. give his friend the information, pretending that it is his own idea

   1.____

2. Assume that, as a sanitarian, you have received an order from a person of high authority in the Department of Health. This order conflicts with instructions which you have received from your immediate supervisor.
   Of the following, the MOST advisable action for you to take FIRST is to

   A. carry out the order given you by higher authority
   B. inform your supervisor of the situation
   C. proceed according to your supervisor's instructions
   D. send a written memorandum to the person who gave you the order, indicating the conflict with your immediate supervisor's instructions

   2.____

3. Of the following statements concerning reports prepared by a sanitarian, the one which is LEAST valid is:

   A. A case report submitted by a sanitarian should contain factual material to support conclusions made
   B. An extremely detailed report may be of less value than a brief report giving the essential facts
   C. Highly technical language should be avoided as far as possible in preparing a report to be used at a court trial
   D. The position of the important facts in a report does not influence the emphasis placed on them by the reader

   3.____

4. Assume that, as a sanitarian, you are to leave the restaurant after having concluded an inspection of the premises. However, the operator begins a detailed story concerning his business experiences.
   Of the following, the MOST advisable course of action for you to take is to

   A. leave immediately to avoid being delayed by listening to the story
   B. listen for a few minutes and then excuse yourself on the ground that you have other duties
   C. listen quietly to what he has to say, but be noncommittal in making replies
   D. tell the operator that the job of sanitarian does not permit indulgence in personal relationships with operators

   4.____

5. Suppose that a story concerning an investigation conducted by the Department of Health has appeared in the newspapers. A reporter approaches a sanitarian and asks for details concerning this investigation.
Of the following, the MOST advisable way for the sanitarian to handle the situation is to

   A. give the reporter complete information regarding the investigation
   B. refer the reporter to the official of the department responsible for public relations
   C. refuse to speak to the reporter
   D. tell the reporter to make his own investigation of the matter

6. The operator of an establishment tells you that he intends to register a complaint against you, the sanitarian, with the Department of Health. He claims that you are impeding his operations because you insist upon a minute inspection of every piece of equipment. You feel that your methods are justified.
Of the following, the MOST advisable course of action for you to take is to

   A. continue the inspection, and ignore the complaint because you feel that your methods are correct
   B. continue the inspection, but tell the operator that owners of similar establishments do not complain concerning the same type of inspection
   C. explain the reasons for your actions to the operator and inform him that he has the right to complain if he wishes
   D. try to cut down on some of the details of the inspection in order to maintain a good relationship with the operator

7. Assume that, as a sanitarian, you are inspecting the premises of a certain establishment. The owner tells you of his disagreement with certain provisions of the new Health Code which affect his business.
Of the following, the MOST advisable course of action for you to take is to

   A. tell him that most such complaints are groundless
   B. tell him that your workload does not permit you to spend time discussing the new Health Code
   C. tell him to make his complaint in person to the Department of Health
   D. try to explain the reasons for the inclusion of these provisions

8. Suppose that, as a sanitarian, you realize that you have made an error in a report that has been forwarded to another unit. You know that this error is not likely to be discovered for some time.
Of the following, the MOST advisable course of action for you to take is to

   A. approach the supervisor of the other unit on an informal basis and ask him to correct the error
   B. say nothing about it since most likely one error will not invalidate the entire report
   C. tell your supervisor immediately that you have made an error so that it may be corrected, if necessary
   D. wait until the error is discovered and then admit that you have made it

9. Suppose that you have become friendly with one of the other sanitarians in your unit. You notice that recently he has been doing very poor work and you know that the rest of the staff is aware of the situation.
Of the following, the MOST advisable course of action for you to take is to

A. seek an opportunity to speak privately to your friend and ask if you can help in any way
B. speak to the other members of the staff when you have an opportunity, and try to minimize the situation
C. speak to your supervisor and tell him that he ought to transfer this man to another unit
D. tell your friend that you are willing to share some of his workload for a while

10. Assume that, as a sanitarian, you realize that you have unjustly reprimanded the owner of an establishment while making an inspection.
Of the following, the MOST advisable course of action for you to take is to

   A. admit your mistake and apologize to the owner
   B. attempt to justify the reprimand on some other basis
   C. ignore the matter in order to maintain your authority
   D. overlook some other offense you may notice

10.____

Question 11.

DIRECTIONS: Question 11 is to be answered SOLELY on the basis of the following passage from the Health Code.

A drug or device shall be deemed to be misbranded:

1. If any word, statement, or other information required by this article to appear on the label or labeling is not prominently placed thereon with such conspicuousness, as compared with other words, statements, designs or emblems in the labeling, and in such terms as to render it likely to be read and understood by the ordinary individual under customary conditions of purchase and use; or,

2. If it is a drug and is not designated solely by a name recognized in an official compendium unless its label bears the common or usual name of the drug, if it has one, and, if it is fabricated from two or more ingredients, the common or usual name of each active ingredient, including the kind and quantity by percentage or amount of any alcohol; or,

3. Unless its labeling bears adequate directions for use, except that a drug or device may be exempted from this requirement by the Commissioner when he finds that it is not necessary for the protection of the public health, and such adequate warnings against use in those pathological conditions or by children where its use may be dangerous to health, or against unsafe dosage or methods or duration of administration or application, in such manner and form, as are necessary for the protection of users.

11. According to the above passage, the LEAST accurate of the following statements is:

   A. Certain drugs must have labels which give their names as found in an official compendium
   B. Drugs or devices are not necessarily misbranded if their labels carry warnings against use in certain pathological conditions
   C. Labels on drugs liable to deterioration must state the precautions necessary to prevent deterioration
   D. Required information on a drug label should be at least as conspicuous as other statements on the label

11.____

Questions 12-13.

DIRECTIONS: Questions 12 and 13 are to be answered SOLELY on the basis of the following passage from the Health Code.

(a) The Commissioner shall not consent to the use or proposed use of a food additive if the data before him:
 (1) fail to establish that the proposed use of the additive under the conditions of use specified will be safe; or,
 (2) show that the proposed use of the additive would otherwise result in adulteration or in misbranding of food within the meaning of this Code.

(b) If, in the opinion of the Commissioner, based on the data before him, a tolerance limitation is required in order to assure that the proposed use of an additive will be safe, the Commissioner:
 (1) shall not fix such tolerance limitation at a level higher than he finds to be reasonably required to accomplish the physical or other technical effect for which such additive is intended; and,
 (2) shall not consent to the proposed use of the additive if he finds that the data do not establish that such use would accomplish the intended physical or other technical effect.

(c) In determining whether a proposed use of a food additive is safe, the Commissioner shall consider among other relevant factors:
 (1) the probable consumption of the additive and of any substance formed in the food because of the use of the additive; and,
 (2) the cumulative effect of such additive in the diet of man or animals.

12. If the data indicate that the proposed use of a food additive will be safe if the amount added is limited to 5 milligrams per gram of the food, the Commissioner shall fix the tolerance limitation at

 A. 5 milligrams per gram of the food
 B. 4 milligrams per gram of the food if this is the amount that can be expected to produce the desired effect
 C. less than 5 but more than 4 milligrams per gram of the food if 4 milligrams is the amount that can be expected to produce the desired effect
 D. less than 5 milligrams per gram of the food

13. According to the above passage, the LEAST accurate of the following statements is:

 A. Some food additives may, in some cases, be considered as adulterants
 B. The Commissioner should consider all relevant factors in determining whether the proposed use of a food additive is safe
 C. The Commissioner may not prohibit the use of an additive if the data show that its use is safe within certain tolerance limitations
 D. The Commissioner may prohibit the use of an additive even if the data indicate that its use would be safe within certain tolerance limitations

14. Of the following, a LIKELY reason for the inclusion of section (b)(2) given above is that   14.____

    A. food additives used within their tolerance limitations are likely to be unsafe
    B. producers may tend to add more than the safe amount if the tolerance limitation does not permit the accomplishment of the intended physical or other technical effect
    C. the probable consumption of the additive cannot be determined if it does not accomplish the intended physical or other technical effect
    D. use of a food additive that does not accomplish the intended physical or other technical effect is uneconomical

Questions 15-16.

DIRECTIONS: Questions 15 and 16 are to be answered SOLELY on the basis of the following passage from the Health Code.

The new Health Code governs such aspects of the food industry as pertain to cleanliness of apparatus, equipment, and utensils used in the preparation and service of food and sanitation of food establishment premises.

This revision marks a considerable shift in emphasis from detailed specific standards to broad performance standards and the imposition of greater obligation on industry to carry out well-formulated inspection procedures under its own direction and under continuing supervision of the Department. The emphasis is on clean and sanitary food products produced, sold or served in clean and sanitary food establishments.

The emphasis on generalized performance standards serves the important purpose of encouraging, through less restrictive regulations, the development of new processes in food sanitation and food manufacture. The advances in food technology practices, new chemical aids and new sanitary designs of machinery, have already pointed the way to getting the job done better and without the need for restrictive detailed regulations. This article is not only designed to permit progress of this kind to the fullest, but it also reflects the view that such industry growth should receive constant stimulation so that there is less need for official policing and more and more self-sanitation and self-supervision.

15. According to the above passage, the new Health Code   15.____

    A. requires detailed specific standards rather than broad performance standards
    B. is intended to provide for ultimate complete self-supervision by the food industry
    C. places less emphasis on self-inspection than on generalized performance standards
    D. is designed to take cognizance of the effects of new developments on food industry practices

16. According to the above passage, the new Health Code does NOT   16.____

    A. consider continued supervision of the food industry by the Department to be of great importance
    B. consider that advances in food technology indicate the need for less restrictive regulations

C. emphasize coercion but seeks voluntary compliance by the food industry
D. obligate the food industry to carry out well-formulated inspection procedures under its own direction

Questions 17-18.

DIRECTIONS: Questions 17 and 18 are to be answered SOLELY on the basis of the following passage.

The beginnings of hygiene can be traced back to antiquity in the sanitary laws of the Hebrews. Preventive medicine began with the first primitive idea of contagion. Even in the time when epidemics were explained as due to the wrath of the gods or visitations of evil spirits, it was observed that certain illnesses apparently spread from person to person. Gradually, the idea of contagiousness was associated with a number of diseases. Fracastorium, in his book, DE CONTAGIONE, published in 1554, proposed a classification of diseases into those which were contagious and those which were not. For three centuries following this publication, the medical profession was divided into two camps: the non-contagionists, who believed that the causative agents of epidemic disease were inanimate and gaseous in nature and associated with emanations from decomposing organic matter, effluvia, and miasma; and the much smaller group, the contagionists, who identified contagiousness with germs of some kind.

Looking backward, this confusion is understandable. That some diseases were contagious was fairly obvious, but some apparently arose spontaneously without a traceable source. The confusion was finally resolved in the latter part of the nineteenth century by the work of Pasteur, Koch, and their followers. The causative relationship of specific microorganisms for one after another of the infectious diseases was established and the part played by carriers, missed cases, common water and food supplies, arthropod vectors, and animal reservoirs in transmission was gradually elucidated.

17. The above passage IMPLIES that

    A. all infectious diseases were highly contagious
    B. the contagionists of the early 19th century had identified the specific microorganisms causing certain diseases
    C. the role of animal reservoirs contributed to the confusion which once existed concerning disease transmission
    D. the sanitary laws of the ancient Hebrews show that they had some scientific knowledge of the causes of disease

18. According to the above passage, the MOST accurate of the following statements is:

    A. Fracastorius believed that all diseases could be caused by miasma
    B. It is still believed by scientists that certain infectious diseases arise spontaneously
    C. Nothing was accomplished in disease prevention until the germ theory was established
    D. Preventive medicine was practiced to some extent in early times even though epidemics may have been attributed to evil spirits

Questions 19-20.

DIRECTIONS: Questions 19 and 20 are to be answered SOLELY on the basis of the following paragraph.

Microorganisms are living things so small that they can be seen only with the aid of a microscope. They are widely distributed in nature and are responsible for many physical and chemical changes of importance to the life of plants, of animals, and of human beings. Altogether too many people believe that all *microbes* or *germs* are harmful, and that they are an entirely undesirable group of living things. While it is true that some microorganisms produce disease, the great majority of them do not. In fact, the activities of these hosts of non-disease-producing microorganisms make possible the continued existence of plants and animals on the earth. In addition, many kinds of microorganisms are used in industries to manufacture products of great value to man. But the activities of non-disease-producing microorganisms are not always desirable. Fabrics and fibers may be rotted, fermentation processes may be upset by undesirable organisms and other harmful effects may occur. From a practical point of view, we are interested in the microorganisms because of the things that they do and the physical and chemical changes which they produce. Also, we are interested in ways and means to control undesirable organisms and to put the useful ones to work; but a study of the activities and the means for control of microorganisms must be based upon knowledge of their nature and life processes.

19. The one of the following which is the MOST suitable title for the above paragraph is   19._____

    A. BACTERIA CAN BE USEFUL
    B. MICROORGANISMS AND THE PUBLIC HEALTH SANITARIAN
    C. THE CONTROL OF MICROBES
    D. THE RELATIONSHIP OF MICROORGANISMS TO MAN AND HIS ENVIRONMENT

20. According to the above paragraph, the MOST accurate of the following statements is: 20._____

    A. All non-disease-producing microorganisms are beneficial to mankind
    B. *Microbes* or *germs* are terms which are synonymous with *bacteria*
    C. The activities of useful bacteria need no controls
    D. Without microorganisms, life on earth would be virtually impossible

KEY (CORRECT ANSWERS)

1.	A	11.	C
2.	B	12.	B
3.	D	13.	C
4.	B	14.	B
5.	B	15.	D
6.	C	16.	C
7.	D	17.	C
8.	C	18.	D
9.	A	19.	D
10.	A	20.	D

TEST 2

DIRECTIONS: Each question or incomplete statement is followed by several suggested answers or completions. Select the one that BEST answers the question or completes the statement. *PRINT THE LETTER OF THE CORRECT ANSWER IN THE SPACE AT THE RIGHT.*

1. Solutions to which relatively large amounts of strong acid or base can be added with ONLY SLIGHT resulting change in pH are called _____ solutions. 1.____

    A. buffered   B. molar   C. normal   D. standard

2. Of the following statements concerning isotopes, the one which is INCORRECT is that isotopes of a given element have 2.____

    A. similar chemical properties
    B. the same atomic number
    C. the same atomic weight
    D. the same nuclear charge

3. Nuclei of atoms are considered to be composed of 3.____

    A. neutrons and protons   B. photons and electrons
    C. positrons and neutrons   D. protons and electrons

4. *Dry Ice* is solid 4.____

    A. ammonia   B. carbolic acid
    C. carbon dioxide   D. freon

5. The pH of a solution in which the apparent hydrogen ion concentration is equal to 1×10^{-8} moles per liter is 5.____

    A. 2   B. 4   C. 6   D. 8

6. Substances in solutions which change color at a particular pH are termed 6.____

    A. catalysts   B. desiccants
    C. indicators   D. mordants

7. The amount of 2.0 N KOH required to neutralize 40 ml. of 0.5 N HCl is _____ ml. 7.____

    A. 2   B. 4   C. 5   D. 10

8. The term *anion* refers to a 8.____

    A. *negatively* charged electrode
    B. *negatively* charged ion
    C. *positively* charged electrode
    D. *positively* charged ion

9. If the concentration of a salt solution is given as 0.7243 grams per liter, it may also be expressed as _____ grams per liter. 9.____

    A. 7.243×10^{-2} B. 72.43×10^{-1}
    C. 72.43×10^{-2} D. 724.3×10^{-2}

10. Invertase is a type of

    A. carbohydrate
    B. enzyme
    C. fat
    D. protein

11. An enzyme that acts upon starches is said to be

    A. aminolytic
    B. amylolytic
    C. lipolytic
    D. proteolytic

12. The structural formula $H_2N-\underset{H}{\overset{H}{C}}-C\underset{OH}{\overset{O}{\diagup}}$ represents a(n)

    A. ketone
    B. alcohol
    C. amino acid
    D. ester

13. The one of the following which is a PRODUCT of the saponification of a fat is

    A. glycerol   B. glycine   C. lecithin   D. sterol

14. Synthetic detergents can be used INSTEAD of natural soaps because both

    A. are organic compounds
    B. have the same chemical composition
    C. lower the surface tension of water
    D. raise the surface tension of water

15. A Bourdon gage is used to measure

    A. electrical resistance
    B. gas pressure
    C. internal diameters
    D. relative humidity

16. A specific gravity bottle weighs 150 g when empty, 250 g when filled with water, and 385 g when filled with another liquid.
    The specific gravity of the liquid is MOST NEARLY

    A. 1.67   B. 2.35   C. 2.57   D. 3.85

17. At sea level, the number of degrees between the freezing point and the boiling point of water on the Centigrade temperature scale is

    A. 32   B. 100   C. 180   D. 212

18. The general gas law for a given mass of gas, where P stands for pressure, V stands for volume, and T stands for absolute temperature may be stated as

    A. P = KVT   B. PK = VT   C. PT = KV   D. PV = KT

19. If a mercury column barometer is constructed with a tube twice the diameter of a standard barometer, the reading will be _____ that of the standard barometer.

    A. one-fourth of
    B. one-half of
    C. twice
    D. the same as

20. The watt is a unit of electrical

    A. current
    B. inductance
    C. potential
    D. power

21. Bacteria are classified with the

    A. Bryophytes
    B. Protozoa
    C. Pteridophytes
    D. Thallophytes

22. The scientific name of a certain microorganism is Clostridium butyricum. The second word of this name indicates the

    A. class
    B. genus
    C. phylum
    D. species

23. Suppose that 100 ml of a water sample are added to 1900 ml of dilution water, and that 1 ml of this dilution is added to 49 ml of dilution water. The dilution of the original water sample in the second mixture is 1:

    A. 900
    B. 950
    C. 1000
    D. 1250

24. Spheroid shaped bacteria which look like chains of beads under the microscope are known as

    A. sarcinas
    B. spirilla
    C. staphylococci
    D. streptococci

25. In addition to alcohol, the fermentation of glucose by yeast yields

    A. carbon dioxide
    B. citric acid
    C. hydrogen
    D. oxygen

KEY (CORRECT ANSWERS)

1. A
2. C
3. A
4. C
5. D
6. C
7. D
8. B
9. C
10. B
11. B
12. C
13. A
14. C
15. B
16. B
17. B
18. D
19. D
20. D
21. D
22. D
23. C
24. D
25. A

TEST 3

DIRECTIONS: Each question or incomplete statement is followed by several suggested answers or completions. Select the one that BEST answers the question or completes the statement. *PRINT THE LETTER OF THE CORRECT ANSWER IN THE SPACE AT THE RIGHT.*

1. The one of the following which is NOT an antibiotic is
   - A. actinomycin
   - B. trypsin
   - C. streptothricin
   - D. tyrothricin

2. Vaccination confers _____ acquired immunity.
   - A. *active* artificially
   - B. *active* naturally
   - C. *passive* artificially
   - D. *passive* naturally

3. The one of the following which is NOT used as a disinfectant or antiseptic is
   - A. ethyl acetate
   - B. phenol
   - C. potassium permanganate
   - D. silver nitrate

4. The vector responsible for the transmission of yellow fever is the
   - A. flea
   - B. louse
   - C. mosquito
   - D. tick

5. Typhus fever is caused by microorganisms of the genus
   - A. Escherichia
   - B. Proteus
   - C. Rickettsia
   - D. Salmonella

6. The one of the following diseases which is caused by a virus is
   - A. encephalitis
   - B. malaria
   - C. Q fever
   - D. tetanus

7. The one of the following diseases which is considered to be infectious is
   - A. angina pectoria
   - B. diabetes
   - C. glaucoma
   - D. psittacosis

8. The one of the following diseases in which rats do NOT act as intermediate hosts is
   - A. amoebic dysentery
   - B. endemic typhus
   - C. plague
   - D. Weil's disease

9. The Kahn test is used to diagnose
   - A. gonorrhea
   - B. syphilis
   - C. tuberculosis
   - D. typhoid fever

10. The one of the following BEST known for his work in connection with antibiotics is
    - A. Löffler
    - B. Rivers
    - C. Waksman
    - D. Welch

11. Of the following constituents of milk, the one which is present in the LEAST proportion is
    - A. fat
    - B. mineral ash
    - C. protein
    - D. sugar

12. Casein occurs in fresh milk in the form of a(n)

    A. colloidal solution	B. foam
    C. emulsion	D. true solution

13. One type of lactometer used for determining the specific gravity of milk is graduated from 0 to 29 degrees to indicate a certain range of specific gravity. Another type is graduated from 0 to 100 degrees to indicate the same range.
    If the specific gravity is determined from the reading of the first type by the formula, $1 + \frac{reading}{1000}$, then the formula to be used with the second type is

    A. $1 + (\frac{reading}{1000} \times \frac{1}{.29})$	B. $1 + (\frac{reading}{1000} \times .29)$
    C. $(\frac{reading}{1000} \times .29) - 1$	D. $(\frac{reading}{1000} \times \frac{1}{.29}) - 1$

14. If milk is adulterated by the addition of water, its

    A. specific gravity will be decreased
    B. specific gravity will be increased
    C. relative fat content will be increased
    D. relative mineral content will be increased

15. The *Holding* method and the *High Temperature Short Time* method of milk pasteurization require, respectively, _____ minutes and _____ seconds.

    A. 15; 15	B. 15; 30	C. 30; 30	D. 30; 15

16. Of the following, the one which is NOT used for testing milk is the _____ test.

    A. methylene blue reduction
    B. phosphatase
    C. precipitin
    D. sediment

17. The one of the following which is ordinarily NOT considered to be a disease transmissible through milk is

    A. scarlet fever	B. septic sore throat
    C. spotted fever	D. brucellosis

18. The one of the following which would ordinarily NOT be used in sterilizing milk plant equipment is

    A. chlorine solution	B. sodium fluoroacetate
    C. hot water	D. live steam

19. The legal requirement for butter is that its butterfat content shall be NOT less than

    A. 95%	B. 90%	C. 85%	D. 80%

20. Of the following, the one which is COMMONLY used as a stabilizer for ice cream is

    A. albumin	B. benzoic acid
    C. gelatin	D. sucrose

21. Of the following, the one which is NOT a factor used in grading butter is   21.____

    A. body   B. butterfat content
    C. color   D. salt

22. When fortifying milk with vitamin D, the minimum number of vitamin D units required per   22.____
    quart is USUALLY

    A. 400   B. 600   C. 800   D. 1000

23. Milk is USUALLY tested for adequacy of homogenization by   23.____

    A. allowing it to stand for 48 hours and then observing the percentage of butterfat
       which rises to the upper portion
    B. employing a modified Babcock test
    C. noting the time required for coagulation of the milk
    D. using a centrifuge

24. Rennet, used in cheese manufacture, is obtained   24.____

    A. by chemical synthesis   B. from bacterial cultures
    C. from calves' stomachs   D. from goats' milk

25. A *starter* used in making cheese is a(n)   25.____

    A. bacterial culture   B. mechanical agitator
    C. enzyme   D. organic acid

26. The term *process cheese* refers to cheese   26.____

    A. made by old European methods not readily duplicated in the United States
    B. made from one or more varieties of cheese which have been reworked into a mixture with a smooth texture
    C. which is manufactured by a patented method
    D. which is permitted to ripen for a considerable length of time

27. Curing preserves meat PRIMARILY because of the   27.____

    A. high temperatures at which the curing process is carried on
    B. low temperatures at which the curing process is carried on
    C. use of salt in fairly high concentration
    D. use of spices in low concentration

28. In commercial canning of low-acid food, appropriate *heat processing* is used in order to   28.____

    A. destroy spore-forming bacteria
    B. expel air and other gases from the product
    C. fix the natural color of the product
    D. remove raw flavors from the foods

29. Custard-filled baked goods are FREQUENTLY involved in cases of food poisoning primarily because   29.____

    A. harmful preservatives are sometimes used in custards
    B. many people are allergic to some of the ingredients used in custard
    C. the custard forms a good medium for growth of certain harmful bacteria
    D. the ingredients may be stale

30. An unsexed male chicken (usually under 10 months of age) is called a 30._____
    A. broiler B. capon C. fryer D. stag

KEY (CORRECT ANSWERS)

1.	B	16.	C
2.	A	17.	C
3.	A	18.	B
4.	C	19.	D
5.	C	20.	C
6.	A	21.	B
7.	D	22.	A
8.	A	23.	A
9.	B	24.	C
10.	C	25.	A
11.	B	26.	B
12.	A	27.	C
13.	B	28.	A
14.	A	29.	C
15.	D	30.	B

TEST 4

DIRECTIONS: Each question or incomplete statement is followed by several suggested answers or completions. Select the one that BEST answers the question or completes the statement. *PRINT THE LETTER OF THE CORRECT ANSWER IN THE SPACE AT THE RIGHT.*

1. An unopened can containing spoiled food which CANNOT be detected by its external appearance is called a

    A. flat sour
    B. flipper
    C. springer
    D. swell

    1.____

2. The one of the following which is usually NOT a factor considered in determining the grade of canned fruit is the

    A. color of the fruit
    B. density of the syrup
    C. texture of the fruit
    D. uniformity of size

    2.____

3. The term *marbling*, as used in connection with the grading of beef, refers to

    A. a hardened condition of the bones
    B. coarseness in the texture of the meat
    C. the external fat covering the meat
    D. the network of intramuscular fat visible in the cut surface of the meat

    3.____

4. Food poisoning is MOST likely to be caused by bacteria of the genus

    A. Neisseria
    B. Pasteurella
    C. Salmonella
    D. Treponema

    4.____

5. When candling eggs, the characteristic which indicates eggs of SUPERIOR quality is

    A. germ development
    B. large air cell
    C. slightly defined yolk outline
    D. weak white

    5.____

6. *Enriched bread* is thus designated because it contains added

    A. eggs
    B. minerals and vitamins
    C. shortening
    D. sugar

    6.____

7. Oysters may be involved in outbreaks of disease PRIMARILY because they may

    A. contain parasitic worms
    B. have been eaten while still immature
    C. have been taken from polluted waters
    D. have been transplanted to water containing less salt than the original bed

    7.____

8. The one of the following which is NOT a vitamin of the B complex is

    A. carotene
    B. pantothenic acid
    C. riboflavin
    D. thiamine

    8.____

9. The department that enforces the Federal Food, Drug, and Cosmetic Act is the Department of

   A. Agriculture
   B. Commerce
   C. Health, Education and Welfare
   D. the Interior

10. The CHIEF purpose for regulating the sale of barbiturates is to

    A. be able to check the amount of stock of barbiturates a dispenser has on hand
    B. be able to identify purchasers
    C. discourage their use and sale
    D. prevent their use by irresponsible persons

11. The one of the following diseases which is NOT considered to be transmissible through water is

    A. anthrax
    B. bacillary dysentery
    C. cholera
    D. typhoid fever

12. The one of the following which is NOT used as a coagulant in water purification is

    A. aluminum sulfate
    B. ferric chloride
    C. ferric sulfate
    D. sodium phosphate

13. Routine bacteriological examination of water tests for the presence of coliform organisms.
    This is done because

    A. absence of coliforms warrants the assumption that water-borne pathogens are absent
    B. the coliforms are the easiest to collect in a water sample
    C. the coliforms are the most highly pathogenic water-borne organisms
    D. there are no other tests available for isolating other pathogens from water

14. Sodium thiosulfate is added to bottles used for collecting water samples from swimming pools for bacteriological counts in order to

    A. facilitate subsequent plate counts
    B. neutralize residual chlorine
    C. reduce the turbidity of the water
    D. sterilize the bottles

15. The orthotolidine test used for determining residual chlorine in swimming pool water is a _____ test.

    A. bacteriological
    B. colorimetric
    C. microscopic
    D. precipitation

16. An operator of a swimming pool is ordinarily NOT required to test for

    A. bacterial count per ml of the water
    B. clearness of the water
    C. pH of the water
    D. residual chlorine

17. Imhoff tanks used for sewage disposal are PRIMARILY dependent upon the action of   17.____

    A. bacterial decomposition   B. chemical disinfectants
    C. high temperatures   D. water dilution

18. One of the purposes of a vent pipe used in connection with a plumbing system is to   18.____

    A. carry off discharge from wash basins
    B. carry off discharge from water closets
    C. protect trap seals
    D. provide a means of cleaning house drains

19. The term *cross connection,* as used in reference to plumbing systems, is to   19.____

    A. a connecting pipe which joins two other pipes of the same line
    B. a connection between a potable water line and a waste or sewer line
    C. the connection between a house drain and a house sewer
    D. the joining of waste pipes from several fixtures

20. Of the following, the one which is NOT used as a rodenticide is   20.____

    A. Antu   B. methoxychlor
    C. sodium fluoroacetate   D. Warfarin

21. In rodent control, the PRIMARY method of producing permanent results is   21.____

    A. fumigating   B. poisoning
    C. proofing   D. trapping

22. The use of DDT insecticide as a residual spray is EFFECTIVE because it is a   22.____

    A. contact poison   B. fumigant
    C. respiratory poison   D. stomach poison

23. The one of the following which is NOT used as an insect repellent is   23.____

    A. dimethyl phthalate   B. Indalone
    C. Rutgers 6-12   D. 1080

24. The one of the following which is ordinarily NOT used as a fumigant is   24.____

    A. ethylene oxide   B. hydrogen cyanide
    C. methyl bromide   D. phosphorus pentoxide

25. Certification of coal-tar hair dyes to be used in beauty parlors is made in accordance with   25.____
    the provisions of the

    A. Federal Food, Drug and Cosmetic Act
    B. Federal Labeling Act
    C. State Agriculture and Markets Law
    D. State Education Law

26. The unit used to express the MAXIMUM permissible weekly dose of ionizing radiation for   26.____
    human beings is the

    A. eV   B. MKS   C. MPN   D. REM

27. The half-life of a radioactive element is a measure of its

    A. atomic weight
    B. biological effect
    C. penetrating ability
    D. rate of decay

28. Alpha particles are considered to be the SAME as

    A. cathode rays
    B. heavy hydrogen nuclei
    C. helium nuclei
    D. x-rays

29. The formula, $E = mc^2$, is known as

    A. Einstein's Equation
    B. Newton's second law of motion
    C. Planck's Equation
    D. Raoult's Law

30. Of the following, the one generally NOT used for the detection of radioactivity is the

    A. geiger counter
    B. ionization chamber
    C. photographic film
    D. polarimeter

KEY (CORRECT ANSWERS)

1.	A	16.	A
2.	B	17.	A
3.	D	18.	C
4.	C	19.	B
5.	C	20.	B
6.	B	21.	C
7.	C	22.	A
8.	A	23.	D
9.	C	24.	D
10.	D	25.	A
11.	A	26.	D
12.	D	27.	D
13.	A	28.	C
14.	B	29.	A
15.	B	30.	D

EXAMINATION SECTION
TEST 1

DIRECTIONS: Each question or incomplete statement is followed by several suggested answers or completions. Select the one that BEST answers the question or completes the statement. *PRINT THE LETTER OF THE CORRECT ANSWER IN THE SPACE AT THE RIGHT.*

1. Assume that you have been assigned to inspect a building reported to be infested by rats and to prepare a written report thereon.
   Of the following items covered in the report, the LEAST important one is *probably* the

   A. fact that rats appear to be feeding on the garbage of a luncheonette which adjoins the building
   B. name and address of the building owner
   C. record of past violations by the owner
   D. statement made by tenants regarding the presence of rats

   1.____

2. After completing an inspection of a food manufacturing plant, you submit a report of your findings to your supervisor. A few days later, you receive a memorandum from your supervisor indicating that the head of the bureau found your report inadequate. You are to re-inspect the establishment immediately. Your supervisor's memorandum lists the areas which he feels your report did not cover adequately. You, however, are convinced that your report is adequate.
   The BEST course of action for you to take at this time is to

   A. refrain from re-inspecting the food establishment unless directed to do so personally by the head of the bureau
   B. re-inspect the premises, submit another report, and then discuss the matter with your supervisor
   C. telephone your supervisor and insist that the matter be fully discussed before you proceed further with a re-inspection
   D. write a letter to the head of the bureau explaining why you feel your report was adequate, and wait for a reply before you re-inspect

   2.____

3. Assume that you have a close relative who is engaged in the practice of accounting. Following your inspection of a restaurant which is not in violation of the health code, you inform the owner that your relative is an accountant. You hand the owner the accountant's business card and suggest that your relative be considered for any accounting work needed. The owner then tells you that he would like to have your relative take over his accounting work.
   Your action in securing the restaurant's accounting work for your relative is

   A. *improper;* you should have discussed the matter with the restaurant owner after your regular working hours
   B. *improper;* you should not have suggested your relative for the owner's accounting work
   C. *proper* as long as the owner remains in full compliance with the health code
   D. *proper* provided that your relative does not discuss the owner's business with you

   3.____

4. A tenant of an apartment house telephones the department of health to complain that no heat is being furnished to her apartment. The complaint is referred to you with instructions to make a field visit. When you arrive at the apartment house, the tenant partly opens her door but refuses to allow you to enter the apartment. You explain the situation to the tenant, but she persists in her refusal to allow you to enter the apartment.
The BEST thing for you to do in these circumstances is to

   A. notify the tenant that if she refuses you admittance to her apartment, you may be required to obtain a court order directing her to allow you to enter
   B. place the complaint in your pending file and return to the apartment the next time you are in the neighborhood
   C. prepare a report setting forth that the tenant refused to allow you to enter the apartment
   D. take a reading of the temperature in the hallway and then estimate the temperature in the apartment

5. In the course of your inspection of a luncheonette, you note a violation of a provision of the health code relating to the unsanitary condition of food containers. You point out the condition to the owner as you begin to prepare a notice of violation. The owner becomes very angry and declares that the food containers are clean. To illustrate his point, he shows the food containers to two patrons seated at the lunch counter. Both patrons declare that the food containers are clean and suggest that you not *pick* on the owner. The owner then tells you that if you make trouble for him, he will make trouble for you.
Of the following, the BEST course of action for you to take is to

   A. inform the owner that you will return at a later date to complete your notice of violation
   B. refrain from giving the owner a notice of violation since he has witnesses to support his position
   C. serve the owner with a notice of violation
   D. telephone your supervisor, tell him of the condition of the food containers, and ask him whether you should give the owner a notice of violation

6. A provision of the health code requires food handlers to take a course in food handling sanitation. Your supervisor requests that when you visit food establishments in your district, you remind them of the code requirement. Your supervisor stresses that your visit is to be an educational one and that you are not to emphasize the mandatory aspect of this provision. Later, you visit a restaurant owner in your district who expresses strong reservations as to the practicability of releasing food handlers to take such a course.
The one statement which you should NOT make to the owner under any circumstances is that if his food handlers take such a course,

   A. future violations of the health code by the owner will receive special treatment since he is cooperating with the department
   B. his profits may rise since patrons prefer to eat in a place where food sanitation standards are high
   C. the possibility of food poisoning with attendant possible economic loss to the owner will be decreased
   D. the requirement of the health code is mandatory in this respect and must be complied with

7. During your inspection of a multiple dwelling, you find a serious violation of a provision of the health code. The owner claims that at one time the particular provision in question was sensible, but circumstances have changed and the provision should now be repealed. After listening to the owner, you are convinced that the health code should be changed as indicated by the owner. The CORRECT course of action for you to take is to

   A. give the owner a notice of violation and refrain from making any report to your office concerning the provision in question
   B. give the owner a notice of violation and suggest to your superior that the provision be reviewed as to its continued usefulness
   C. refrain from giving the owner a notice of violation since the provision is obviously outdated
   D. refrain from giving the owner a notice of violation until the courts rule on the constitutionality of the provision

8. Assume that you are in the apartment of a tenant who has complained that the landlord is not furnishing sufficient heat. Your thermometer shows that the landlord is furnishing sufficient heat to comply with the pertinent provision of the health code. You so inform the tenant. The tenant excitedly declares that you are using a *fake* thermometer and that you may be on the landlord's *payroll.*
   Under these circumstances, you should state that

   A. if the tenant has any allegation to make concerning your inspection or character, she should contact your department
   B. if these, allegations are repeated, you will refer the tenant for psychiatric examination
   C. the allegations constitute defamation of the character of a public officer, and that you will so notify the police department
   D. you will ask the landlord to speak to the tenant to vouch for your honesty

9. You have been assigned to investigate a complaint with regard to a certain fruit and vegetable stand. Your investigation does not disclose any violation. Upon informing the owner of the stand of your findings, he offers you a bag of fruit as a gift. You decline it. He then offers to sell you the bag of fruit below the retail price - at cost to him. You SHOULD

   A. accept the offer, but refrain from visiting the establishment again
   B. accept the offer, provided you are satisfied that the fruit is being sold to you at cost
   C. decline the offer because it is not possible to calculate the wholesale cost of the fruit
   D. decline the offer since acceptance would be improper

10. The term *FT/SEC* is a unit of

    A. density   B. length   C. mass   D. speed

11. A container can hold 100 pounds of water or 70 pounds of an *unknown* liquid. The specific gravity of the *unknown* liquid is

    A. .30   B. .70   C. 1.0   D. 1.4

12. A *calorie* may be defined as the amount of heat required to raise one

    A. gram of water $1°C$
    B. gram of water $1°F$
    C. pound of water $1°C$
    D. pound of water $1°F$

13. The acidity of vinegar is due to the presence of _____ acid.

    A. acetic   B. carbonic   C. citric   D. hydrochloric

14. The cleansing action of a soap solution is due PRIMARILY to its

    A. acid reaction
    C. neutral reaction
    B. increased surface tension
    D. reduced surface tension

15. Titration refers to a process of

    A. determining the normality of an acid solution
    B. determining the refractive index of a crystal
    C. extracting oxygen from water
    D. measuring the quantity of salt present in a saline solution

16. Which one of the following types of compounds ALWAYS includes carbon, hydrogen, and oxygen?

    A. Carbohydrates
    C. Hydrates
    B. Carbonates
    D. Hydrocarbons

17. The formula for nitric acid is

    A. HNO_2 B. HNO_3 C. NO_2 D. N_2O

18. Gastric juice owes its acidity, *for the most part*, to the presence of _____ acid.

    A. carbonic   B. hydrochloric   C. nitric   D. sulfuric

19. Insulin is a type of

    A. enzyme   B. hormone   C. sugar   D. vitamin

20. The organ which prevents food from entering the windpipe during the act of swallowing is the

    A. epiglottis   B. larynx   C. pharynx   D. trachea

21. Casein is a type of

    A. carbohydrate   B. enzyme   C. fat   D. protein

22. The MAIN function of the kidneys is to remove wastes formed as a result of the oxidation of

    A. carbohydrates   B. fats   C. proteins   D. vitamins

23. Vitamin C is ALSO known as _____ acid.

    A. ascorbic   B. citric   C. glutamic   D. lactic

24. Light passes through the crystalline lens in the eye and focuses on the

    A. cornea   B. iris   C. pupil   D. retina

25. An electron weighs

    A. less than a neutron
    B. more than a neutron
    C. the same as a neutron
    D. the same as a proton

25.____

KEY (CORRECT ANSWERS)

1. C
2. B
3. B
4. C
5. C

6. A
7. B
8. A
9. D
10. D

11. B
12. A
13. A
14. D
15. A

16. A
17. B
18. B
19. B
20. A

21. D
22. C
23. A
24. D
25. A

TEST 2

DIRECTIONS: Each question or incomplete statement is followed by several suggested answers or completions. Select the one that BEST answers the question or completes the statement. *PRINT THE LETTER OF THE CORRECT ANSWER IN THE SPACE AT THE RIGHT.*

1. An electron has a _____ charge. 1._____
   A. negative   B. positive   C. variable   D. zero

2. Isotopes are atoms of elements which have _____ atomic weight(s). 2._____
   A. different atomic numbers and different
   B. different atomic numbers but the same
   C. the same atomic number and the same
   D. the same atomic number but different

3. In the Einstein equation $E = mc^2$, E, m, and c^2 stand for, respectively, 3._____
   A. electrons, molecules, and (centimeters)^2
   B. energy, mass, and (light velocity)^2
   C. energy, mass, and (radioactivity)^2
   D. energy, molecules, and (light velocity)^2

4. Photosynthesis entails the absorption of 4._____
   A. carbon dioxide and oxygen and release of water
   B. carbon dioxide and water and release of oxygen
   C. oxygen and release of carbon dioxide and water
   D. water and release of carbon dioxide and oxygen

5. Ordinary body temperature is approximately 37 on the _____ scale. 5._____
   A. absolute   B. A.P.I.   C. centigrade   D. Fahrenheit

6. Bacteria are _____ chlorphyll. 6._____
   A. multicellular organisms containing
   B. multicellular organisms that do not contain
   C. unicellular organisms containing
   D. unicellular organisms that do not contain

7. The immunity acquired as a result of an injection of tetanus antitoxin is termed _____ immunity. 7._____
   A. artificially acquired active
   B. artificially acquired passive
   C. naturally acquired active
   D. naturally acquired passive

8. A virus is the causative agent of 8._____
   A. diphtheria   B. smallpox   C. syphilis   D. tuberculosis

9. Typhus fever epidemics are caused by

   A. bacteria   B. rickettsiae   C. viruses   D. yeasts

10. The one of the following tests used to determine susceptibility to scarlet fever is the _____ test.

    A. Dick   B. Schick   C. Wasserman   D. Widal

11. Generally, the type of individual immunity to disease which is of the LONGEST duration is brought about by

    A. antibody production stimulated by killed microorganisms
    B. antibody production stimulated by live microorganisms
    C. transfer of antibodies during pregnancy from an immune mother to her unborn child by placental transfer
    D. transfer of antibodies from one adult to another

12. Diabetes is considered to be a(n) _____ disease.

    A. communicable   B. contagious
    C. noninfectious   D. infectious

13. The genus *Mycobacterium* contains a species responsible for

    A. diphtheria   B. gonorrhea
    C. tuberculosis   D. whooping cough

14. The pH of a neutral solution is

    A. 3   B. 5   C. 7   D. 9

15. Of the following, the pair that is NOT a set of equivalents is

    A. .014% .00014   B. 1/5% .002
    C. 1.5% 3/200   D. 115% .115

16. 10^{-2} is equal to

    A. 0.001   B. 0.01   C. 0.1   D. 100.0

17. $10^2 \times 10^3$ is equal to

    A. 10^5 B. 10^6 C. 100^5 D. 100^6

18. The length of two objects are in the ratio of 2:1. If each were 3 inches shorter, the ratio would be 3:1. The longer object is _____ inches.

    A. 8   B. 10   C. 12   D. 14

19. If the weight of water is 62.4 pounds per cubic foot, the weight of the water that fills a rectangular container 6 inches by 6 inches by 1 foot is _____ pounds.

    A. 7.8   B. 15.6   C. 31.2   D. 46.8

20. *Dry-ice* is solid

    A. ammonia   B. carbon dioxide
    C. freon   D. sulfur dioxide

21. The fat content of normal milk is *approximately* 21.____

    A. 1%   B. 4%   C. 10%   D. 16%

22. The one of the following acids GENERALLY responsible for the natural souring of milk is 22.____
    _____ acid.

    A. acetic   B. amino   C. citric   D. lactic

23. From a nutritional standpoint, milk is *deficient* in 23.____

    A. iron
    C. mineral salts
    B. lactose
    D. protein

24. The man who is USUALLY known as the father of chemotherapy is 24.____

    A. Paul Ehrlich
    C. Louis Pasteur
    B. Elie Metchnikoff
    D. John Tyndall

25. The success of this country in building the Panama Canal was due to the successful conquest of yellow fever. 25.____
    The man who directed the study which led to this conquest was

    A. Joseph Lister
    C. Theobold Smith
    B. Walter Reed
    D. William Welch

KEY (CORRECT ANSWERS)

1.	A	11.	B
2.	D	12.	C
3.	B	13.	C
4.	B	14.	C
5.	C	15.	D
6.	D	16.	B
7.	B	17.	A
8.	B	18.	C
9.	B	19.	B
10.	A	20.	B

21. B
22. D
23. A
24. A
25. B

TEST 3

DIRECTIONS: Each question or incomplete statement is followed by several suggested answers or completions. Select the one that BEST answers the question or completes the statement. *PRINT THE LETTER OF THE CORRECT ANSWER IN THE SPACE AT THE RIGHT.*

1. The *Babcock test* is used in milk analysis to determine _____ content. 1._____

    A. butterfat   B. mineral   C. protein   D. vitamin

2. The phosphatase test is used to determine whether milk 2._____

    A. has an objectionable odor
    B. has been adequately pasteurized
    C. has been adulterated
    D. is too alkaline

3. A lactometer is used in milk inspection work to determine the 3._____

    A. acidity of milk
    B. color of milk
    C. percentage of milk solids
    D. specific gravity of milk

4. Milk samples collected at milk plants should be taken from milk cans, the contents of which have 4._____

    A. not been stirred so that sediment does not appear in the sample
    B. not been stirred so that the growth of bacteria which thrive on oxygen is not encouraged
    C. been stirred in order to obtain a representative sample
    D. been stirred so that the percentage of dissolved oxygen meets required standards

5. In the holding process, milk should be pasteurized for at least 30 minutes at a temperature of about 5._____

    A. 115° F   B. 145° F   C. 180° F   D. 212° F

6. Undulant fever, which may be contracted from milk, is caused by an organism known as 6._____

    A. Bacillus subtilis
    B. Brucella abortus
    C. Staphylococcus aureus
    D. Streptococcus pyogenes

7. The presence of *milk stone* or *water stone* in dairy equipment is 7._____

    A. *desirable;* it indicates that dairy equipment is modern
    B. *desirable;* it indicates that milking machines have been sterilized
    C. *undesirable;* it will increase the bacterial count of milk that comes in contact with it
    D. *undesirable;* it will greatly increase the percentage of water in the final milk product

8. The type of dairy barn flooring which is LEAST desirable from a sanitarian's point of view is 8._____

    A. asphalt
    B. compressed cork and asphalt
    C. concrete
    D. wood

9. *Curds* and *whey* are substances encountered in the manufacture of cheese. Of the two substances, usually one 9._____

A. is made into cheese; the other is a by-product used to feed animals
B. is made into cheese; the other is made into butter
C. is made into hard cheese; the other is made into soft cheese
D. refers to bacteria-ripened cheese; the other refers to mold-ripened cheese

10. Botulism food poisoning in the United States is USUALLY caused by 10.____

    A. eating fish caught in polluted waters
    B. failure to wash raw fruit before eating
    C. improper home-canning of fruits and vegetables
    D. tapeworms found in beef or sheep

11. The growth of pathogenic bacteria in preserved dates and figs is *inhibited* because these foods have a high _____ content. 11.____

    A. acid   B. mineral   C. protein   D. sugar

12. In the heating of the following foods during canning, the one which generally requires the LOWEST temperature to prevent microbiological activity is 12.____

    A. fish   B. fruit   C. meat   D. milk

13. Food poisoning cases in the United States are USUALLY characterized by _____ followed by death. 13.____

    A. long periods of illness
    B. long periods of illness rarely
    C. short periods of illness
    D. short periods of illness rarely

14. In the United States, food poisoning due to eating mushrooms is LARGELY attributable to 14.____

    A. failure to cook mushrooms
    B. failure to wash mushrooms
    C. mushrooms which are blue in color
    D. mushrooms which have not been cultivated domestically

15. Of the following, the food whose flavor is NOT improved by the addition of monosodium glutamate is 15.____

    A. cooked vegetables   B. fruit juice
    C. meats   D. seafood and chowders

16. A NEW method of food preservation involves preservation by 16.____

    A. chemicals   B. drying   C. heat   D. radiation

17. In grading meat, the term *finish* refers to 17.____

    A. distribution of fat   B. muscle hardness
    C. presence of tapeworm   D. symmetry of the carcass

18. Of the following preservatives, the one which may NOT be legally used in the preservation of meat is

    A. benzoic acid
    B. salt
    C. sugar
    D. wood smoke

19. A vitamin known to be effective in the prevention of pellagra is

    A. ascorbic acid
    B. niacin
    C. riboflavin
    D. thiamin

20. Eggs are *candled* for the purpose of determining

    A. calcium content
    B. size of the egg
    C. the presence of blood spots
    D. weight of the egg

KEY (CORRECT ANSWERS)

1.	A	11.	D
2.	B	12.	B
3.	D	13.	D
4.	C	14.	D
5.	B	15.	B
6.	B	16.	D
7.	C	17.	A
8.	D	18.	A
9.	A	19.	B
10.	C	20.	C

TEST 4

DIRECTIONS: Each question or incomplete statement is followed by several suggested answers or completions. Select the one that BEST answers the question or completes the statement. *PRINT THE LETTER OF THE CORRECT ANSWER IN THE SPACE AT THE RIGHT.*

1. Foodstuffs such as cereal and flour do not readily spoil as a result of bacterial action because such foodstuffs usually have a low _____ content.

    A. acid B. ash C. sodium D. water

    1.____

2. The presence of bacteria responsible for typhoid fever in a public water supply is PROBABLY traceable to

    A. fecal contamination
    B. excessive water aeration
    C. pus from skin lesions
    D. rotting animal and fish remains

    2.____

3. Objectionable tastes and odors in public water supplies are, in the great majority of cases, due to the presence of

    A. algae and protozoa
    B. animal remains
    C. dissolved oxygen
    D. yeasts and molds

    3.____

4. Atmospheric pressure as indicated by the mercury barometer at sea level is GENERALLY about _____ inches.

    A. 10 B. 15 C. 30 D. 45

    4.____

5. The CHIEF objective of a sewage treatment and disposal system is to

    A. alter sewage by chemical treatment so that it may be sold as commercial fertilizer
    B. convert liquid sludge so that it may be used as drinking water
    C. convert sewage into a form usable as land fill
    D. remove or decompose the organic matter

    5.____

6. *Warfarin* is GENERALLY used in the control of

    A. ants B. flies C. lice D. rats

    6.____

7. The control of the common housefly has been regarded as important because houseflies

    A. are a great nuisance although they are not responsible for the transmission of diseases
    B. may transmit diseases by biting humans
    C. may transmit diseases by contaminating food with pathogenic organisms
    D. may transmit diseases by injecting pathogenic organisms into the bloodstream of animals which are later eaten by man

    7.____

8. The term *Anopheles* refers to a type of

    A. ant B. louse C. mosquito D. termite

    8.____

9. Galvanized iron is made by coating iron with

   A. chromium   B. lead   C. tin   D. zinc

10. The amount of oxygen in the air of a properly ventilated room, expressed as a percentage of volume, is APPROXIMATELY

    A. 5%   B. 10%   C. 15%   D. 20%

11. Field control of hay fever generally depends upon the effective use of a(n)

    A. bacteriostatic agent
    B. fungicide
    C. insect spray
    D. weed killer

12. An orthotolidine testing set may be used to determine the presence of

    A. bacterial growth in milk cans and pails
    B. chlorine in wash and rinse waters
    C. DDT dust in foods such as flour and sugar
    D. organisms responsible for the spoilage of shucked oysters

13. The one of the following which is NOT a characteristic of carbon monoxide gas is that it

    A. causes nausea and vomiting
    B. has a strong irritating odor
    C. interferes with the oxygen-carrying power of the blood
    D. is a common constituent of manufactured gas

Question 14.

DIRECTIONS: Question 14 is based on the following statement.

The rise of science is the most important fact of modern life. No student should be permitted to complete his education without understanding it. From a scientific education, we may expect an understanding of science. From scientific investigation, we may expect scientific knowledge. We are confusing the issue and demanding what we have no right to ask if we seek to learn from science the goals of human life and of organized society.

14. The foregoing statement implies MOST NEARLY that

    A. in a democratic society, the student must determine whether to pursue a scientific education
    B. organized society must learn from science how to meet the needs of modern life
    C. science is of great value in molding the character and values of the student
    D. scientific education is likely to lead the student to acquire an understanding of scientific processes

Questions 15-16.

DIRECTIONS: Questions 15 and 16 are based on the following statement.

Since sewage is a variable mixture of substances from many sources, it is to be expected that its microbial flora will fluctuate both in types and numbers. Raw sewage may contain millions of bacteria per milliliter. Prominent among these are the coliforms. strepto-

cocci, anaerobic spore forming bacilli, the Proteus group, and other types which have their origin in the intestinal tract of man. Sewage is also a potential source of pathogenic intestinal organisms. The poliomyelitis virus has been demonstrated to occur in sewage; other viruses are readily isolated from the same source. Aside from the examination of sewage to demonstrate the presence of some specific microorganism for epidemiological purposes, bacteriological analysis provides little useful information because of the magnitude of variations known to occur with regard to both numbers and kinds.

15. According to the above passage,

    A. all sewage contains pathogenic organisms
    B. bacteriological analysis of sewage is routinely performed in order to determine the presence of coliform organisms
    C. microorganisms found in sewage vary from time to time
    D. poliomyelitis epidemics are due to viruses found in sewage

16. The title which would be MOST suitable for the above passage is:

    A. Disposal of Sewage by Bacteria
    B. Microbes and Sewage Treatment
    C. Microbiological Characteristics of Sewage
    D. Sewage Removal Processes

Questions 17-18.

DIRECTIONS: Questions 17 and 18 are based on the following statement.

Most cities carrying on public health work exercise varying degrees of inspection and control over their milk supplies. In some cases, it consists only of ordinances, with little or no attempt at enforcement. In other cases, good control is obtained through wise ordinances and an efficient inspecting force and laboratory. While inspection alone can do much toward controlling the quality and production of milk, there must also be frequent laboratory tests of the milk.

The bacterial count of the milk indicates the condition of the dairy and the methods of milk handling. The counts, therefore, are a check on the reports of the sanitarian. High bacterial counts of milk from a dairy reported by a sanitarian to be "good" may indicate difficulty not suspected by the sanitarian such as infected udders, inefficient sterilisation of utensils, or poor cooling.

17. According to the above passage, the MOST accurate of the following statements is:

    A. The bacterial count of milk will be low if milk-producing animals are free from disease.
    B. A high bacterial count of milk can be reduced by pasteurization.
    C. The bacterial count of milk can be controlled by the laboratory.
    D. The bacterial count of milk will be low if the conditions of milk production, processing and handling are good.

18. The following conclusion may be drawn from the above passage: 18.____
    A. Large centers of urban population usually exercise complete control over their milk supplies.
    B. Adequate legislation is an important adjunct of a milk supply control program.
    C. Most cities should request the assistance of other cities prior to instituting a milk supply control program.
    D. Wise laws establishing a milk supply control program obviate the need for the enforcement of such laws provided that good laboratory techniques are employed.

Question 19-20.

DIRECTIONS: Questions 19 and 20 are based upon the following excerpt from the health code.

Article 101 Shellfish and Fish
Section 101. 03 Shippers of shellfish; registration
(a) No shellfish shall be shipped into the city unless the shipper of such shellfish is registered with the department.
(b) Application for registration shall be made on a form furnished by the department.
(c) The following shippers shall be eligible to apply for registration :
   1. A shipper of shellfish located in the state but outside the city who holds a shellfish shipper's permit issued by the state conservation department; or
   2. A shipper of shellfish located outside the state, or located in Canada, who holds a shellfish certificate of approval or a permit issued by the state or provincial agency having control of the shellfish industry of his state or province, which certificate of approval or permit appears on the current list of interstate shellfish shipper permits published by the United States Public Health Service.
(d) The commissioner may refuse to accept the registration of any applicant whose past observance of the shellfish regulations is not satisfactory to the commissioner.
(e) No applicant shall ship shellfish into the city unless he has been notified in writing by the department that his application for registration has been approved.
(f) Every registration as a shipper of shellfish, unless sooner revoked, shall terminate on the expiration date of the registrant's state shellfish certificate or permit.

19. The above excerpt from the health code provides that 19.____
    A. permission to register may not be denied to a shellfish shipper meeting the standards of his own jurisdiction
    B. permission to register will not be denied unless the shipper's past observances of shellfish regulations has not been satisfactory to the U.S. Public Health Service
    C. the commissioner may suspend the regulations applicable to registration if requested to do so by the governmental agency having jurisdiction over the shellfish shipper
    D. an applicant for registration as a shellfish shipper may ship shellfish into the city when notified by the department in writing that his application has been approved

20. The above excerpt from the health code provides that 20.____
    A. applications for registration will not be granted to out-of-state shippers of shellfish who have already received permission to sell shellfish from another jurisdiction
    B. shippers of shellfish located outside of the city may not ship shellfish into the city unless the shellfish have passed inspection by the jurisdiction in which the shellfish shipper is located
    C. a shipper of shellfish located in Canada is eligible for registration provided that he holds a shellfish permit issued by the appropriate provincial agency and that such permit appears on the current list of shellfish shipper permits published by the U.S. Public Health Service
    D. a shipper of shellfish located in Canada whose shellfish permit has been revoked by the provincial agency may ship shellfish into the city until such time as he is notified in writing by the department that his shellfish registration has been revoked

KEY (CORRECT ANSWERS)

1.	D	11.	D
2.	A	12.	B
3.	A	13.	B
4.	C	14.	D
5.	D	15.	C
6.	D	16.	C
7.	C	17.	D
8.	C	18.	B
9.	D	19.	D
10.	D	20.	C

EXAMINATION SECTION

TEST 1

DIRECTIONS: Each question or incomplete statement is followed by several suggested answers or completions. Select the one that BEST answers the question or completes the statement. *PRINT THE LETTER OF THE CORRECT ANSWER IN THE SPACE AT THE RIGHT.*

1. What type of lymphocyte is produced in the bone marrow and synthesizes and secretes antibodies in response to the presence of a foreign substance?
   A. T-lymphocyte
   B. B-lymphocyte
   C. Macrophages
   D. Eosinophils

   1.____

2. Which of the following are substances that increase in concentration in various tissues of living organisms as they take in contaminated air, water, or food because the substances are very slowly metabolized or excreted?
   A. Bioaccumulants
   B. Biohazards
   C. Bioequivalents
   D. Biotoxins

   2.____

3. _____ is the use of living organisms to clean up oil spills or remove other pollutants from soil, water, or wastewater, such as using non-harmful insects to remove agricultural pests
   A. Biotechnology
   B. Bioremediation
   C. Nanotechnology
   D. Bioconsolidation

   3.____

4. Which of the following is an epidemiologic method of identifying two groups of individuals, one which has received the exposure of interest and one which has not and following both groups forward for the outcome of interest?
   A. Case study
   B. Longitudinal study
   C. Double-blind study
   D. Cohort study

   4.____

5. Which of the following is the basic unit used to describe the intensity of radioactivity in a sample of material?
   A. Sievert   B. Becquerel   C. Curie   D. Gray

   5.____

6. _____ is the study of human characteristics for the appropriate design of the living and working environment.
   A. Ergonomics   B. Bionomics   C. Autonomics   D. Physiologics

   6.____

7. Which of the following would be considered a heavy metal which can damage living things at low concentrations and tend to accumulate in the food chain?
   A. Aluminum   B. Cadmium   C. Magnesium   D. Technetium

   7.____

8. Beef and pork tapeworms, the largest of the heminths, are a member of which species?
   A. Schistosomes   B. Trematodes   C. Cestodes   D. Nematodes

   8.____

9. _____ occurs when a layer of warm air prevents the rise of cooling air and traps pollutants beneath it and causes an air pollution episodes.
   A. Inversion B. Erosion C. Subversion D. Chemisorption

10. Which of the following is the time from the first exposure of a chemical until the appearance of a toxic effect?
    A. Latency B. Patency C. Half-life D. Reactivity

11. Which of the following is the process by which soluble constituents are dissolved and filtered through the soil by a percolating fluid?
    A. Osmosis B. Absorption C. Leaching D. Emission

12. Which of the following are large, amoeboid and phagocytic cells that are found in many tissues, especially in areas of inflammation?
    A. Monocytes
    B. Lymphocytes
    C. Eosinophils
    D. Macrophages

13. Microscopic fungi that grow as single cells are known as
    A. yeasts B. molds C. helminths D. prions

14. An agent that causes a permanent genetic change in a cell other than that which occurs during normal group is
    A. carcinogen B. antigen C. mutagen D. pathogen

15. What type of radiation does not change the structure of atoms but does heat tissue and may cause harmful biologic effects?
    A. Ionizing
    B. Electromagnetic
    C. Ultraviolet
    D. Gamma

16. Which of the following refers to the length of time a compound stays in the environment once it is introduced?
    A. Half-life
    B. Persistence
    C. Permeability
    D. Sustainability

17. Which of the following refers to a measurable or visible discharge of a contaminant from a given point of origin which can be visible or thermal in water or visible in the air?
    A. Fumes B. Plume C. Leak D. Exhaust

18. In electricity, the quality of having two oppositely charged poles, one positive and one negative, is referred to as which of the following?
    A. Molarity B. Osmolality C. Polarity D. Linearity

19. _____ is defined as the number of existing disease cases in a defined population during a specific time period.
    A. Prevalence B. Incidence C. Morbidity D. Mortality

20. Which of the following refers to one-celled animals that are larger and more complex than bacteria and may cause disease?
    A. Fungi B. Molds C. Protozoa D. Prions

20.____

21. _____ refers to the ongoing, systematic collection, analysis, and interpretation of health data.
    A. Persistence
    B. Surveillance
    C. Remittance
    D. Adherence

21.____

22. Which of the following is a systematic collection of information on persons exposed to a specific substance or having specific diseases?
    A. Census B. Registry C. Database D. Population

22.____

23. The process of evaluating and selecting alternative regulatory and non-regulatory responses to risk is known as risk
    A. assessment
    B. communication
    C. management
    D. reduction

23.____

24. Which of the following occurs during or after treatment of a primary infection because the normal bacterial flora is destroyed, therefore allowing yeast to flourish?
    A. Secondary infection
    B. Nosocomial infection
    C. Latent infection
    D. Chronic infection

24.____

25. A liquid capable of dissolving or dispersing another substance is known as a
    A. solvent B. substrate C. solution D. solute

25.____

KEY (CORRECT ANSWERS)

1.	B	11.	C
2.	A	12.	D
3.	B	13.	A
4.	D	14.	C
5.	C	15.	B
6.	A	16.	B
7.	B	17.	B
8.	C	18.	C
9.	A	19.	A
10.	A	20.	C

21. B
22. B
23. C
24. A
25. A

TEST 2

DIRECTIONS: Each question or incomplete statement is followed by several suggested answers or completions. Select the one that BEST answers the question or completes the statement. *PRINT THE LETTER OF THE CORRECT ANSWER IN THE SPACE AT THE RIGHT.*

1. In order to protect both human health and welfare, the USEPA has established standards for certain pollutants found in indoor air known as criteria air pollutants. Which of the following represent criteria air pollutants? Particulate matter, _____, sulfur oxides, nitrogen oxides, and lead.
   A. ground-level ozone, carbon monoxide
   B. stratospheric ozone, carbon monoxide
   C. ground-level ozone, carbon dioxide
   D. stratospheric ozone, carbon dioxide

   1._____

2. The treatment of drinking water involves all of the following EXCEPT
   A. removal of organic materials
   B. killing of microorganisms
   C. removal of all dissolved chemicals
   D. removal of large inorganic particles

   2._____

3. Which of the following is the MOST favored method for waste management?
   A. Source reduction   B. Offsite composting
   C. Landfilling   D. Waste combustion

   3._____

4. What piece of legislation provided for the "Superfund"?
   A. Hazardous and Solid Waste Amendment Act of 1984
   B. Toxic Substances Control Act of 1976
   C. Resource Conservation and Recovery Act of 1976
   D. Comprehensive Environmental Response, Compensation, and Liability Act of 1980

   4._____

5. Which of the following is an acceptable definition for risk?
   A. The capacity of a substance to causes an adverse effect in a specific organ or system
   B. The probability that a hazard will occur under specific exposure conditions
   C. The weighing of policy alternatives and selection of the most appropriate regulatory actions
   D. A measure of the intensity, frequency, and duration of human exposure to agents

   5._____

6. Which of the following is the PRIMARY risk factor for food-borne illness?
   A. Contamination
   B. Improper holding time and temperature
   C. Inadequate preparation
   D. Food from unsafe sources

   6._____

7. _____ immunity is defined as the resistance of a population to an infectious disease.
   A. Herd   B. Natural   C. Artificial   D. Acquired

8. An epidemic is defined as a
   A. disease that is controlled in the world
   B. disease that is regionally uncontrolled
   C. newly discovered disease
   D. contagious, non-fatal disease rapidly spreading throughout the world

9. Which of the following is defined as "the number of lives lost due to a disease?
   A. Risk ratio   B. Prevalence   C. Morbidity   D. Mortality

10. Which of the following groups were once considered to be at a high risk of acquiring HIV/AIDS but is no longer considered to be?
    A. IV drug users
    B. Homosexuals
    C. Hemophiliacs
    D. Individuals with chronic illness

11. What type of radiation can be stopped by a sheet of paper and cannot penetrate human skin but can cause highly concentrated local damage if inhaled or ingested?
    A. Alpha   B. Beta   C. Gamma   D. Positron

12. _____ is defined as the use of enzymes in chemical synthesis to produce chemical compounds of a desired stereochemistry.
    A. Bioaccumulation
    B. Bioactivation
    C. Biotechnology
    D. Biotransformation

13. Which of the following is defined as an agent that results in an alteration in the fetus leading to a birth defect?
    A. Antigen   B. Pathogen   C. Teratogen   D. Carcinogen

14. A chemical believed to initiate carcinogenicity or mutagenicity is referred to as a
    A. catalyst   B. promoter   C. antagonist   D. agonist

15. The surface on which an organism grows or to which it is attached is referred to as the
    A. analyte   B. substrate   C. solvent   D. host

16. Which of the following refers to the scientific discipline involving the study of the actual or potential danger presented by the harmful effects of substances on living organisms and ecosystems?
    A. Microbiology
    B. Epidemiology
    C. Toxicology
    D. Virology

17. Which of the following is the process in which normal cells are changed so that they are able to form tumors?
    A. Carcinogenesis
    B. Tumor initiation
    C. Tumor progression
    D. Tumor promotion

    17.____

18. A substance that is either present in an environment where it does not belong or is present at levels that might cause harmful health effects is known as a(n)
    A. contaminant
    B. toxicant
    C. vector
    D. antagonist

    18.____

19. Oxidation, reduction, and hydrolysis occurs in which phase of biotransformation?
    A. I
    B. II
    C. III
    D. IV

    19.____

20. The lethal dose that kills 50% of the test animals (LD50) and the No Observed Adverse Health Effect Level (NOAEL) are examples of _____ used to evaluate health effects in humans.
    A. Regulations
    B. Benchmarks
    C. Policies
    D. Procedures

    20.____

21. A _____ can be any measurement that characterizes exposure, susceptibility, or response in a biological system.
    A. biomarker
    B. bioburden
    C. body burden
    D. risk assessment

    21.____

22. A(n) _____ is an attempt to quantitatively determine the relationship between exposure to a toxicant and disease.
    A. dose-response evaluation
    B. exposure assessment
    C. risk assessment
    D. feasibility study

    22.____

23. A(n) _____ involves the development of a quantitative estimate of the magnitude, duration, frequency, and timing of an exposure to the toxicant of concern.
    A. dose-response evaluation
    B. exposure assessment
    C. risk assessment
    D. feasibility study

    23.____

24. Which of the following is a common by-product of water disinfection?
    A. Trihalomethanes
    B. Organochlorines
    C. Pyrethroids
    D. Carbamates

    24.____

25. Municipal effluent is disinfected prior to discharge to reduce the pathogen load primarily by which process?
    A. Fluoridation
    B. Chlorination
    C. Hydrolysis
    D. Oxidation

    25.____

KEY (CORRECT ANSWERS)

1. A
2. C
3. A
4. D
5. B

6. B
7. A
8. B
9. D
10. C

11. A
12. D
13. C
14. B
15. B

16. C
17. B
18. A
19. A
20. B

21. A
22. A
23. B
24. A
25. B

TEST 3

DIRECTIONS: Each question or incomplete statement is followed by several suggested answers or completions. Select the one that BEST answers the question or completes the statement. *PRINT THE LETTER OF THE CORRECT ANSWER IN THE SPACE AT THE RIGHT.*

1. Which of the following is a historic compound associated with occupational asthma?
   A. Tri-nitrotoluene
   B. Tri-hydroxybenzene
   C. Myeloperoxidase
   D. Toluene di-isocyanate

2. Which is primary risk management focused on?
   A. Prevention   B. Intervention   C. Assessment   D. Management

3. Hazard Analysis Critical Control Point (HAACP) is a food safety system employed to serve what purpose?
   A. Detect bacterial contamination in food after it happens
   B. Identify and control problems that may cause foodborne illness before they happen
   C. Isolate and identify bacterial pathogens from a foodborne illness outbreak
   D. Set temperature limits for foods containing eggs

4. Which of the following is the MOST commonly occurring mosquito-borne disease in the United States?
   A. West Nile Virus Neuroinvasive Disease
   B. Malaria
   C. Dengue fever
   D. Yellow fever

5. Which of the following is the "Greenhouse Gas" of primary concern in global warming?
   A. Chlorofluorocarbons
   B. Carbon monoxide
   C. Sulfur dioxide
   D. Carbon dioxide

6. A(n) _____ is defined as the habitual presence of disease within a given geographic area.
   A. epidemic   B. endemic   C. pandemic   D. outbreak

7. Which of the following measures the severity of disease and is the ratio of deaths within a designated population of people with a particular condition over a certain period of time?
   A. Case fatality rate
   B. Crude mortality rate
   C. Cause-specific mortality rate
   D. Age-specific mortality rate

8. Which of the following is an example of analytic epidemiology?
   A. Comparison of people who develop a condition with people who do not
   B. Routine analysis of vital statistics, communicable disease reports, and notifiable events
   C. Comparing information to look for differences and patterns
   D. Specialized surveys to establish prevalence of a medical condition

   8.____

9. Which of the following is an example of descriptive epidemiology?
   A. A comparison of people who develop a condition with people who do not
   B. A comparison of people with and without a characteristic in relation to a health related event
   C. A comparison of a subsequent experience exhibited by people to whom a treatment of preventive intervention has been given to that of people not provided that intervention
   D. Periodic surveys of health status, knowledge, belief, attitudes, practices, behavior, environmental exposures, and health care encounters

   9.____

10. _____ of a study is defined as the probability that a study will find a statistically significant difference when a difference of a given magnitude truly exists.
    A. Bias   B. Power   C. Significance   D. Validity

    10.____

11. _____ is a systematic error due to incorrect definition, measurement, or classification of variables of interest which results in the misclassification of the study of participants with respect to disease or exposure status.
    A. Selection bias   B. Information bias
    C. Differential misclassification   D. Non-differential misclassification

    11.____

12. Which of the following occurs when the probability of misclassification of exposure is different in diseased and non-diseased persons?
    A. Selection bias   B. Information bias
    C. Differential misclassification   D. Non-differential misclassification

    12.____

13. _____ is defined as the process of killing and removing all forms of life including bacteria and their spores, fungi, and viruses.
    A. Disinfection   B. Decontamination
    C. Sterilization   D. Ionization

    13.____

14. What organism is transmitted to humans due to unpasteurized milk?
    A. Bovine tuberculosis   B. Streptococcus thermophiles
    C. Lactobacillus bugaricus   D. Penicillium roquefortii

    14.____

15. Which of the following grows on peanuts and other grains that produces the potent carcinogen aflatoxin?
    A. Streptococcus thermophiles B. Aspergillus flavus
    C. Aspergillus oryzae   D. Saccharomyces cerevisiae

    15.____

16. _____ is an enterotoxin that is a common cause of food poisoning which is found in cream-filled pastries, ham and pork sausage and is often associated with inadequate refrigeration and workers touching the food.
    A. Clostridium perfringens
    B. Staphylococcus aureus
    C. Bacillus cereus
    D. Clostridium botulinum

17. Which of the following is the one organism that causes food poisoning by releasing a neurotoxin rather than an enterotoxin?
    A. Clostridium perfringens
    B. Staphylococcus aureus
    C. Bacillus cereus
    D. Clostridium botulinum

18. _____ is defined as the capability of a microorganism to cause disease.
    A. Persistence
    B. Virulence
    C. Resonance
    D. Purulence

19. Which organism, which tends to be found in cheese due to lack of pasteurization, is particularly harmful to pregnant females because it produces a toxin that is able to cross the placenta?
    A. Listeria monocytogenes
    B. Streptococcus pyrogenes
    C. Neisseria meningitis
    D. Haemophilus influenzae

20. Which of the following is the BEST process if you are attempting to eliminate cryptosporidium, giardia, or amoebic cysts?
    A. Ionization
    B. Fluoridation
    C. Chlorination
    D. Ozonation

21. _____ is defined as the reduction in the number of organisms to a level in which they no longer pose danger.
    A. Disinfection
    B. Sterilization
    C. Pasteurization
    D. Decontamination

22. A _____ is defined as a particle that is transferred from an infected organism to an uninfected organism causing infection.
    A. Pathogen
    B. Antigen
    C. Contagion
    D. Carcinogen

23. _____ is controlled biological decomposition of organic matter such as food and yard wastes into a soil-like material.
    A. Recycling
    B. Incinerating
    C. Composting
    D. Reusing

24. Infants younger than the age of 4 who are fed formula reconstituted with well water are at HIGHEST risk of blue baby syndrome due to excessive levels of
    A. carbon monoxide
    B. mercury
    C. nitrates
    D. sulfur dioxide

25. A significant percentage of a population is complaining of nausea, vomiting, and a sensation of pins and needles in the hands and feet. Which metal contaminant could cause these symptoms?
    A. Arsenic
    B. Benzene
    C. Cadmium
    D. Zinc

KEY (CORRECT ANSWERS)

1. D
2. A
3. B
4. A
5. D

6. B
7. A
8. A
9. D
10. B

11. B
12. C
13. C
14. A
15. B

16. B
17. D
18. B
19. A
20. D

21. A
22. C
23. C
24. C
25. A

TEST 4

DIRECTIONS: Each question or incomplete statement is followed by several suggested answers or completions. Select the one that BEST answers the question or completes the statement. *PRINT THE LETTER OF THE CORRECT ANSWER IN THE SPACE AT THE RIGHT.*

1. During an inspection of a food facility, you notice mouse droppings in a remote area of the building. What solution would you use to clean this contamination?
    A. 3% sodium chloride
    B. 10% bleach
    C. 5% hydrogen peroxide
    D. 20% rubbing alcohol

    1.____

2. During a routine inspection of a restaurant, everything appears to be in order until you turn the tap on the hand sink and realize there is no water. What is the FIRST thing you should do in this situation?
    A. Check for another water supply.
    B. Determine why water is not available at that sink.
    C. Write up an infraction and tell the operator to repair the water supply.
    D. Close the premises immediately.

    2.____

3. If you are asked to perform a routine inspection of a barbershop, with what type of illnesses should you be MOST concerned?
    A. Water-borne
    B. Airborne
    C. Blood-borne
    D. Vector-borne

    3.____

4. Upon inspection of a restaurant, you notice a raw chicken breast and a large pot of cooked rice sitting on the counter. What would be your FIRST action?
    A. Take the internal temperature of the food.
    B. Discuss cooking and cooling procedures with the owner.
    C. Discuss safe temperatures and shallow pans.
    D. Immediately dispose of the food.

    4.____

5. During a routine inspection, you uncover botulism contamination. Which solution would you use to inactivate botulism?
    A. 3% sodium chloride
    B. 10% bleach
    C. 5% hydrogen peroxide
    D. 0.1% sodium hypochlorite

    5.____

6. If you receive a call from a physician regarding a confirmed case of hepatitis A in a person who is a food handler, what should be done within two weeks of exposure?
    A. A complete inspection of the facility in which the food handler works
    B. The restaurant be closed immediately pending an investigation
    C. Immunoglobulin should be administered to all other food handlers in the facility
    D. Begin surveillance measures regarding an outbreak of hepatitis A

    6.____

7. If you instruct a municipal water treatment facility to add fluoride into their water, what is the MOST important factor when calculating the dose?
    A. Volume of water
    B. Concentration of fluoride
    C. Temperature of the water
    D. Turbidity of the water

8. If you were to compare prostate screening rates between Caucasian and African-American men and 60% of Caucasian men and 40% of African-American men report undergoing appropriate screening, what test would be MOST appropriate to analyze this data?
    A. Spearman correlation test
    B. Two-sample t-test
    C. Pearson chi-square test
    D. Paired t-test

9. If a public health issue arises for which there is no evidence base to suggest a response strategy, what is the MOST appropriate action?
    A. Implement several strategies to see which is most effective
    B. Issue is able to be dismissed
    C. Do nothing until this issue arises again
    D. Actively collect additional data and perform community-based research

10. If you are asked to calculate the infant mortality rate of several states, which method would be MOST appropriate to use to adjust for racial differences in infant mortality rates among the states?
    A. Linear regression
    B. Logistic regression
    C. Direct standardization
    d. Paired t-test

11. If you are dispatched to a natural disaster, which of the following would be the SAFEST source of drinking water?
    A. Toilet tank
    B. Open cistern
    C. Water heater
    D. Swimming pool

12. You are asked to inspect a public swimming pool in which the water has turned a reddish-brown color. Which of the following is the MOST likely contaminant?
    A. Iron
    B. Manganese
    C. Copper
    D. Algae

13. Several people in a community are experiencing skin rashes following soaking in a public whirlpool. What microorganism is commonly associated with skin rashes?
    A. Staphylococcus aureus
    B. Pseudomonas aeruginosa
    C. Escherichia coli
    D. Clostridium perfringens

14. Several people who attended the same church banquet began experiencing vertigo, headache, diplopia, and some nerve paralysis. Which of the following would you suspect to be the cause?
    A. Vibrio parahaemolyticus
    B. Staphylococcus aureus
    C. Clostridium botulinum
    D. Shigella

15. If you obtain a positive result from a blue ring milk test, this result indicates the presence of
    A. brucellosis
    B. shigellosis
    C. salmonellosis
    D. ornithosis

16. You are assigned to monitor milk-borne diseases in the community. All of the following diseases fall under this category EXCEPT
    A. tuberculosis
    B. Escherichia coli
    C. brucellosis
    D. cryptosporidiosis

17. Establishing funding for rural ambulance services, acute trauma centers at hospitals, and brain injury rehabilitation centers are examples of what type of preventative effort?
    A. Primary preventative effort
    B. Secondary preventative effort
    C. Tertiary preventative effort
    D. Occupational prevention

18. Which type of study is considered to have the HIGHEST level of statistical power and is listed at the top of the evidence pyramid?
    A. Cohort study
    B. Case study
    C. Mixed-methods analysis
    D. Meta-analysis

19. If you perform a study and the ρ-value is determined to be 0.9, what information can you gather from this ρ-value?
    A. The data is significant as it is very close to the null value of 1.
    B. Statisticians agree that 90% is a statistically significant variance from the normal.
    C. Statisticians only accept ρ-values that are 0.05 or less and, therefore, this data is not reliable.
    D. The null value of studies is generally 0 and the data shows definite correlation.

20. _____ is defined as the aggregation of two or more diseases in a population in which there is some level of positive biological interaction that exacerbates the negative health effect of any or all of the diseases. For example, substance abuse, violence, and AIDS (SAVA), which are three conditions that disproportionately affect those living in poverty in U.S. cities.
    A. Epidemic
    B. Endemic
    C. Pandemic
    D. Syndemic

21. Which study design is generally considered to be the "Gold Standard", but is limited in that it is the best suited for studying only one variable and is very expensive to complete?
    A. Meta-analysis
    B. Interventional studies
    C. Cohort studies
    D. Case control studies

22. If you are performing a study investigating the possible relationship of an exposure to a disease and the relative risk is calculate to be 0.48, what information can you deduce from this statistic?
    A. The exposure is definitely related to the disease being studied.
    B. The exposure shows no relationship to the disease as 0.5 is the null value.
    C. There appears to be a protective or negative association between exposure and risk.
    D. The values are insignificant because they are not at the 0.05 level or below.

22.____

23. The installation of stop signs at intersections is an example of what type of prevention?
    A. Primary   B. Secondary   C. Tertiary   D. Community

23.____

24. Which theory of patient behavior features perceived susceptibility, perceived severity, perceived benefits, and perceived barriers?
    A. The Ecological Model   B. The Trans-theoretical Model
    C. The Health Belief Model   D. The Community Outreach Model

24.____

25. If you are analyzing research that describes risk differences between two groups, when can you infer that there is no significant difference between the two groups?
    When the number is
    A. equal to 0   B. equal to 1
    C. greater than 1   D. less than 1

25.____

KEY (CORRECT ANSWERS)

1.	B	11.	C
2.	A	12.	A
3.	C	13.	B
4.	A	14.	C
5.	D	15.	A
6.	C	16.	D
7.	C	17.	C
8.	C	18.	D
9.	D	19.	C
10.	C	20.	D

21.	B
22.	C
23.	A
24.	C
25.	A

EXAMINATION SECTION
TEST 1

DIRECTIONS: Each question or incomplete statement is followed by several suggested answers or completions. Select the one that BEST answers the question or completes the statement. *PRINT THE LETTER OF THE CORRECT ANSWER IN THE SPACE AT THE RIGHT.*

1. The laboratory test that is MOST accurate in determining the efficiency of pasteurization is

   A. phosphorylase
   B. the standard plate test
   C. the coliform count
   D. the CF test

   1.____

2. You ate some canned ham with NO effect. You reheated the remaining ham the following evening. 6-8 hours later you got nausia and diarrhea as well as other symptoms. This is MOST likely _____ food poisoning.

   A. staphylococcus
   C. salmonella
   B. streptococcus
   D. klebsiella

   2.____

3. To dispose of a cow carcass with eosinophilic myositis you MUST

   A. condemn the entire carcass
   B. pass it for cooking
   C. remove lesions and pass the remainder of the carcass unrestricted
   D. pass the head and condemn the rest

   3.____

4. Pasteurization of milk

   A. kills all bacteria
   B. kills all pathogenic bacteria
   C. reduces the number of all bacteria
   D. reduces the number of pathogenic bacteria to a safer level

   4.____

5. If a person is bitten by a dog it is BEST to

   A. kill the dog and examine the brain for evidence of rabies
   B. keep the dog under observation for rabies
   C. examine the saliva of the dog for evidence of rabies
   D. take NO precautions

   5.____

6. The usual pressure of steam sterilization is _____ pounds.

   A. 2.75   B. 1   C. 15   D. 7.2

   6.____

7. Serum is BEST sterilized

   A. in an autoclave
   B. flowing stream
   C. by filtration
   D. by heating to an appropriate temperature

   7.____

8. The coliform count in pasteurized milk *usually* indicates

   A. contamination after pasteurization
   B. contamination prior to pasteurization
   C. poor pasteurization
   D. none of the above

9. A container of pasteurized milk was found positive to the coliform test. The MOST likely cause is

   A. a contaminated water supply
   B. a broken bathroom steel
   C. improper time or temperature of pasteurization
   D. post-pasteurization contamination

10. Boiling a can of vegetables in anticipation of eliminating the possibility of botulism

    A. will prolong the shelf-life
    B. kills the organism
    C. alters the harmful toxin to a harmless toxin
    D. kills the toxin

11. The proper way to send porcine brain to the diagnostic lab for tests is

    A. refrigerated
    B. frozen
    C. in 10% formalin
    D. in saline suspension

12. An animal that has been designated a reactor to the tuberculin test

    A. may be retested in 60 days by the accredited veterinarian
    B. may be isolated and retested by a regularly employed state or federal veterinarian
    C. MUST be tagged and branded and promptly removed from the herd
    D. should be kept until the calf is weaned

13. For effective disinfection, a 1% solution of sodium orthopenylphena should be applied at

    A. a temperature of 60 degrees F or *higher* and preceded by cleaning with lye
    B. a temperature at or *below* 60 degrees F preceded by cleaning with *highly* alkaline solutions
    C. a temperature at or *above* 60 degrees F NOT preceded by cleaning with *highly* alkaline solutions
    D. 120 degrees F and mixed with sodium hydroxide solution

14. Three head of purebred dairy heifers originating on a farm near St. Louis, Missouri are to be exported to Haiti.
    Which of the following statements is true?

    A. These animals may be exported to Haiti by air from St. Louis after proper veterinary inspection and issuance and endorsement of proper health certificates
    B. These animals must be moved from the premises of origin in cleaned and disinfected conveyances if such conveyances previously were used to haul livestock
    C. The conveyances need not be cleaned and disinfected when moved from the premises of origin under government seal provided vehicle is leak-proof
    D. All of the above statements are correct

15. Tissues submitted to a laboratory for histopathological examination should be

   A. preserved by refrigeration
   B. placed in sterile saline solution to keep the tissue from drying
   C. fixed in a preservative with 10 times as much fixing fluid as tissue
   D. shipped in buffered glycerine

15.____

16. Vesicular conditions and other animal diseases NOT readily recognized or easily diagnosed should be reported to state and federal livestock sanitary officials promptly and without fail because

   A. increased world traffic by air and surface routes is multiplying the danger of foreign animal diseases entering the country
   B. of international tension, there is danger that animal diseases will be used as a method of biological warfare
   C. it is necessary to test the efficiency of state-federal emergency disease eradication organizations
   D. indemnity money may be available

16.____

17. When scrapie is suspected, the MOST important procedure to follow is to

   A. treat the sheep symptomatically
   B. recommend immediate slaughter of infected animals
   C. report it immediately to state or federal livestock sanitary officials
   D. cull and ship for slaughter

17.____

18. Beef products may be imported into the U.S. from a country infested with foot and mouth disease without restriction if

   A. the animals from which the product is derived are vaccinated
   B. effective and acceptable processing has been done in the country of origin
   C. the shipment is moved *directly* to the port of entry
   D. the product is in tight containers

18.____

19. Anaplasmosis, an infectious and transmissible disease of cattle characterized by destruction of the erythrocytes

   A. is an example of another livestock disease that has been eradicated from the United States by the efforts of accredited veterinarians and cooperating state and federal regulatory officials
   B. has been reported in a majority of the states and movement of infected animals is subject to state and federal restrictions
   C. has shown no response to broad-spectrum antibiotic treatment
   D. has been kept out of the United States by prompt application of control measures in the Hawaiian Islands in 1955

19.____

20. How may animals be certified by an accredited veterinarian for movement from an area of seasonal screwworm infestation into a free area?

   A. By a special screwworm health certificate
   B. On a regular health certificate, following examinations, with the certification that the animals are free of screwworms

20.____

C. Without a health certificate, but with a visual inspection 36 hours prior to movement
D. There are NO specific requirements

21. For effective disinfection, a 1% solution of sodium orthophenylphenate should be applied at

    A. a temperature at or *above* 60° F not preceded by cleaning with highly alkaline solutions
    B. a temperature at or *below* 60° F preceded by cleaning with highly alkaline solutions
    C. a temperature of 60° F or *above* and preceded by cleaning with lye
    D. 120° F and mixed with sodium hydroxide solution

22. Disinfection

    A. is the mechanical destruction of pathogenic organisms
    B. MUST be followed by effective cleaning
    C. is the chemical destruction of pathogenic organisms through contact
    D. is achieved in the presence of organic matter

23. Canned ham says, *perishable, keep refrigerated*. This means that

    A. its all right to leave the ham out as long as it does not get warmer than room temperature
    B. the ham has been kept at a plant for 10 days to check its stability
    C. the ham is pasteurized
    D. you must thoroughly cook the meat to avoid a chance of trichina infection

24. The time-temperature relationship of pasteurization is MOST concerned with

    A. killing milk borne pathogens
    B. delaying spoilage
    C. killing all pathogens
    D. removing reductase

25. The absence of phosphatase in milk indicates

    A. improper sterilization
    B. the milk has not been pasteurized
    C. the milk has been pasteurized
    D. the presense of staphlococcus in mastitic milk

KEY (CORRECT ANSWERS)

1. A
2. A
3. C
4. B
5. B

6. C
7. C
8. A
9. D
10. C

11. C
12. C
13. C
14. B
15. C

16. A
17. C
18. B
19. B
20. B

21. A
22. C
23. A
24. A
25. C

TEST 2

DIRECTIONS: Each question or incomplete statement is followed by several suggested answers or completions. Select the one that BEST answers the question or completes the statement. *PRINT THE LETTER OF THE CORRECT ANSWER IN THE SPACE AT THE RIGHT.*

1. The principal method employed by MOST meat inspection systems in the U.S. to reduce human trichinosis is to

   A. educate the public to avoid eating raw or semicooked pork products
   B. require the killing of trichina larvae in pork products customarily eaten without further cooking
   C. require the cooking of all garbage fed to swine
   D. require the freezing of all raw pork used in sausage
   E. detect pork carcasses with trichina larvae by microscopic examination of musculature

1.___

2. The modern trend in the milk industry to keep the milk longer under refrigeration on the farm and in the plant and to *decrease* the number of deliveries to the consumers has been *increased* by the importance of _____ bacteria.

   A. thermophilic
   B. thermodermic
   C. pathogenic
   D. coliform
   E. psychrophilic

2.___

3. Proper pasteurization of milk requires 161° at _____ seconds.

   A. 5   B. 10   C. 12   D. 15   E. 25

3.___

4. In a high temperature short-time pasteurizer in which ALL milk and heating and cooling liquids are closed to the atmosphere, the milk pump may be located between the

   A. raw milk side of the regenerator and the heater
   B. heater and the holder
   C. holder and the hot milk side of the regenerator
   D. regenerator and the cooler
   E. cooler and the bottler

4.___

5. Many diseases pass meat inspection because there are NO visible lesions, although they should be condemned.
   The condition that is NOT like this is

   A. leukemia (lymphosarcoma)
   B. tetanus
   C. milk fever
   D. railroad sickness
   E. rabies

5.___

6. Before fresh pork can leave an inspected establishment, it

   A. need not be treated in any way to kill trichina
   B. must be heated to an internal temp. of 137°
   C. must be heated to an internal temp of 145°

6.___

D. can be used only for processed products
E. must bear recommended cooking instructions

7. The minimum treatment with steam under pressure by which large bundles of surgical equipment can be completely sterilized is _____ minutes.

   A. 212° F for 15
   B. 212° F for 30
   C. 225° F for 30
   D. 250° F for 15
   E. 250° F for 30

8. The organism that is MOST likely to be found in pasteurized milk is

   A. brucella
   B. lactobacillus dermaphilus
   C. staphlococcus
   D. strep. lactus
   E. anthrax

9. Certified milk must NOT contain a bacterial count of MORE than

   A. 1,000
   B. 10,000
   C. 20,000
   D. 50,000
   E. 5,000,000

10. To protect yourself from the destructive effects of the x-ray during fluoroscopy you should

    A. wear a lead apron and lead gloves
    B. stand behind the control panel
    C. wear a film badge that will warn you against excess radiation
    D. wear fluoroscopic goggles
    E. wear heavy clothing

11. A vat of milk is held at 72°F for several hours prior to pasteurization and being made into cheese.
    An outbreak of food poisoning in persons consuming the cheese is probably due to

    A. E. coli
    B. strep. ag.
    C. aerobacter
    D. salmonella spp.
    E. staph aureus

12. Milk becomes rancid as a result of

    A. an *increase* in sediment
    B. lipase activity
    C. slow cooling
    D. an *increase* in leukocyte content
    E. coliform contamination

13. The U.S. Public Health service milk ordinance and code requires that Grade A pasteurized milk MUST have a bacteria count per ml of NOT more than

    A. 30,000 by *direct* microscopic count and a coliform count of 0
    B. 30,000 by *direct* microscopic count and a coliform count of not more than 10
    C. 20,000 by *plate* count and a coliform count of not more than 10
    D. 50,000 by *plate* count and a coliform count of not more than 10
    E. 50,000 by *direct* microscopic count and a coliform count of not more than 10

14. After a nuclear attack, poultry may represent one of the MOST dependable sources of fresh food of animal origin because

    A. they do not as a rule eat the vegetation likely to be exposed to fallout
    B. they present a small surface for the absorption of fallout
    C. they are the most radioresistant species of domesticated animals
    D. their roosting habits protect them against fallout
    E. their feathers protect them against contamination

15. A smoked ham is prepared and a portion of it consumed without ill effects. The next day the leftover part is heated to a boiling temperature for a few minutes and then served. The persons who eat the ham become ill 6 to 8 hours later. Their symptoms are nausea, vomiting, diarrhea, abdominal cramps, headache, and sweating. They recover within 25 hours.
    This type of food poisoning is MOST likely

    A. streptococcal
    B. ptomaine
    C. staphlococcal
    D. chemical
    E. salmonella

16. A process along with sanitation that has helped to prevent bone sour in cured hams is

    A. freezing before curing
    B. dry curing
    C. vein pumping
    D. soaking hams
    E. smoking hams

17. The *minimum* temperature at which meat affected with trichinosis must be heated is _____ degress F.

    A. 60-70
    B. 70-80
    C. 80-90
    D. 90-100
    E. *greater* than 137

18. An enzyme that is a normal constituent of milk and is used in a laboratory test to check the efficiency of pasteurization is

    A. phosphatase
    B. peroxidase
    C. reductase
    D. calactase
    E. lipase

19. Some conditions require condemnation of the whole carcass yet on autopsy, very few or no lesions are noted.
    One such condition is

    A. rabies
    B. hog cholera
    C. milk fever
    D. tetanus
    E. TB

20. On post mortem, you are presented with a porcine carcass that has diamond shaped lesions mostly on the back. These lesions are about one inch long and 1/4 inch in diameter. Careful examination reveals no other lesions. The MOST recent USDA regulations recommend to

    A. condemn the whole carcass
    B. condemn the skin and pass the rest of the carcass
    C. condemn the skin and pass the carcass for cooking
    D. pass the whole carcass
    E. condemn the head and pass the rest

KEY (CORRECT ANSWERS)

1.	B	11.	E
2.	E	12.	B
3.	D	13.	C
4.	A	14.	C
5.	A	15.	C
6.	E	16.	A
7.	E	17.	E
8.	B	18.	A
9.	A	19.	C
10.	A	20.	B

MICROBIOLOGY

EXAMINATION SECTION
TEST 1

DIRECTIONS: Each question or incomplete statement is followed by several suggested answers or completions. Select the one that BEST answers the question or completes the statement. PRINT THE LETTER OF THE CORRECT ANSWER IN THE SPACE AT THE RIGHT.

1. As a result of using Grain's method for differential staining, the gram-negative organisms become 1.____

   A. blue B. pink C. brown D. colorless

2. The medium used in antibiotic sensitivity testing by the Kirby-Bauer method is 2.____

   A. Brain Heart Infusion agar
   B. Trypticase Soy agar
   C. Mueller-Hinton agar
   D. Thioglycollate agar

3. A yeast-like organism that is easily identified by its large capsule is 3.____

   A. Histoplasma capsulatum
   B. Cryptococcus neoformans
   C. Sporotrichum schenckii
   D. Blastomyces dermatitidis

4. The MOST effective method for sterilization of bacteriological media for laboratory use is to 4.____

   A. heat the media in the hot air oven at 160°C for 30 minutes
   B. boil the media for 30 minutes
   C. autoclave the media at 125°C for 5 minutes
   D. autoclave the media at 121°C for 15 minutes

5. Bacteria that cannot tolerate oxygen are called 5.____

   A. aerobes B. anaerobes C. mesotrophs D. thermophiles

6. The MOST definitive test for the identification of pathogenic Staphylococci involves 6.____

   A. the hemolysis of erythrocytes
   B. mannitol fermentation
   C. the production of coagulase
   D. a tellurite reduction

7. A test for differentiating Salmonella from Proteus is the 7.____

   A. motility test
   B. urease test
   C. colloidal gold test
   D. Hemincrystal test

8. The stain used to indicate the presence of acid-fast bacteria is 8.____

   A. Gram's stain
   B. Giemsa stain
   C. Ziehl-Neelsen stain
   D. Ponder's stain

9. In the classic IMViC reaction, E. coli has the following reaction: 9.____

   A. ++-- B. --++ C. +-+- D. -+-+

10. A test used to differentiate Pneumococcus from Streptococcus viridans is the

    A. coagulase test
    B. oxidase test
    C. catalase test
    D. bile solubility test

11. Staphylococci can be differentiated from Streptococci by means of the

    A. oxidase test
    B. catalase test
    C. coagulase test
    D. bile solubility test

12. A disease that confers immunity is

    A. gonorrhea
    B. syphilis
    C. tuberculosis
    D. scarlet fever

13. Metachromatic granules are demonstrated in Corynebacterium diphtheriae by

    A. Gram's stain
    B. Dorner's stain
    C. Hiss' stain
    D. Ponder's stain

14. Which of the following is a satisfactory enrichment medium for a Salmonella-infected stool specimen?

    A. Blood broth
    B. Selenite broth
    C. Thioglycollate medium
    D. Nutrient broth

15. A medium used for the growth of Hemophilus influenza MUST contain

    A. both the X factor and the V factor
    B. the X factor but not the V factor
    C. the V factor but not the X factor
    D. neither the X factor nor the V factor

16. Serum tellurite agar medium is used for the isolation of pathogenic members of the genus

    A. Streptococcus
    B. Pseudomonas
    C. Corynebacterium
    D. Salmonella

17. Which of the following gram-negative bacteria would BEST be isolated on an alkaline medium (pH 8.4)?

    A. Vibrio comma
    B. Escherichia coli
    C. Neisseria gonorrhoeae
    D. Citrobacter freundii

18. Charcoal agar is used in the isolation of

    A. Bordetella pertussis
    B. Branhamella catarrhalis
    C. Listeria monocytogenes
    D. Streptococcus bovis

19. Blood tellurite and Tinsdale media are used in the isolation of

    A. Neisseria gonorrhoeae
    B. Corynebacterium diphtheriae
    C. Vibrio comma
    D. Mycobacterium tuberculosis

20. A formula calls for 45 grains of dehydrated medium per liter of distilled water. Following this formula, the number of grams of dehydrated medium that would be added to 200 ml of distilled water is, most nearly,

    A. 0.9 gram
    B. 4.5 grams
    C. 9.0 grains
    D. 11.25 grains

21. Room temperature is considered to be

    A. 5-10°C   B. 15-20°C   C. 23-25°C   D. 32-35°C

22. Of the following media, the one that should NOT be stored in the refrigerator is

    A. Blood agar
    B. Chocolate agar
    C. Trypticase soy broth
    D. Thioglycollate

23. A dimorphic fungus is one that has a

    A. mold phase at 23°C and a yeast phase at 37°C
    B. yeast phase at 23°C and a mold phase at 37°C
    C. yeast phase at both 23° and 37°C
    D. mold phase at both 23°C and 37°C

24. Of the following microorganisms, the one that multiplies by budding is

    A. Staphylococcus aureus
    B. Rabies virus
    C. Rickettsia
    D. Candida albicans

25. When stained with Ziehl-Neelsen stain, acid-fast bacteria stain

    A. red   B. blue   C. green   D. purple

KEY (CORRECT ANSWERS)

1. B
2. C
3. B
4. D
5. B

6. C
7. B
8. C
9. A
10. D

11. B
12. D
13. D
14. B
15. A

16. C
17. A
18. A
19. B
20. C

21. C
22. D
23. A
24. D
25. A

TEST 2

DIRECTIONS: Each question or incomplete statement is followed by several suggested answers or completions. Select the one that *BEST* answers the question or completes the statement. *PRINT THE LETTER OF THE CORRECT ANSWER IN THE SPACE AT THE RIGHT.*

1. The decolorizing agent in the Ziehl-Neelsen stain is

   A. 95% ethanol
   B. 50:50 ethanol: acetone
   C. 70% ethanol
   D. 3% HCl in ethanol

   1.____

2. 95°F is equivalent to

   A. 40°C   B. 37°C   C. 35°C   D. 30°C

   2.____

3. Gravis, intermedius, and mitis, are types of

   A. Corynebacterium diphtheriae
   B. Listeria monocytogenes
   C. Hemophilus influenza
   D. Bordetella pertussis

   3.____

4. The Kauffman-White schema is used to identify members of the genus

   A. Klebsiella   B. Salmonella   C. Shigella   D. Pseudomonas

   4.____

5. Gram-negative intracellular and extracellular diplococci from a male urethral smear indicates that the patient has

   A. syphilis
   B. gonorrhea
   C. Lymphogranuloma venerum
   D. chancroid

   5.____

6. Bacitracin sensitivity is a presumptive test for

   A. Group A streptococci
   B. Group D streptococci
   C. Pneumococci
   D. Staphylococcus aureus

   6.____

7. Serum, some carbohydrates, and urea should be sterilized by

   A. boiling for 10 minutes
   B. autoclaving
   C. filtration
   D. addition of acid

   7.____

8. Lowenstein-Jensen and Petragnani's are media used in the cultivation of

   A. Mycobacterium tuberculosis
   B. Mycobacterium leprae
   C. Bordetella pertussis
   D. Pasteurella pestis

   8.____

9. Anaerobic spore-forming bacteria belong to the genus

   A. Bacillus
   B. Clostridium
   C. Listeria
   D. Corynebacterium

   9.____

10. Tularemia is transmitted by

    A. bite of rat lice
    B. direct contact with convalescent patients
    C. mosquito bites
    D. the bite of infected flies and ticks

    10.____

11. Canned foods that are bulging at the ends should NOT be used because they are probably contaminated with

    A. Clostridium botulinum
    B. Bacillus subtilis
    C. Staphylococcus aureus
    D. Salmonella typhi

11.____

12. Many people developed gastroenteritis after eating potato salad that had been kept at room temperature for several hours. The organism MOST likely responsible was

    A. Escherichia coli
    B. Proteus vulgaris
    C. Enterobacter cloacae
    D. Staphylococcus aureus

12.____

13. Of the following organisms, the one which has NOT been successfully grown on artificial media is

    A. Mycobacterium tuberculosis
    B. Mycobacterium leprae
    C. Vibrio cholerae
    D. Brucella abortus

13.____

14. The organisms that cause syphilis are BEST observed by

    A. phase contrast microscopy
    B. fluorescence microscopy
    C. ordinary light microscopy
    D. darkfield microscopy

14.____

15. The pH indicator in MacConkey's agar is

    A. phenol red
    B. purple brown cresol
    C. neutral red
    D. bromthymol blue

15.____

16. A gram stain of a sputum showed many gram-positive diplococci. The organisms present is MOST likely

    A. Neisseria catarrhalis
    B. Diplococcus pneumoniae]
    C. Klebsiella pneumoniae
    D. Staphylococcus aureus

16.____

17. Rocky mountain spotted fever is caused by a

    A. bacterium   B. virus   C. rickettsia   D. fungus

17.____

18. The organism that causes syphilis is

    A. Treponema pallidum
    B. Treponema pertenue
    C. Borrelia recurrentis
    D. Sporotrichum schenckii

18.____

19. The tine test is a test for

    A. syphilis   B. gonorrhea   C. tuberculosis   D. diphtheria

19.____

20. Colonies of Pseudomonas aeruginosa on MacConkey's agar appear to be

    A. pink   B. black   C. red   D. colorless

20.____

21. The equivalent of 0.04 g is

    A. 0.40 mg   B. 4.0 mg   C. 40 mg   D. 400 mg

21.____

22. The organism that usually indicates fecal contamination is

    A. Proteus vulgaris
    B. Alcaligenes faecalis
    C. Enterobacter aerogenes
    D. Escherichis coli

22.____

23. The cause of bubonic plague is

    A. Vibrio comma
    B. Francisella tularensis
    C. Bacillus anthracis
    D. Pasteurella pestis

24. Littman's, Sabouraud's, and Mycosel agars are all used in the identification of

    A. fungi   B. bacteria   C. Chamydia   D. Rickettsia

25. Thayer-Martin medium is used in the isolation of

    A. Mycobacterium tuberculosis
    B. Corynebacterium diphtheriae
    C. Streptococcus hemolyticus
    D. Neisseria gonorrhaeae

KEY (CORRECT ANSWERS)

1.	D	11.	A
2.	C	12.	D
3.	A	13.	B
4.	B	14.	D
5.	B	15.	C
6.	A	16.	B
7.	C	17.	C
8.	A	18.	A
9.	B	19.	C
10.	D	20.	D

21.	C
22.	D
23.	D
24.	A
25.	D

EXAMINATION SECTION
TEST 1

DIRECTIONS: Each question or incomplete statement is followed by several suggested answers or completions. Select the one that BEST answers the question or completes the statement. *PRINT THE LETTER OF THE CORRECT ANSWER IN THE SPACE AT THE RIGHT.*

1. Of the following, the one which is LEAST satisfactory as a differential coliform test is

   A. citrate utilization
   B. gelatin liquefaction
   C. methyl-red
   D. Voges-Proskauer

2. The cholera vibrio is

   A. atrichous
   B. amphitrichous
   C. monotrichous
   D. perltrichous

3. The tetanus bacilli are classified as

   A. aerobes
   B. facultative anaerobes
   C. micro-aerophiles
   D. obligate anaerobes

4. Milk is pasteurized in order to destroy all

   A. bacteria
   B. non-spore forming bacteria
   C. non-spore forming pathogens
   D. spore forming pathogens

5. The IMVIC for typical strains of E.coli is

   A. + + + +   B. + + − −   C. − − + +   D. − − − −

6. The term *peritrichous* means having

   A. a single flagellum at one pole
   B. a tuft of flagella at one pole
   C. flagella at both poles
   D. flagella completely surrounding the body

7. Bacteria belonging to the genus Thiothrix are GENERALLY called _____ bacteria.

   A. iron
   B. nitrifying
   C. sulfate-reducing
   D. sulfur

8. Bacteria belonging to the genus Crenothrix are GENERALLY termed _____ bacteria.

   A. iron
   B. nitrifying
   C. sulfate-reducing
   D. sulfur

9. The one of the following which is NOT characteristic of the coliform group is

   A. ferment lactose
   B. Gram-negative
   C. non-gas former
   D. non-spore former

10. The organism, Aerobacter aerogenes, is USUALLY considered to be a(n) _____ coliform organism.

    A. fecal
    B. intestinal
    C. non-fecal
    D. pathogenic

11. The term *plankton* includes all organisms that are microscopic or barely visible to the naked eye, with the exception of the

    A. bacteria
    B. Crustacea
    C. protozoa
    D. rotifera

12. The one of the following methods GENERALLY associated with the concentration of water samples for water analysis is the _____ method.

    A. Kjeldahl
    B. Sedgwick-Rafter
    C. Winkler
    D. Zeolite

13. The ortho-tolidine method is GENERALLY used to measure

    A. copper
    B. nitrite nitrogen
    C. orthophosphate
    D. residual chlorine

14. A study of water-borne epidemics in the United States reveals that the disease responsible for the GREATEST number of cases is

    A. anthrax
    B. Asiatic cholera
    C. dysentery
    D. tuberculosis

15. The name of the organism causing non-bacillary dysentery is

    A. Endameba coli
    B. Endameba histolytica
    C. Escherichia coli
    D. Shigella sonnei

16. The immunity acquired against tuberculosis by prophylactic vaccination with BCG is _____ acquired _____ immunity.

    A. artificially; active
    B. artificially; passive
    C. naturally; active
    D. naturally; passive

17. The optimum temperature of growth for MOST pathogenic bacteria is APPROXIMATELY

    A. 20° C
    B. 20° F
    C. 37° C
    D. 37° F

18. Of the following diseases, the one NOT caused by an acid-fast organism is

    A. Johne's disease
    B. leprosy
    C. pertussis
    D. tuberculosis

19. The presence of Vi antibodies in the human serum is indicative of an infection of

    A. cholera
    B. salmonellosis
    C. shigellosis
    D. typhoid fever

20. The causative agents of salmonellosis are gram-_____, lactose _____ rods.

    A. negative; negative
    B. negative; positive
    C. positive; negative
    D. positive; positive

21. Of the following, the organism MOST resistant to disinfecting agents is the one causing 21.____
    A. amebic dysentery
    B. bacillary dysentery
    C. cholera
    D. typhoid

22. The FIRST step in the recommended procedure for cleaning glassware containing infectious material is 22.____
    A. rinsing
    B. scraping
    C. sterilizing
    D. washing

23. The MOST heat-resistant of the pathogens *generally* found in milk is 23.____
    A. Salmonella typhosa
    B. Mycobacterium tuberculosis
    C. Shigella sonnei
    D. Streptococcus pyogenes

24. The hydrogen-ion concentration of culture media increases during sterilization. The USUAL decrease in the pH reading as a result of sterilization is *approximately* 24.____
    A. 0.3   B. 0.8   C. 1.4   D. 2.7

25. The PRINCIPAL ingredients of nutrient broth are 25.____
    A. beef extract and peptone
    B. beef extract and glucose
    C. ground beef and peptone
    D. ground beef and glucose

KEY (CORRECT ANSWERS)

1. B		11. A	
2. C		12. B	
3. D		13. D	
4. C		14. C	
5. B		15. B	
6. D		16. A	
7. D		17. C	
8. A		18. C	
9. C		19. D	
10. C		20. A	

21. A
22. C
23. B
24. A
25. A

TEST 2

DIRECTIONS: Each question or incomplete statement is followed by several suggested answers or completions. Select the one that BEST answers the question or completes the statement. *PRINT THE LETTER OF THE CORRECT ANSWER IN THE SPACE AT THE RIGHT.*

1. The solidifying point of agar is APPROXIMATELY

    A. 25° C B. 40° C C. 55° C D. 70° C

    1.____

2. The one of the following NOT contained in Krumwiede Triple Sugar Agar is

    A. dextrose B. lactose C. maltose D. sucrose

    2.____

3. The indicator GENERALLY used in Krumwiede Triple Sugar Agar is

    A. bromcresol purple B. litmus
    C. methyl orange D. phenol red

    3.____

4. The one of the following which is NOT an ingredient of Endo medium is

    A. agar B. basic fuchsin
    C. glucose D. lactose

    4.____

5. Endo medium when cooled is

    A. blue B. colorless C. green D. yellow

    5.____

6. The color of the colonies produced by Escherichia coli on Endo medium is

    A. blue B. brown C. green D. red

    6.____

7. The gas produced in the fermentation of lactose is ESSENTIALLY

    A. CO B. CO_2 C. H_2 D. H_2O

    7.____

8. The Barrett method is GENERALLY used to determine production of

    A. acetyl-methyl-carbinol B. hydrogen sulfide
    C. indol D. urea

    8.____

9. The color of the test reagent in a positive indol test is

    A. dark blue B. dark red
    C. light green D. light yellow

    9.____

10. Indol is a decomposition product of

    A. amyl alcohol
    B. lactose
    C. paradimethylaminobenzaldehyde
    D. tryptophane

    10.____

11. A sodium citrate positive test is indicated if, after 96 hours of incubation, there is

    A. a red color B. a yellow color
    C. no growth D. visible growth

    11.____

12. A positive Voges-Proskauer test is GENERALLY indicated by the appearance of a _____ color.

    A. blue   B. green   C. red   D. yellow

13. Phosphate is added to the test medium used for the methyl red test to provide a(n)

    A. buffer
    B. food supply
    C. indicator
    D. inhibitor

14. The Kjeldahl method is used to analyze for

    A. chlorine   B. copper   C. iron   D. nitrogen

15. Amino acids are formed in the hydrolysis of

    A. disaccharides
    B. fats
    C. monosaccharides
    D. proteins

16. The one of the following that is NOT classified as a disaccharide is

    A. glucose   B. lactose   C. maltose   D. sucrose

17. The process of culturing bacteria by providing them with the necessary conditions for growth is known as

    A. incubation
    B. inoculation
    C. sterilization
    D. staining

18. Blood typing is necessary in the transfusion of

    A. amino acids
    B. dextrose
    C. plasma
    D. whole blood

19. The BEST method of preventing the spread of the common cold is to treat the patient by

    A. injecting antitoxin
    B. isolating him
    C. administering sulfa drugs
    D. vaccinating him

20. Requiring food handlers to undergo a periodic health examination might reduce the number of cases of

    A. scurvy
    B. tetanus
    C. typhoid fever
    D. yellow fever

21. Jumping at a sudden noise is an example of a

    A. habit
    B. simple reflex
    C. conditioned reflex
    D. voluntary act

22. Which vitamin is MOST easily destroyed by heat or air?

    A. A   B. B   C. C   D. D

23. Which is a product of fermentation by yeasts?

    A. Alcohol   B. Oxygen   C. Nitrogen   D. Starch

24. A drop of milk was placed on each of several culture medium preparations and then incubated for several days. No bacterial colonies developed.
   The milk MOST probably had been
   A. boiled
   B. pasteurized
   C. refrigerated
   D. skimmed

   24.____

25. MOST antibodies have been isolated from organisms that live in

   25.____

   A. water   B. air   C. soil   D. animals

KEY (CORRECT ANSWERS)

1. B
2. C
3. D
4. C
5. B

6. D
7. B
8. A
9. B
10. D

11. D
12. C
13. A
14. D
15. D

16. A
17. A
18. D
19. B
20. C

21. A
22. C
23. A
24. A
25. C

EXAMINATION SECTION
TEST 1

DIRECTIONS: Each question or incomplete statement is followed by several suggested answers or completions. Select the one that BEST answers the question or completes the statement. *PRINT THE LETTER OF THE CORRECT ANSWER IN THE SPACE AT THE RIGHT.*

1. The one of the following which is the BEST description of a properly objective investigator is one who

    A. is friendly and sensitive to the client's feelings, without becoming emotionally involved
    B. is distant and impersonal, remaining unaffected by what the client says
    C. lets personal emotions enter as far as the client's situation calls for them
    D. becomes emotionally involved with the client's situation but without showing this involvement

2. The one of the following which is MOST necessary for successfully interviewing a person who belongs to a culture different from that of the investigator is for the investigator to

    A. have some appreciation of the other culture
    B. ignore those cultural differences which lead to bias
    C. stay away from sensitive, "touchy" issues
    D. assume the mannerisms of people in the other cultures

3. In fact-finding interviews, it is generally assumed that the smaller the number of interviewees, the greater the increase of reliability with the addition of others. The PROPER number of interviewees needed to insure the accuracy of information obtained *generally* depends upon the

    A. educational level of those interviewed
    B. number of people who have the required information
    C. directness of the questions asked
    D. variability of the information received

4. The one of the following which is generally MOST likely to be accurately described in an interview by an interviewee is

    A. the presence of a large painting in the investigator's office
    B. the number of people in the investigator's waiting room
    C. space relations
    D. duration of time

5. The one of the following which is *generally* the BEST course of action for an investigator to take when interviewing a person who is reluctant to tell what he knows about a matter under investigation is to

    A. be curt and abrupt and threaten the person with the consequences of his withholding information
    B. be firm and severe and pressure the person into telling the needed information
    C. be patient and candid with the person being questioned about the investigation since doing otherwise is not ethical

D. give the person false information about the investigation so he will give the needed information without realizing its importance

6. It is often recommended that an investigator prepare in advance a list of questions or topics to be covered in an interview. The MAIN reason for using such a check list is to

   A. allow investigations to be assigned to less efficient investigators
   B. eliminate a large amount of follow-up paper work
   C. aid the investigator in remembering to cover all important topics
   D. aid the investigator in maintaining an objective distance from the person interviewed

7. Usually, the CHIEF advantage of a directive approach in an interview is that

   A. the investigator maintains control over the course of the interview
   B. the person interviewed is more likely to be put at ease
   C. the person interviewed is generally left free to direct the interview
   D. the investigator will not suggest answers to the person interviewed

8. Usually, the CHIEF advantage of a non-directive approach by an investigator in conducting an interview is that

   A. the investigator generally conceals what he is looking for in the interview
   B. the person interviewed is more likely to express his true feelings about the topic under discussion
   C. the person interviewed is more likely to follow an idea introduced by the investigator
   D. the investigator can keep the discussion limited to topics he believes to be relevant

9. The one of the following which is generally the *least likely* to be accurate in a description of an event given to an investigator is a statement about

   A. the presence of an object
   B. the number of people, when their number is small
   C. locations of people
   D. duration of time

10. Assume that you, an investigator, are conducting a character investigation. In an interview, the one of the following character traits of the person being interviewed which can USUALLY be determined with a *good* degree of reliability is

    A. honesty
    B. dependability
    C. forcefulness
    D. perseverance

11. As an investigator, you have been assigned the task of obtaining a family's social history. The BEST place for you to interview members of the family while obtaining this social history would *generally* be in

    A. the family's home
    B. your agency's general offices
    C. the home of a friend of the family
    D. your own private office

12. You, an investigator, are checking someone's work history. The way for you to get the MOST reliable information from a previous employer is to

   A. send personal letters; the employer will respond to the personal attention
   B. send form letters; the employer will cooperate readily since little time or effort is asked of him
   C. arrange a personal interview; the employer may offer information he would not care to put in a letter or speak over the phone
   D. telephone; this method is as effective as a personal interview and is much more convenient

13. The effect that attestation, or the formal taking of an oath, has on witness testimony is to

   A. decrease accuracy, since a witness under oath is more nervous about what is said
   B. make little difference, since the witness is not too swayed by an oath
   C. increase accuracy, since a witness under oath feels more responsibility for what is said
   D. eliminate inaccuracy unless there is deliberate perjury on the part of the witness

14. If an investigator obtains testimony from persons in interviews by means of interrogation or asking questions rather than by letting the person freely relate the testimony, what is said will GENERALLY be

   A. greater in range and less accurate
   B. greater in range and more accurate
   C. about the same in range and less accurate
   D. about the same in range and more accurate

15. Experienced investigators have learned to phrase their questions carefully in order to obtain the desired response. Of the following, the question which would *usually* elicit the MOST accurate answer is:

   A. "How old are you?"
   B. "What is your income?"
   C. "How are you today?"
   D. "What is the date of your birth?"

16. The one of the following questions which would *generally* lead to the LEAST reliable answer is

   A. "Did you see a wallet?"
   B. "Was the German Shepherd gray?"
   C. "Didn't you see the stop sign?"
   D. "Did you see the guard on duty?"

17. Some investigators may make a practice of observing details of the surroundings when interviewing in someone's home or office. Such a practice is *generally* considered

   A. *undesirable,* mainly because such snooping is an unwarranted, unethical invasion of privacy
   B. *undesirable,* mainly because useful information is rarely, if ever, gained this way
   C. *desirable,* mainly because, useful insights into the character of the person interviewed may be gained

D. *desirable,* mainly because it is impossible to evaluate a person adequately without such observation of his environment

18. The one of the following questions which will MOST often lead to a reliable answer is: 18.____

    A. "Was his hair very dark?"
    B. "Wasn't there a clock on the wall?"
    C. "Was the automobile white or gray?"
    D. "Did you see a motorcycle?"

19. The one of the following which can MOST accurately be determined by an investigator by means of interviewing is 19.____

    A. a persons's intelligence
    B. factual information about an event
    C. a person's aptitude for a specific task
    D. a person's perceptions of his own abilities

20. The one of the following which is *most likely* to help a person being interviewed feel at ease is for the investigator to 20.____

    A. let him start the conversation
    B. give him an abundance of time
    C. be relaxed himself
    D. open the interview by telling a joke

21. If the interviewee is to perceive some goal for himself in the interview and thus be motivated to participate in it, it is important that he clearly understand some of the aspects of the interview. Of the following aspects, the one the interviewee needs LEAST to understand is 21.____

    A. the purpose of the interview
    B. the mechanics of interviewing
    C. the use made of the information he contributes
    D. what will be expected of him in the interview

22. As an investigator working on a project requiring inter-agency cooperation, you find that employees of an agency involved in the project are constantly making it difficult for you to obtain necessary information. Of the following, the BEST action for you to take FIRST is to 22.____

    A. discuss the problem with your supervisor
    B. speak with your counterpart in the other agency
    C. discuss the problem with the head of the uncooperative agency
    D. contact the head of your agency

23. The investigator is justified in misleading the interviewee only when, in the investigator's judgment, this is clearly required by the problem being investigated. Such practice is 23.____

    A. *necessary;* there are times when complete honesty will impede a successful investigation
    B. *unnecessary ;* such a tactic is unethical and should never be employed
    C. *necessary;* an investigator must be guided by success rather than ethical considerations in an investigation

D. *unnecessary;* it is clearly doubtful whether such a practice will help the investigator conclude the investigation successfully

24. Assume that, in investigating a case of possible welfare fraud, it becomes necessary to hold an interview in the client's home in order to observe family interaction and conditions. Upon arriving, the investigator finds that the client's living room is noisy and crowded, with neighbors present and children running in and out. Of the following, the BEST course of action for the investigator to take is to

    A. conduct the interview in the living room after telling the children to behave, and asking the neighbors to leave
    B. tell the client that it is impossible to conduct the interview in the apartment, and make an appointment for the next day in the investigator's office
    C. suggest that they move from the living room into the kitchen where there is a table on which he can write
    D. try his best to conduct the interview in the noisy and crowded living room

24.____

25. You, an investigator, are giving testimony in court about a matter you have investigated. An attorney is questioning you in an abrasive, badgering way, and, in an insulting manner, calls into doubt your ability as an investigator. You lose your temper and respond angrily, telling the attorney to stop harassing and insulting you. Of the following, the BEST description of such a response is that it *is generally*

    A. *appropriate;* as a witness in court, you do not have to take insults from anybody, including an attorney
    B. *inappropriate; losing your* temper will show that you are weak and cannot be trusted as an investigator
    C. *appropriate;* a judge and jury will usually respect someone who responds strongly to unjust provocation
    D. *inappropriate;* such conduct is unprofessional and may unfavorably impress a judge and jury

25.____

KEY (CORRECT ANSWERS)

1.	A	11.	A
2.	A	12.	C
3.	D	13.	C
4.	A	14.	A
5.	C	15.	D
6.	C	16.	B
7.	A	17.	C
8.	B	18.	D
9.	D	19.	D
10.	C	20.	C

21. B
22. A
23. A
24. C
25. D

TEST 2

DIRECTIONS: Each question or incomplete statement is followed by several suggested answers or completions. Select the one that BEST answers the question or completes the statement. *PRINT THE LETTER OF THE CORRECT ANSWER IN THE SPACE AT THE RIGHT.*

1. The reliability of information obtained increases with the number of persons interviewed. The more the interviewees differ in their statements, the more persons it is necessary to interview to ascertain the true facts. According to this statement, the dependability of the information about an occurrence obtained from interviews is related to

   A. how many people are interviewed
   B. how soon after the occurrence an interview can be arranged
   C. the individual technique of the interviewer
   D. the interviewer's ability to detect differences in the statements of interviewees

   1.____

2. An investigator interviews members of the public at his desk. The attitude of the public toward this department will probably be LEAST affected by this investigator's

   A. courtesy   B. efficiency
   C. height   D. neatness

   2.____

3. The *one* of the following which is NOT effective in obtaining complete testimony from a witness during an interview is to

   A. ask questions in chronological order
   B. permit the witness to structure the interview
   C. make sure you fully understand the response to each question
   D. review questions to be asked beforehand

   3.____

4. The person MOST likely to be a good interviewer is one who

   A. is able to outguess the person being interviewed
   B. tries to change the attitudes of the persons he interviews
   C. controls the interview by skillfully dominating the conversation
   D. is able to imagine himself in the position of the person being interviewed

   4.____

5. When you are interviewing someone to obtain information, the BEST of the following reasons for you to repeat certain of his exact words is to

   A. *assure* him that appropriate action will be taken
   B. *encourage* him to elaborate on a point he has made
   C. *assure* him that you agree with his point of view
   D. *encourage* him to switch to another topic of discussion

   5.____

6. You are interviewing a client who has just been assaulted. He has trouble collecting his thoughts and telling his story coherently. Which of the following represents the MOST effective method of questioning under these circumstances?

   A. Ask questions which structure the client's story chronologically into units, each with a beginning, middle and end.
   B. Ask several questions at a time to structure the interview.

   6.____

C. Ask open-ended questions which allow the client to respond in a variety of ways.
D. Begin the interview with several detailed questions in order to focus the client's attention on the situation.

7. You are conducting an initial interview with a witness who expresses reluctance, even hostility, to being questioned. You feel it would be helpful to take some notes during the interview.
In this situation, it would be BEST to

   A. put off note-taking until a follow-up interview, and concentrate on establishing rapport with the witness
   B. explain the necessity of note-taking, and proceed to take notes during the interview
   C. make notes from memory after the witness has left
   D. take notes, but as unobtrusively as possible

7.____

8. You are interviewing the owner of a stolen car about facts relating to the robbery. After completing his statement, the car owner suddenly states that some of the details he has just related are not correct. You realize that this change might be significant.
Of the following, it would be BEST for you to

   A. ask the owner what other details he may have given incorrectly
   B. make a note of the discrepancy for discussion at a later date
   C. repeat your questioning on the details that were misstated until you have covered that area completely
   D. explain to the owner that because of his change of testimony, you will have to repeat the entire interview

8.____

9. Assume that you have been asked to get all the pertinent information from an employee who claims that she witnessed a robbery.
Which of the following questions is *least likely* to influence the witness's response?

   A. "Can you describe the robber's hair?"
   B. "Did the robber have a lot of hair?"
   C. "Was the robber's hair black or brown?"
   D. "Was the robber's hair very dark?"

9.____

10. In order to obtain an accurate statement from a person who has witnessed a crime, it is BEST to question the witness

    A. as soon as possible after the crime was committed
    B. after the witness has discussed the crime with other witnesses
    C. after the witness has had sufficient time to reflect on events and formulate a logical statement
    D. after the witness has been advised that he is obligated to tell the whole truth

10.____

11. Assume that your superior assigns you to interview an individual who, he warns, seems to be hightly "introverted." You should be aware that, during an interview, such a person is likely to

    A. hold views which are highly controversial in nature
    B. be domineering and try to control the direction of the interview
    C. resist answering personal questions regarding his background
    D. give information which is largely fabricated

11.____

12. A young woman was stabbed in the hand in her home by her estranged boyfriend. Her mother and two sisters were at home at the time.
Of the following, it would generally be BEST to interview the young woman in the presence of

    A. her mother *only*
    B. all members of her immediate family
    C. members of the family who actually observed the crime
    D. the official authorities

13. The one of the following statements concerning interviewing which is LEAST valid is that

    A. skill in interviewing can be improved by knowledge of the basic factors involving relations between people
    B. interviewing should become a routine and mechanical practice to the skilled and experienced interviewer
    C. genuine interest in people is essential for successful interviewing
    D. certain psychological traits characterize most people most of the time

14. The initial interview will normally be more of a problem to the interviewer than any subsequent interviews he may have with the same person because

    A. the interviewee is likely to be hostile
    B. there is too much to be accomplished in one session
    C. he has less information about the client than he will have later
    D. some information may be forgotten when later making record of this first interview

15. Continuous taking of notes during an interview is generally

    A. *desirable* because no important facts will be forgotten
    B. *undesirable* because it gives the person being interviewed a clue to the importance of the information being obtained from him
    C. *desirable* because the interviewer cannot write as fast as the person being interviewed can speak
    D. *undesirable* because it may put the person being interviewed ill at ease

16. "Carefully planned interviews tend to impose restrictions which leave little room for spontaneity." A flaw in this criticism of the planned interview is that it does NOT take into account that

    A. a planned interview obviates the need for spontaneity
    B. even the planned interview may be flexible
    C. not all planned interviews impose restrictions
    D. restrictions that result from planning are undesirable

17. Writing up the interview into a systematic report is BEST done

    A. in the presence of the subject, so that mistakes can be corrected immediately
    B. within a reasonably short time after the interview, so that nothing is forgotten
    C. no sooner than several days after the interview, so that the interviewer will have had plenty of time to think about it
    D. with the help of someone not present at the interview, so that an objective view can be obtained

18. While you are conducting an interview, the telephone on your desk rings. Of the following, it would be BEST for you to

    A. ask the interviewer at the next desk to answer your telephone and take the message for you
    B. excuse yourself, pick up the telephone, and tell the person on the other end you are busy and will call him back later
    C. ignore the ringing telephone and continue with the interview
    D. use another telephone to inform the operator not to put calls through to you while you are conducting an interview

19. An interviewee is at your desk, which is quite near to desks where other people work. He beckons you a little closer and starts to talk in a low voice as though he does not want anyone else to hear him. Under these circumstances, the BEST thing for you to do is to

    A. ask him to speak a little louder so that he can be heard
    B. cut the interview short and not get involved in his problems
    C. explain that people at other desks are not eavesdroppers
    D. listen carefully to what he says and give it consideration

20. Of the following, the BEST way for a person to develop competence as an interviewer is to

    A. attend lectures on interviewing techniques
    B. practice with employees on the job
    C. conduct interviews under the supervision of an experienced instructor
    D. attend a training course in counseling

21. During the course of an interview, it would be LEAST desirable for the investigator to

    A. correct immediately any grammatical errors made by an interviewee
    B. express himself in such a way as to be clearly understood
    C. restrict the interviewee to the subject of the interview
    D. make notes in a way that will not disturb the interviewee

22. Suppose that you are interviewing an eleven year old boy. The CHIEF point among the following for you to keep in mind is that a child, as compared with an adult, is generally

    A. more likely to attempt to conceal information
    B. a person of lower intelligence
    C. more garrulous
    D. more receptive to suggestive questions

23. In interviewing a person, "suggestive questions" should be avoided because, among the following,

    A. the answers to leading questions are not admissible in evidence
    B. an investigator must be fair and impartial
    C. the interrogation of a witness must be formulated according to his mentality
    D. they are less apt to lead to the truth

24. Among the following, it is generally desirable to interview a person outside his home or office because

A. the presence of relatives and friends may prevent him from speaking freely
B. a person's surroundings tend to color his testimony
C. the person will find less distraction outside his home or office
D. a person tends to dominate the interview when in familiar surroundings

25. For the interviewing process to be MOST successful, the interviewer should generally   25.____

   A. remind the person being interviewed that false statements will constitute perjury and will be prosecuted as such
   B. devise a single and unvarying pattern for all interviewing situations
   C. let the individual being interviewed control the content of the interview but not its length
   D. vary his interviewing approach as the situation requires it

KEY (CORRECT ANSWERS)

1.	A	11.	C
2.	C	12.	D
3.	B	13.	B
4.	D	14.	C
5.	B	15.	D
6.	A	16.	B
7.	B	17.	B
8.	C	18.	B
9.	A	19.	D
10.	A	20.	C

21.	A
22.	D
23.	D
24.	A
25.	D

SCIENCE READING COMPREHENSION
EXAMINATION SECTION
TEST 1

DIRECTIONS: Each question or incomplete statement is followed by several suggested answers or completions. Select the one that BEST answers the question or completes the statement. *PRINT THE LETTER OF THE CORRECT ANSWER IN THE SPACE AT THE RIGHT.*

PASSAGE

    Photosynthesis is a complex process with many intermediate steps. Ideas differ greatly as to the details of these steps, but the general nature of the process and its outcome are well established. Water, usually from the soil, is conducted through the xylem of root, stem and leaf to the chlorophyl-containing cells of a leaf. In consequence of the abundance of water within the latter cells, their walls are saturated with water. Carbon dioxide, diffusing from the air through the stomata and into the intercellular spaces of the leaf, comes into contact with the water in the walls of the cells which adjoin the intercellular spaces. The carbon dioxide becomes dissolved in the water of these walls, and in solution diffuses through the walls and the plasma membranes into the cells. By the agency of chlorophyl in the chloroplasts of the cells, the energy of light is transformed into chemical energy. This chemical energy is used to decompose the carbon dioxide and water, and the products of their decomposition are recombined into a new compound. The compound first formed is successively built up into more and more complex substances until finally a sugar is produced.

Questions 1-8.

1. The union of carbon dioxide and water to form starch results in an excess of   1.____

    A. hydrogen   B. carbon   C. oxygen
    D. carbon monoxide   E. hydrogen peroxide

2. Synthesis of carbohydrates takes place   2.____

    A. in the stomata
    B. in the intercellular spaces of leaves
    C. in the walls of plant cells
    D. within the plasma membranes of plant cells
    E. within plant cells that contain chloroplasts

3. In the process of photosynthesis, chlorophyl acts as a   3.____

    A. carbohydrate   B. source of carbon dioxide
    C. catalyst   D. source of chemical energy
    E. plasma membrane

4. In which of the following places are there the GREATEST number of hours in which photosynthesis can take place during the month of December?   4.____

    A. Buenos Aires, Argentina   B. Caracas, Venezuela
    C. Fairbanks, Alaska   D. Quito, Ecuador
    E. Calcutta, India

5. During photosynthesis, molecules of carbon dioxide enter the stomata of leaves because   5.___

   A. the molecules are already in motion
   B. they are forced through the stomata by the son's rays
   C. chlorophyl attracts them
   D. a chemical change takes place in the stomata
   E. oxygen passes out through the stomata

6. Besides food manufacture, another USEFUL result of photosynthesis is that it   6.___

   A. aids in removing poisonous gases from the air
   B. helps to maintain the existing proportion of gases in the air
   C. changes complex compounds into simpler compounds
   D. changes certain waste products into hydrocarbons
   E. changes chlorophyl into useful substances

7. A process that is almost the exact reverse of photosynthesis is the   7.___

   A. rusting of iron   B. burning of wood
   C. digestion of starch   D. ripening of fruit
   E. storage of food in seeds

8. The leaf of the tomato plant will be unable to carry on photosynthesis if the   8.___

   A. upper surface of the leaf is coated with vaseline
   B. upper surface of the leaf is coated with lampblack
   C. lower surface of the leaf is coated with lard
   D. leaf is placed in an atmosphere of pure carbon dioxide
   E. entire leaf is coated with lime

TEST 2

DIRECTIONS: Each question or incomplete statement is followed by several suggested answers or completions. Select the one that BEST answers the question or completes the statement. *PRINT THE LETTER OF THE CORRECT ANSWER IN THE SPACE AT THE RIGHT.*

PASSAGE

The only carbohydrate which the human body can absorb and oxidize is the simple sugar glucose. Therefore, all carbohydrates which are consumed must be changed to glucose by the body before they can be used. There are specific enzymes in the mouth, the stomach, and the small intestine which break down complex carbohydrates. All the monosaccharides are changed to glucose by enzymes secreted by the intestinal glands, and the glucose is absorbed by the capillaries of the villi.

The following simple test is used to determine the presence of a reducing sugar. If Benedict's solution is added to a solution containing glucose or one of the other reducing sugars and the resulting mixture is heated, a brick-red precipitate will be formed. This test was carried out on several substances and the information in the following table was obtained. "P" indicates that the precipitate was formed and "N" indicates that no reaction was observed.

Material Tested	Observation
Crushed grapes in water	P
Cane sugar in water	N
Fructose	P
Molasses	N

Questions 1-2.

1. From the results of the test made upon crushed grapes in water, one may say that grapes contain

    A. glucose   B. sucrose   C. a reducing sugar
    D. no sucrose   E. no glucose

    1.____

2. Which one of the following foods probably undergoes the LEAST change during the process of carbohydrate digestion in the human body?

    A. Cane sugar   B. Fructose   C. Molasses
    D. Bread   E. Potato

    2.____

TEST 3

DIRECTIONS: Each question or incomplete statement is followed by several suggested answers or completions. Select the one that BEST answers the question or completes the statement. *PRINT THE LETTER OF THE CORRECT ANSWER IN THE SPACE AT THE RIGHT.*

PASSAGE

The British pressure suit was made in two pieces and joined around the middle in contrast to the other suits, which were one-piece suits with a removable helmet. Oxygen was supplied through a tube, and a container of soda lime absorbed carbon dioxide and water vapor. The pressure was adjusted to a maximum of 2 1/2 pounds per square inch (130 millimeters) higher than the surrounding air. Since pure oxygen was used, this produced a partial pressure of 130 millimeters, which is sufficient to sustain the flier at any altitude.

Using this pressure suit, the British established a world's altitude record of 49,944 feet in 1936 and succeeded in raising it to 53,937 feet the following year. The pressure suit is a compromise solution to the altitude problem. Full sea-level pressure can not be maintained, as the suit would be so rigid that the flier could not move arms or legs. Hence a pressure one third to one fifth that of sea level has been used. Because of these lower pressures, oxygen has been used to raise the partial pressure of alveolar oxygen to normal.

Questions 1-9.

1. The MAIN constituent of air not admitted to the pressure suit described was

   A. oxygen B. nitrogen C. water vapor
   D. carbon dioxide E. hydrogen

2. The pressure within the suit exceeded that of the surrounding air by an amount equal to 130 millimeters of

   A. mercury B. water C. air
   D. oxygen E. carbon dioxide

3. The normal atmospheric pressure at sea level is

   A. 130 mm B. 250 mm C. 760 mm
   D. 1000 mm E. 1300 mm

4. The water vapor that was absorbed by the soda lime came from

   A. condensation
   B. the union of oxygen with carbon dioxide
   C. body metabolism
   D. the air within the pressure suit
   E. water particles in the upper air

5. The HIGHEST altitude that has been reached with the British pressure suit is about

   A. 130 miles B. 2 1/2 miles C. 6 miles
   D. 10 miles E. 5 miles

1.___

2.___

3.___

4.___

5.___

6. If the pressure suit should develop a leak, the 6.____
    A. oxygen supply would be cut off
    B. suit would fill up with air instead of oxygen
    C. pressure within the suit would drop to zero
    D. pressure within the suit would drop to that of the surrounding air
    E. suit would become so rigid that the flier would be unable to move arms or legs

7. The reason why oxygen helmets are unsatisfactory for use in efforts to set higher altitude records is that 7.____
    A. it is impossible to maintain a tight enough fit at the neck
    B. oxygen helmets are too heavy
    C. they do not conserve the heat of the body as pressure suits do
    D. if a parachute jump becomes necessary, it can not be made while such a helmet is being worn
    E. oxygen helmets are too rigid

8. The pressure suit is termed a compromise solution because 8.____
    A. it is not adequate for stratosphere flying
    B. aviators can not stand sea-level pressure at high altitudes
    C. some suits are made in two pieces, others in one
    D. other factors than maintenance of pressure have to be accommodated
    E. full atmospheric pressure can not be maintained at high altitudes

9. The passage implies that 9.____
    A. the air pressure at 49,944 feet is approximately the same as it is at 53,937 feet
    B. pressure cabin planes are not practical at extremely high altitudes
    C. a flier's oxygen requirement is approximately the same at high altitudes as it is at sea level
    D. one-piece pressure suits with removable helmets are unsafe
    E. a normal alveolar oxygen supply is maintained if the air pressure is between one third and one fifth that of sea level

TEST 4

DIRECTIONS: Each question or incomplete statement is followed by several suggested answers or completions. Select the one that BEST answers the question or completes the statement. *PRINT THE LETTER OF THE CORRECT ANSWER IN THE SPACE AT THE RIGHT.*

PASSAGE

Chemical investigations show that during muscle contraction the store of organic phosphates in the muscle fibers is altered as energy is released. In doing so, the organic phosphates (chiefly adenoisine triphosphate and phospho-creatine) are transformed anaerobically to organic compounds plus phosphates. As soon as the organic phosphates begin to break down in muscle contraction, the glycogen in the muscle fibers also transforms into lactic acid plus free energy; this energy the muscle fiber uses to return the organic compounds plus phosphates into high-energy organic phosphates ready for another contraction. In the presence of oxygen, the lactic acid from the glycogen decomposition is changed also. About one-fifth of it is oxidized to form water and carbon dioxide and to yield another supply of energy. This time the energy is used to transform the remaining four-fifths of the lactic acid into glycogen again.

Questions 1-5.

1. The energy for muscle contraction comes directly from the   1.__

   A. breakdown of lactic acid into glycogen
   B. resynthesis of adenosine triphosphate
   C. breakdown of glycogen into lactic acid
   D. oxidation of lactic acid
   E. breakdown of the organic phosphates

2. Lactic acid does NOT accumulate in a muscle that   2.__

   A. is in a state of lacking oxygen
   B. has an ample supply of oxygen
   C. is in a state of fatigue
   D. is repeatedly being stimulated
   E. has an ample supply of glycogen

3. The energy for the resynthesis of adenosine triphosphate and phospho-creatine comes from the   3.__

   A. oxidation of lactic acid
   B. synthesis of organic phosphates
   C. change from glycogen to lactic acid
   D. resynthesis of glycogen
   E. change from lactic acid to glycogen

4. The energy for the resynthesis of glycogen comes from the   4.__

   A. breakdown of organic phosphates
   B. resynthesis of organic phosphates
   C. change occurring in one-fifth of the lactic acid

D. change occurring in four-fifths of the lactic acid
E. change occurring in four-fifths of glycogen

5. The breakdown of the organic phosphates into organic compounds plus phosphates is an   5._____

    A. anobolic reaction   B. aerobic reaction
    C. endothermic reaction   D. exothermic reaction
    E. anaerobic reaction

TEST 5

DIRECTIONS: Each question or incomplete statement is followed by several suggested answers or completions. Select the one that BEST answers the question or completes the statement. *PRINT THE LETTER OF THE CORRECT ANSWER IN THE SPACE AT THE RIGHT.*

PASSAGE

And with respect to that theory of the origin of the forms of life peopling our globe, with which Darwin's name is bound up as closely as that of Newton with the theory of gravitation, nothing seems to be further from the mind of the present generation than any attempt to smother it with ridicule or to crush it by vehemence of denunciation. "The struggle for existence," and "natural selection," have become household words and everyday conceptions. The reality and the importance of the natural processes on which Darwin founds his deductions are no more doubted than those of growth and multiplication; and, whether the full potency attributed to them is admitted or not, no one is unmindful of or at all doubts their vast and far-reaching significance. Wherever the biological sciences are studied, the "Origin of Species" lights the path of the investigator; wherever they are taught it permeates the course of instruction. Nor has the influence of Darwinian ideas been less profound beyond the realms of biology. The oldest of all philosophies, that of evolution, was bound hand and foot and cast into utter darkness during the millennium of theological scholasticism. But Darwin poured new life-blood into the ancient frame; the bonds burst, and the revivified thought of ancient Greece has proved itself to be a more adequate expression of the universal order of things than any of the schemes which have been accepted by the credulity and welcomed by the superstition of seventy later generations of men.

Questions 1-7.

1. Darwin's theory of the origin of the species is based on

   A. theological deductions
   B. the theory of gravitation
   C. Greek mythology
   D. natural processes evident in the universe
   E. extensive reading in the biological sciences

2. The passage implies that

   A. thought in ancient Greece was dead
   B. the theory of evolution is now universally accepted
   C. the "Origin of Species" was seized by the Church
   D. Darwin was influenced by Newton
   E. the theories of "the struggle for existence" and "natural selection" are too evident to be scientific

3. The idea of evolution

   A. was suppressed for 1,000 years
   B. is falsely claimed by Darwin
   C. has swept aside all superstition
   D. was outworn even in ancient Greece
   E. has revolutionized the universe

4. The processes of growth and multiplication

   A. have been replaced by others discovered by Darwin
   B. were the basis for the theory of gravitation
   C. are "the struggle for existence" and "natural selection"
   D. are scientific theories not yet proved
   E. are accepted as fundamental processes of nature

4._____

5. Darwin's treatise on evolution

   A. traces life on the planets from the beginning of time to the present day
   B. was translated from the Greek
   C. contains an ancient philosophy in modern, scientific guise
   D. has had a profound effect on evolution
   E. has had little notice outside scientific circles

5._____

6. The theory of evolution

   A. was first advanced in the "Origin of Species"
   B. was suppressed by the ancient Greeks
   C. did not get beyond the monasteries during the millennium
   D. is philosophical, not scientific
   E. was elaborated and revived by Darwin

6._____

7. Darwin has contributed GREATLY toward

   A. a universal acceptance of the processes of nature
   B. reviving the Greek intellect
   C. ending the millennium of theological scholasticism
   D. a satisfactory explanation of scientific theory
   E. easing the struggle for existence

7._____

TEST 6

DIRECTIONS: Each question or incomplete statement is followed by several suggested answers or completions. Select the one that BEST answers the question or completes the statement. *PRINT THE LETTER OF THE CORRECT ANSWER IN THE SPACE AT THE RIGHT.*

PASSAGE

The higher forms of plants and animals, such as seed plants and vertebrates, are similar or alike in many respects but decidedly different in others. For example, both of these groups of organisms carry on digestion, respiration, reproduction, conduction, growth, and exhibit sensitivity to various stimuli. On the other hand, a number of basic differences are evident. Plants have no excretory systems comparable to those of animals. Plants have no heart or similar pumping organ. Plants are very limited in their movements. Plants have nothing similar to the animal nervous system. In addition, animals can not synthesize carbohydrates from inorganic substances. Animals do not have special regions of growth, comparable to terminal and lateral meristems in plants, which persist through-out the life span of the organism. And, finally, the animal cell "wall" is only a membrane, while plant cell walls are more rigid, usually thicker, and may be composed of such substances as cellulose, lignin, pectin, cutin, and suberin. These characteristics are important to an understanding of living organisms and their functions and should, consequently, be carefully considered in plant and animal studies

Questions 1-7.

1. Which of the following do animals lack?

    A. Ability to react to stimuli
    B. Ability to conduct substances from one place to another
    C. Reproduction by gametes
    D. A cell membrane
    E. A terminal growth region

2. Which of the following statements is false?

    A. Animal cell "walls" are composed of cellulose.
    B. Plants grow as long as they live.
    C. Plants produce sperms and eggs.
    D. All vertebrates have hearts.
    E. Wood is dead at maturity.

3. Respiration in plants takes place

    A. only during the day
    B. only in the presence of carbon dioxide
    C. both day and night
    D. only at night
    E. only in the presence of certain stimuli

4. An example of a vertebrate is the

    A. earthworm   B. starfish   C. amoeba
    D. cow   E. insect

5. Which of the following statements is true?   5.____

    A. All animals eat plants as a source of food.
    B. Respiration, in many ways, is the reverse of photo-synthesis.
    C. Man is an invertebrate animal.
    D. Since plants have no hearts, they can not develop high pressures in their cells.
    E. Plants can not move.

6. Which of the following do plants lack?   6.____

    A. A means of movement
    B. Pumping structures
    C. Special regions of growth
    D. Reproduction by gametes
    E. A digestive process

7. A substance that can be synthesized by green plants but NOT by animals is   7.____

    A. protein   B. cellulose   C. carbon dioxide
    D. uric acid   E. water

TEST 7

DIRECTIONS: Each question or incomplete statement is followed by several suggested answers or completions. Select the one that BEST answers the question or completes the statement. *PRINT THE LETTER OF THE CORRECT ANSWER IN THE SPACE AT THE RIGHT.*

PASSAGE

Sodium chloride, being by far the largest constituent of the mineral matter of the blood, assumes special significance in the regulation of water exchanges in the organism. And, as Cannon has emphasized repeatedly, these latter are more extensive and more important than may at first thought appear. He points out "there are a number of circulations of the fluid out of the body and back again, without loss." Thus, by example, it is estimated that from a quart and one-half of water daily "leaves the body" when it enters the mouth as saliva; another one or two quarts are passed out as gastric juice; and perhaps the same amount is contained in the bile and the secretions of the pancreas and the intestinal wall. This large volume of water enters the digestive processes; and practically all of it is reabsorbed through the intestinal wall, where it performs the equally important function of carrying in the digested foodstuffs. These and other instances of what Cannon calls "the conservative use of water in our bodies" involve essentially osmotic pressure relationships in which the concentration of sodium chloride plays an important part.

Questions 1-11.

1. This passage implies that

    A. the contents of the alimentary canal are not to be considered within the body
    B. sodium chloride does not actually enter the body
    C. every particle of water ingested is used over and over again
    D. water can not be absorbed by the body unless it contains sodium chloride
    E. substances can pass through the intestinal wall in only one direction

2. According to this passage, which of the following processes requires MOST water? The

    A. absorption of digested foods
    B. secretion of gastric juice
    C. secretion of saliva
    D. production of bile
    E. concentration of sodium chloride solution

3. A body fluid that is NOT saline is

    A. blood   B. urine   C. bile
    D. gastric juice   E. saliva

4. An organ that functions as a storage reservoir from which large quantities of water are reabsorbed into the body is the

    A. kidney   B. liver   C. large intestine
    D. mouth   E. pancreas

5. Water is reabsorbed into the body by the process of

   A. secretion
   B. excretion
   C. digestion
   D. osmosis
   E. oxidation

6. Digested food enters the body PRINCIPALLY through the

   A. mouth
   B. liver
   C. villi
   D. pancreas
   E. stomach

7. The metallic element found in the blood in compound form and present there in larger quantities than any other metallic element is

   A. iron
   B. calcium
   C. magnesium
   D. chlorine
   E. sodium

8. An organ that removes water from the body and prevents its reabsorption for use in the body processes is the

   A. pancreas
   B. liver
   C. small intestine
   D. lungs
   E. large intestine

9. In which of the following processes is sodium chloride removed MOST rapidly from the body?

   A. Digestion
   B. Breathing
   C. Oxidation
   D. Respiration
   E. Perspiration

10. Which of the following liquids would pass from the alimentary canal into the blood MOST rapidly?

    A. A dilute solution of sodium chloride in water
    B. Gastric juice
    C. A concentrated solution of sodium chloride in water
    D. Digested food
    E. Distilled water

11. The reason why it is unsafe to drink ocean water even under conditions of extreme thirst is that it

    A. would reduce the salinity of the blood to a dangerous level
    B. contains dangerous disease germs
    C. contains poisonous salts
    D. would greatly increase the salinity of the blood
    E. would cause salt crystals to form in the blood stream

TEST 8

DIRECTIONS: Each question or incomplete statement is followed by several suggested answers or completions. Select the one that BEST answers the question or completes the statement. *PRINT THE LETTER OF THE CORRECT ANSWER IN THE SPACE AT THE RIGHT.*

PASSAGE

The discovery of antitoxin and its specific antagonistic effect upon toxin furnished an opportunity for the accurate investigation of the relationship of a bacterial antigen and its antibody. Toxin-antitoxin reactions were the first immunological processes to which experimental precision could be applied, and the discovery of principles of great importance resulted from such studies. A great deal of the work was done with diphtheria toxin and antitoxin and the facts elucidated with these materials are in principle applicable to similar substances.

The simplest assumption to account for the manner in which an antitoxin renders a toxin innocuous would be that the antitoxin destroys the toxin. Roux and Buchner, however, advanced the opinion that the antitoxin did not act directly upon the toxin, but affected it indirectly through the mediation of tissue cells. Ehrlich, on the other hand, conceived the reaction of toxin and antitoxin as a direct union, analogous to the chemical neutralization of an acid by a base.

The conception of toxin destruction was conclusively refuted by the experiments of Calmette. This observer, working with snake poison, found that the poison itself (unlike most other toxins) possessed the property of resisting heat to 100 degrees C, while its specific antitoxin, like other antitoxins, was destroyed at or about 70 degrees C. Nontoxic mixtures of the two substanues, when subjected to heat, regained their toxic properties. The natural inference from these observations was that the toxin in the original mixture had not been destroyed, but had been merely inactiviated by the presence of the antitoxin and again set free after destruction of the antitoxin by heat.

Questions 1-10.

1. Both toxins and antitoxins ORDINARILY

    A. are completely destroyed at body temperatures
    B. are extremely resistant to heat
    C. can exist only in combination
    D. are destroyed at 180° F
    E. are products of nonliving processes

    1.__

2. MOST toxins can be destroyed by

    A. bacterial action   B. salt solutions
    C. boiling   D. diphtheria antitoxin
    E. other toxins

    2.__

3. Very few disease organisms release a true toxin into the blood stream. It would follow, then, that

    A. studies of snake venom reactions have no value
    B. studies of toxin-antitoxin reactions are of little importance

    3.__

C. the treatment of most diseases must depend upon information obtained from study of a few
D. antitoxin plays an important part in the body defense against the great majority of germs
E. only toxin producers are dangerous

4. A person becomes susceptible to infection again immediately after recovering from

   A. mumps
   B. tetanus
   C. diphtheria
   D. smallpox
   E. tuberculosis

5. City people are more frequently immune to communicable diseases than country people are because

   A. country people eat better food
   B. city doctors are better than country doctors
   C. the air is more healthful in the country
   D. country people have fewer contacts with disease carriers
   E. there are more doctors in the city than in the country

6. The substances that provide us with immunity to disease are found in the body in the

   A. blood serum
   B. gastric juice
   C. urine
   D. white blood cells
   E. red blood cells

7. A person ill with diphtheria would MOST likely be treated with

   A. diphtheria toxin
   B. diphtheria toxoid
   C. dead diphtheria germs
   D. diphtheria antitoxin
   E. live diphtheria germs

8. To determine susceptibility to diphtheria, an individual may be given the

   A. Wassermann test
   B. Schick test
   C. Widal test
   D. Dick test
   E. Kahn test

9. Since few babies under six months of age contract diphtheria, young babies PROBABLY

   A. are never exposed to diphtheria germs
   B. have high body temperatures that destroy the toxin if acquired
   C. acquire immunity from their mothers
   D. acquire immunity from their fathers
   E. are too young to become infected

10. Calmette's findings

    A. contradicted both Roux and Buchner's opinion and Ehrlich's conception
    B. contradicted Roux and Buchner, but supported Ehrlich
    C. contradicted Ehrlich, but supported Roux and Buchner
    D. were consistent with both theories
    E. had no bearing on the point at issue

TEST 9

DIRECTIONS: Each question or incomplete statement is followed by several suggested answers or completions. Select the one that BEST answers the question or completes the statement. *PRINT THE LETTER OF THE CORRECT ANSWER IN THE SPACE AT THE RIGHT.*

PASSAGE

In the days of sailing ships, when voyages were long and uncertain, provisions for many months were stored without refrigeration in the holds of the ships. Naturally no fresh or perishable foods could be included. Toward the end of particularly long voyages the crews of such ships became ill and often many died from scurvy. Many men, both scientific and otherwise, tried to devise a cure for scurvy. Among the latter was John Hall, a son-in-law of William Shakespeare, who cured some cases of scurvy by administering a sour brew made from scurvy grass and water cress.

The next step was the suggestion of William Harvey that scurvy could be prevented by giving the men lemon juice. He thought that the beneficial substance was the acid contained in the fruit.

The third step was taken by Dr. James Lind, an English naval surgeon, who performed the following experiment with 12 sailors, all of whom were sick with scurvy: Each was given the same diet, except that four of the men received small amounts of dilute sulfuric acid, four others were given vinegar and the remaining four were given lemons. Only those who received the fruit recovered.

Questions 1-7.

1. Credit for solving the problem described above belongs to

    A. Hall, because he first devised a cure for scurvy
    B. Harvey, because he first proposed a solution of the problem
    C. Lind, because he proved the solution by means of an experiment
    D. both Harvey and Lind, because they found that lemons are more effective than scurvy grass or water cress
    E. all three men, because each made some contribution

2. A good substitute for lemons in the treatment of scurvy is

    A. fresh eggs   B. tomato juice   C. cod-liver oil
    D. liver   E. whole-wheat bread

3. The number of control groups that Dr. Lind used in his experiment was

    A. one   B. two   C. three   D. four   E. none

4. A substance that will turn blue litmus red is

    A. aniline   B. lye   C. ice
    D. vinegar   E. table salt

5. The hypothesis tested by Lind was:

    A. Lemons contain some substance not present in vinegar.
    B. Citric acid is the most effective treatment for scurvy.

1.___

2.___

3.___

4.___

5.___

C. Lemons contain some unknown acid that will cure scurvy.
D. Some specific substance, rather than acids in general, is needed to cure scurvy.
E. The substance needed to cure scurvy is found only in lemons.

6. A problem that Lind's experiment did NOT solve was: 6._____

   A. Will citric acid alone cure scurvy?
   B. Will lemons cure scurvy?
   C. Will either sulfuric acid or vinegar cure scurvy?
   D. Are all substances that contain acids equally effective as a treatment for scurvy?
   E. Are lemons more effective than either vinegar or sulfuric acid in the treatment of scurvy?

7. The PRIMARY purpose of a controlled scientific experiment is to 7._____

   A. get rid of superstitions
   B. prove a hypothesis is correct
   C. disprove a theory that is false
   D. determine whether a hypothesis is true or false
   E. discover new facts

TEST 10

DIRECTIONS: Each question or incomplete statement is followed by several suggested answers or completions. Select the one that BEST answers the question or completes the statement. *PRINT THE LETTER OF THE CORRECT ANSWER IN THE SPACE AT THE RIGHT.*

PASSAGE

The formed elements of the blood are the red corpuscles or erythrocytes, the white corpuscles or leucocytes, the blood platelets, and the so-called blood dust or hemoconiae. Together, these constitute 30-40 per cent by volume of the whole blood, the remainder being taken up by the plasma. In man, there are normally 5,000,000 red cells per cubic millimeter of blood; the count is somewhat lower in women. Variations occur frequently, especially after exercise or a heavy meal, or at high altitudes. Except in camels, which have elliptical corpuscles, the shape of the mammalian corpuscle is that of a circular, nonnucleated, bi-concave disk. The average diameter usually given is 7.7 microns, a value obtained by examining dried preparations of blood and considered by Ponder to be too low. Ponder's own observations, made on red cells in the fresh state, show the human corpuscle to have an average diameter of 8.8 microns. When circulating in the blood vessels, the red cell does not maintain a fixed shape but changes its form constantly, especially in the small capillaries. The red blood corpuscles are continually undergoing destruction, new corpuscles being formed to replace them. The average life of red corpuscles has been estimated by various investigators to be between three and six weeks. Preceding destruction, changes in the composition of the cells are believed to occur which render them less resistant. In the process of destruction, the lipids of the membrane are dissolved and the hemoglobin which is liberated is the most important, though probably not the only, source of bilirubin. The belief that the liver is the only site of red cell destruction is no longer generally held. The leucocytes, of which there are several forms, usually number between 7000 and 9000 per cubic millimeter of blood. These increase in number in disease, particularly when there is bacterial infection.

Questions 1-10.

1. Leukemia is a disease involving the
   A. red cells   B. white cells   C. plasma
   D. blood platelets   E. blood dust

2. Are the erythrocytes in the blood increased in number after a heavy meal? The paragraph implies that this
   A. is true   B. holds only for camels
   C. is not true   D. may be true
   E. depends on the number of white cells

3. When blood is dried, the red cells
   A. contract   B. remain the same size   C. disintegrate
   D. expand   E. become elliptical

4. Ponder is probably classified as a professional
   A. pharmacist   B. physicist   C. psychologist
   D. physiologist   E. psychiatrist

5. The term "erythema" when applied to skin conditions signifies

    A. redness   B. swelling   C. irritation
    D. pain   E. roughness

6. Lipids are insoluble in water and soluble in such solvents as ether, chloroform and benzene. It may be inferred that the membranes of red cells MOST closely resemble

    A. egg white   B. sugar   C. bone
    D. butter   E. cotton fiber

7. Analysis of a sample of blood yields cell counts of 4,800,000 erythrocytes and 16,000 leucocytes per cubic millimeter. These data suggest that the patient from whom the blood was taken

    A. is anemic
    B. has been injuriously invaded by germs
    C. has been exposed to high-pressure air
    D. has a normal cell count
    E. has lost a great deal of blood

8. Bilirubin, a bile pigment, is

    A. an end product of several different reactions
    B. formed only in the liver
    C. formed from the remnants of the cell membranes of erythrocytes
    D. derived from hemoglobin exclusively
    E. a precursor of hemoglobin

9. Bancroft found that the blood count of the natives in the Peruvian Andes differed from that usually accepted as normal. The blood PROBABLY differed in respect to

    A. leucocytes   B. blood platelets   C. cell shapes
    D. erythrocytes   E. hemoconiae

10. Hemoglobin is probably NEVER found

    A. free in the blood stream
    B. in the red cells
    C. in women's blood
    D. in the blood after exercise
    E. in the leucocytes

TEST 11

Questions 1-7.

DIRECTIONS: Each question or incomplete statement is followed by several suggested answers or completions. Select the one that BEST answers the question or completes the statement. *PRINT THE LETTER OF THE CORRECT ANSWER IN THE SPACE AT THE RIGHT.*

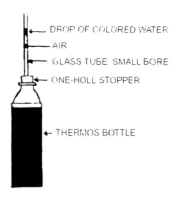

1. The device shown in the diagram above indicates changes that are measured more accurately by a(n)

   A. thermometer B. hygrometer C. anemometer
   D. hydrometer   E. barometer

2. If the device is placed in a cold refrigerator for 72 hours, which of the following is MOST likely to happen?

   A. The stopper will be forced out of the bottle.
   B. The drop of water will evaporate.
   C. The drop will move downward.
   D. The drop will move upward.
   E. No change will take place.

3. When the device was carried in an elevator from the first floor to the sixth floor of a building, the drop of colored water moved about 1/4 inch in the tube. Which of the following is MOST probably true? The drop moved

   A. *downward* because there was a decrease in the air pressure
   B. *upward* because there was a decrease in the air pressure
   C. *downward* because there was an increase in the air temperature
   D. *upward* because there was an increase in the air temperature
   E. *downward* because there was an increase in the temperature and a decrease in the pressure

4. The part of a thermos bottle into which liquids are poured consists of

   A. a single-walled, metal flask coated with silver
   B. two flasks, one of glass and one of silvered metal
   C. two silvered-glass flasks separated by a vacuum
   D. two silver flasks separated by a vacuum
   E. a single-walled, glass flask with a silver-colored coating

5. The thermos bottle is MOST similar in principle to   5.____

   A. the freezing unit in an electric refrigerator
   B. radiant heaters
   C. solar heating systems
   D. storm windows
   E. a thermostatically controlled heating system

6. In a plane flying at an altitude where the air pressure is only half the normal pressure at   6.____
   sea level, the plane's altimeter should read, *approximately,*

   A. 3000 feet   B. 9000 feet   C. 18000 feet
   D. 27000 feet   E. 60000 feet

7. Which of the following is the POOREST conductor of heat?   7.____

   A. Air under a pressure of 1.5 pounds per square inch
   B. Air under a pressure of 15 pounds per square inch
   C. Unsilvered glass
   D. Silvered glass
   E. Silver

TEST 12

DIRECTIONS: Each question or incomplete statement is followed by several suggested answers or completions. Select the one that BEST answers the question or completes the statement. *PRINT THE LETTER OF THE CORRECT ANSWER IN THE SPACE AT THE RIGHT.*

PASSAGE

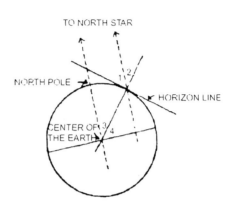

The latitude of any point on the earth's surface is the angle between a plumb line dropped to the center of the earth from that point and the plane of the earth's equator. Since it is impossible to go to the center of the earth to measure latitude, the latitude of any point may be determined indirectly as shown in the accompanying diagram.

It will be recalled that the axis of the earth, if extended out-ward, passes very near the North Star. Since the North Star is, for all practical purposes, infinitely distant, the line of sight to the North Star of an observer on the surface of the earth is virtually parallel with the earth's axis. Angle 1, then, in the diagram represents the angular distance of the North Star above the horizon. Angle 2 is equal to angle 3, because when two parallel lines are intersected by a straight line, the corresponding angles are equal. Angle 1 plus angle 2 is a right angle and so is angle 3 plus angle 4. Therefore, angle 1 equals angle 4 because when equals are subtracted from equals the results are equal.

Questions 1-10.

1. If an observer finds that the angular distance of the North Star above the horizon is 30, his latitude is

    A. 15° N   B. 30° N   C. 60° N   D. 90° N   E. 120° N

    1.___

2. To an observer on the equator, the North Star would be

    A. 30° above the horizon   B. 60° above the horizon
    C. 90° above the horizon   D. on the horizon
    E. below the horizon

    2.___

3. To an observer on the Arctic Circle, the North Star would be

   A. directly overhead
   B. 23 1/2° above the horizon
   C. 66 1/2° above the horizon
   D. on the horizon
   E. below the horizon

3.____

4. The distance around the earth along a certain parallel of latitude is 3600 miles. At that latitude, how many miles are there in one degree of longitude?

   A. 1 mile
   B. 10 miles
   C. 30 miles
   D. 69 miles
   E. 100 miles

4.____

5. At which of the following latitudes would the sun be DIRECTLY overhead at noon on June 21?

   A. 0°
   B. 23 1/2°S
   C. 23 1/2°N
   D. 66 1/2°N
   E. 66 1/2°S

5.____

6. On March 21 the number of hours of daylight at places on the Arctic Circle is

   A. none   B. 8   C. 12   D. 16   E. 24

6.____

7. The distance from the equator to the 45th parallel, measured along a meridian, is, *approximately*,

   A. 450 miles
   B. 900 miles
   C. 1250 miles
   D. 3125 miles
   E. 6250 miles

7.____

8. The difference in time between the meridians that pass through longitude 45°E and longitude 105°W

   A. 6 hours
   B. 2 hours
   C. 8 hours
   D. 4 hours
   E. 10 hours

8.____

9. Which of the following is NOT a great circle or part of a great circle?

   A. Arctic Circle
   B. 100th meridian
   C. Equator
   D. Shortest distance between New York and London
   E. Greenwich meridian

9.____

10. At which of the following places does the sun set EARLIEST on June 21?

    A. Montreal, Canada
    B. Santiago, Chile
    C. Mexico City, Mexico
    D. Lima, Peru
    E. Manila, P.I.

10.____

KEY (CORRECT ANSWERS)

TEST 1

1. C 5. A
2. E 6. B
3. C 7. B
4. A 8. C

TEST 2

1. C
2. B

TEST 3

1. B 6. D
2. A 7. D
3. C 8. E
4. C 9. C
5. D

TEST 4

1. A
2. B
3. C
4. C
5. D

TEST 5

1. D 5. D
2. B 6. E
3. A 7. A
4. E

TEST 6

1. E 5. B
2. A 6. B
3. C 7. B
4. D

TEST 7

1. A 6. C
2. A 7. E
3. D 8. D
4. C 9. E
5. D 10. E
11. D

TEST 8

1. D 6. A
2. C 7. D
3. C 8. B
4. E 9. C
5. D 10. D

TEST 9

1. E 5. D
2. B 6. A
3. B 7. D
4. D

TEST 10

1. B 6. D
2. D 7. B
3. A 8. A
4. D 9. D
5. A 10. E

TEST 11

1. A 5. D
2. C 6. C
3. B 7. A
4. C

TEST 12

1. B 6. C
2. D 7. D
3. C 8. E
4. B 9. A
5. C 10. B

Preparing Written Material

EXAMINATION SECTION
TEST 1

DIRECTIONS: Each short paragraph below is followed by four restatements or summaries of the information contained within it. Select the one that most completely and accurately restates the information or opinion given in the paragraph. *PRINT THE LETTER OF THE CORRECT ANSWER IN THE SPACE AT THE RIGHT.*

1. India's night jasmine, or hurshinghar, is different from most flowering plants, in that its flowers are closed during the day, and open after dark. The scientific reason for this is probably that the plant has avoided competing with other flowers for pollinating insects and birds, and relies instead on the service of nocturnal bats that are drawn to the flower's nectar. According to an old Indian legend, however, the flowers sprouted from the funeral ashes of a beautiful young girl who had fallen hopelessly in love with the sun.

   A. Despite the Indian legend that explains why the hurshinghar's flowers open at dusk, scientists believe it has to do with competition for available pollinators.
   B. The Indian hurshinghar's closure of its flowers during the day is due to a lack of available pollinators.
   C. The hurshinghar of India has evolved an unhealthy dependency on nocturnal bats.
   D. Like most myths, the Indian legend of the hurshinghar's night-flowering has been disproved by science.

1.____

2. Charles Lindbergh's trans-Atlantic flight from New York to Paris made him an international hero in 1927, but he lived nearly another fifty years, and by most accounts they weren't terribly happy ones. The two greatest tragedies of his life—the 1932 kidnapping and murder of his oldest son, and an unshakeable reputation as a Nazi sympathizer during World War II—he blamed squarely on the rabid media hounds who stalked his every move.

   A. Despite the fact that Charles Lindbergh had a hand in the two greatest tragedies of his life, he insisted on blaming the media for his problems.
   B. Charles Lindbergh lived a largely unhappy life after the glory of his 1927 trans-Atlantic flight, and he blamed his unhappiness on media attention.
   C. Charles Lindbergh's later life was marked by despair and disillusionment.
   D. Because of the rabid media attention sparked by Charles Lindbergh's 1927 trans-Atlantic flight, he would later consider it the last happy event of his life.

2.____

3. The United States, one of the world's youngest nations in the early nineteenth century, had yet to spread its wings in terms of foreign affairs, preferring to remain isolated and opposed to meddling in the affairs of others. But the fact remained that as a young nation situated on the opposite side of the globe from Europe, Africa, and Asia, the United States had much work to do in establishing relations with the rest of the world. So, too, as the European colonial powers continued to battle for influence in North and South America, did the United States come to believe that it was proper for them to keep these nations from encroaching into their sphere of influence.

   A. The roots of the Monroe Doctrine can be traced to the foreign policy shift of the United States during the early nineteenth century.

3.____

B. In the early nineteenth century, the United States shifted its foreign policy to reflect a growing desire to actively protect its interests in the Western Hemisphere.
C. In the early nineteenth century, the United States was too young and undeveloped to have devised much in the way of foreign policy.
D. The United States adopted a more aggressive foreign policy in the early nineteenth century in order to become a diplomatic player on the world stage.

4. Hertha Ayrton, a nineteenth-century Englishwoman, pursued a career in science during a time when most women were not given the opportunity to go to college. Her series of successes led to her induction into the Institution of Electrical Engineers in 1899, when she was the first woman to receive this professional honor. Her most noted accomplishment was the research and invention of an anti-gas fan that the British War Office used in the trench warfare of World War I.

    4.____

A. The British Army's success in World War I can be partly attributed to Hertha Ayrton, a groundbreaking British scientist.
B. Hertha Ayrton was the first woman to be inducted into the Institution of Electrical Engineers.
C. The injustices of nineteenth-century England were no match for the brilliant mind of Hertha Ayrton.
D. Hertha Ayrton defied the restrictions of her society by building a successful scientific career.

5. Scientists studying hyenas in Tanzania's Ngorongoro Crater have observed that hyena clans have evolved a system of territoriality that allows each clan a certain space to hunt within the 100-square-mile area. These territories are not marked by natural boundaries, but by droppings and excretions from the hyenas' scent glands. Usually, the hyenas take these boundary lines very seriously; some hyena clans have been observed abandoning their pursuit of certain prey after the prey has crossed into another territory, even though no members of the neighboring clan are anywhere in sight.

    5.____

A. The hyenas of Ngorongoro Crater illustrate that the best way to peacefully coexist within a limited territory is to strictly delineate and defend territorial borders.
B. While most territorial boundaries are marked using geographical features, the hyenas of Ngorongoro Crater have devised another method.
C. The hyena clans of Ngorongoro Crater, in order to co-exist within a limited hunting territory, have developed a method of marking strict territorial boundaries.
D. As with most species, the hyenas of Ngorongoro Crater have proven the age-old motto: "To the victor go the spoils."

6. The flood control policy of the U.S. Army Corps of Engineers has long been an obvious feature of the American landscapethe Corps seeks to contain the nation's rivers with an enormous network of dams and levees, "channelizing" rivers into small, confined routes that will stay clear of settled floodplains when rivers rise. As a command of the U.S. Army, the Corps seems to have long seen the nation's rivers as an enemy to be fought; one of the agency's early training films speaks of the Corps' "battle" with its adversary, Mother Nature.

    6.____

A. The dams and levees built by the U.S. Army Corps of Engineers have at least defeated their adversary, Mother Nature.

B. The flood control policy of the U.S. Army Corps of Engineers has often reflected a military point of view, making the nation's rivers into enemies that must be defeated.
C. When one realizes that the flood policy of the U.S. Army Corps of Engineers has always relied on a kind of military strategy, it is only possible to view the Corps' efforts as a failure.
D. By damming and channelizing the nation's rivers, the U.S. Army Corps of Engineers have made America's floodplains safe for farming and development.

7. Frogs with extra legs or missing legs have been showing up with greater frequency over the past decade, and scientists have been baffled by the cause. Some researchers have concluded that pesticide runoff from farms is to blame; others say a common parasite, the trematode, is the culprit. Now, a new study suggests that both these factors in combination have disturbed normal development in many frogs, leading to the abnormalities. 7._____

   A. Despite several studies, scientists still have no idea what is causing the widespread incidence of deformities among aquatic frogs.
   B. In the debate over what is causing the increase in frog deformities, environmentalists tend to blame pesticide runoff, while others blame a common parasite, the trematode.
   C. A recent study suggests that both pesticide runoff and natural parasites have contributed to the increasing rate of deformities in frogs.
   D. Because of their aquatic habitat, frogs are among the most susceptible organisms to chemical and environmental change, and this is illustrated by the increasing rate of physical deformities among frog populations.

8. The builders of the Egyptian pyramids, to insure that each massive structure was built on a completely flat surface, began by cutting a network of criss-crossing channels into the pyramid's mapped-out ground space and partly filling the channels with water. Because the channels were all interconnected, the water was distributed evenly throughout the channel system, and all the workers had to do to level their building surface was cut away any rock above the waterline. 8._____

   A. The modern carpenter's level uses a principle that was actually invented several centuries ago by the builders of the Egyptian pyramids.
   B. The discovery of the ancient Egyptians' sophisticated construction techniques is a quiet argument against the idea that they were built by slaves.
   C. The use of water to insure that the pyramids were level mark the Egyptians as one of the most scientifically advanced of the ancient civilizations.
   D. The builders of the Egyptian pyramids used a simple but ingenious method for ensuring a level building surface with interconnected channels of water.

9. Thunderhead Mountain, a six-hundred-foot-high formation of granite in the Black Hills of South Dakota, is slowly undergoing a transformation that will not be finished for more than a century, when what remains of the mountain will have become the largest sculpture in the world. The statue, begun in 1947 by a Boston sculptor named Henry Ziolkowski, is still being carved and blasted by his wife and children into the likeness of Crazy Horse, the legendary chief of the Sioux tribe of American natives. The enormity of the sculpture the planned length of one of the figure's arms is 263 feet is understandable, given the historical greatness of Crazy Horse. 9._____

A. Only a hero as great as Crazy Horse could warrant a sculpture so large that it will take more than a century to complete.
B. In 1947, sculptor Henry Ziolkowski began work on what he imagined would be the largest sculpture in the world—even though he knew he would not live to see it completed.
C. The huge Black Hills sculpture of the great Sioux chief Crazy Horse, still being carried out by the family of Henry Ziolkowski, will some day be the largest sculpture in the world.
D. South Dakota's Thunderhead Mountain will soon be the site of the world's largest sculpture, a statue of the Sioux chief Crazy Horse.

10. Because they were some of the first explorers to venture into the western frontier of North America, the French were responsible for the naming of several native tribes. Some of these names were poorly conceived—the worst of which was perhaps Eskimo, the name for the natives of the far North, which translates roughly as "eaters of raw flesh." The name is incorrect; these people have always cooked their fish and game, and they now call themselves the Inuit, a native term that means "the people."

    A. The first to explore much of North America's western frontier were the French, and they usually gave improper or poorly-informed names to the native tribes.
    B. The Eskimos of North America have never eaten raw flesh, so it is curious that the French would give them a name that means "eaters of raw flesh."
    C. The Inuit have fought for many years to overcome the impression that they eat raw flesh.
    D. Like many native tribes, the Inuit were once incorrectly named by French explorers, but they have since corrected the mistake themselves.

11. Of the 30,000 species of spiders worldwide, only a handful are dangerous to human beings, but this doesn't prevent many people from having a powerful fear of all spiders, whether they are venomous or not. The leading scientific theory about arachnophobia, as this fear is known, is that far in our evolutionary past, some species of spider must have presented a serious enough threat to people that the sight of a star-shaped body or an eight-legged walk was coded into our genes as a danger signal.

    A. Scientists theorize that peoples' widespread fear of spiders can be traced to an ancient spider species that was dangerous enough to trigger this fearful reaction.
    B. The fear known as arachnophobia is triggered by the sight of a star-shaped body or an eight-legged walk.
    C. Because most spiders have a uniquely shaped body that triggers a human fear response, many humans are afflicted with the fear of spiders known as arachnophobia.
    D. Though only a few of the planet's 30,000 spider species are dangerous to people, many people have an unreasonable fear of them.

12. From the 1970s to the 1990s, the percentage of Americans living in the suburbs climbed from 37% to 47%. In the latter part of the 1990s, a movement emerged that questioned the good of such a population shift—or at least, the good of the speed and manner in which this suburban land was being developed. Often, people began to argue, the planning of such growth was flawed, resulting in a phenomenon that has become known as suburban "sprawl," or the growth of suburban orbits around cities at rates faster than infrastructures could support, and in ways that are damaging to the environment.

A. The term "urban sprawl" was coined in the 1990s, when the movement against unchecked suburban development began to gather momentum.
B. In the 1980s and 1990s, home builders benefited from a boom in their most favored demographic segment-suburban new-home buyers.
C. Suburban development tends to suffer from poor planning, which can lead to a lower quality of life for residents.
D. The surge in suburban residences in the late twentieth century was criticized by many as "sprawl" that could not be supported by existing resources.

13. Medicare, a $200 billion-a-year program, processes 1 billion claims annually, and in the year 2000, the computer system that handles these claims came under criticism. The General Accounting Office branded Medicare's financial management system as outdated and inadequateone in a series of studies and reports warning that the program is plagued with duplication, overcharges, double billings and confusion among users. 13.____

A. The General Accounting Office's 2000 report proves that Medicare is a bloated bureaucracy in need of substantial reform.
B. Medicare's confusing computer network is an example of how the federal government often neglects the programs that mean the most to average American citizens.
C. In the year 2000, the General Accounting Office criticized Medicare's financial accounting network as inefficient and outdated.
D. Because it has to handle so many claims each year, Medicare's financial accounting system often produces redundancies and errors.

14. The earliest known writing materials were thin clay tablets, used in Mesopotamia more than 5,000 years ago. Although the tablets were cheap and easy to produce, they had two major disadvantages: they were difficult to store, and once the clay had dried and hardened a person could not write on them. The ancient Egyptians later discovered a better writing materialthe thin bark of the papyrus reed, a plant that grew near the mouth of the Nile River, which could be peeled into long strips, woven into a mat-like layer, pounded flat with heavy mallets, and then dried in the sun. 14.____

A. The Egyptians, after centuries of frustration with clay writing tablets, were finally forced to invent a better writing surface.
B. With the bark of the papyrus reed, ancient Egyptians made a writing material that overcame the disadvantages of clay tablets.
C. The Egyptian invention of the papyrus scroll was necessitated in part by a relative lack of available clay.
D. The word "paper" can be traced to the innovations of the Egyptians, who made the first paper-like writing material from the bark of papyrus plant.

15. In 1850, the German pianomaker Heinrich Steinweg and his family stepped off an immigrant ship in New York City, threw themselves into competition with dozens of other established craftsmen, and defeated them all by reinventing the instrument. The company they created commanded the market for nearly the next century and a half, while their competitorssome of the most acclaimed pianomakers in the businessfaded into obscurity. And all the while, Steinway & Sons, through their sponsorship and encouragement of the world's most distinguished pianists, helped define the cultural life of the young United States. 15.____

A. The Steinways capitalized on weak competition during the mid-nineteenth century to capture the American piano market.
B. Because of their technical and cultural innovations, the Steinways had an advantage over other American pianomakers.
C. Heinrich Steinweg founded the Steinway piano empire in 1850.
D. From humble immigrant origins, the Steinway family rose to dominate both the pianomaking industry and American musical culture.

16. Feng Shui, the ancient Chinese science of studying the natural environment's effect on a person's well-being, has gained new popularity in the design and decoration of buildings. Although a complex area of study, a basic premise of Feng Shui is that each building creates a unique field of energy which affects the inhabitants of that building or home. In recent years, decorators and realtors have begun to offer services which include a diagnosis of a building's Feng Shui, or energy.   16._____

   A. Feng Shui, the Chinese science of balancing environmental energies, has been given more aesthetic quality by recent practitioners.
   B. Generally, practitioners of Feng Shui work to create balance within a room, carefully arranging sharp and soft surfaces to create a positive environment that suits the room's primary purpose.
   C. The idea behind the Chinese "science" of Feng Shui—that objects give off certain energies that affect a building's inhabitants—has been a difficult one for most Westerners to accept, but it is gaining in popularity.
   D. The ancient Chinese science of Feng Shui, which studies the balance of energies in a person's environment, has become popular among those who design and decorate buildings.

17. Because the harsh seasonal variations of the Kansas plains make survival difficult for most plant life, the area is dominated by tall, sturdy grasses. The only tree that has been able to survive-and-prosper throughout the wide expanse of prairie is the cottonwood, which can take root and grow in the most extreme climatic conditions. Sometimes a storm will shear off a living branch and carry it downstream, where it may snag along a sandbar and take root.   17._____

   A. Among the plant life of the Kansas plains, the only tree is the cotton-wood.
   B. The only prosperous tree on the Kansas plains is the cottonwood, which can take root and grow in a wide range of conditions.
   C. Only the cottonwood, whose branches can grow after being broken off and washed down a river, is capable of surviving the climatic extremes of the Kansas plains.
   D. Because it is the most widespread and hardiest tree on the Kansas plains, the cottonwood had become a symbol of pioneer grit and fortitude.

18. In the twenty-first century, it's easy to see the automobile as the keystone of American popular culture. Subtract linen dusters, driving goggles, and women's *crepe de chine* veils from our history, and you've taken the Roaring out of the Twenties. Take away the ducktail haircuts, pegged pants and upturned collars from the teen Car Cult of the Fifties, and the decade isn't nearly as Fabulous. Were the chromed and tailfinned muscle cars of the automobile's Golden Age modeled after us, or were we mimicking them?   18._____

   A. Ever since its invention, the automobile has shaped American culture.
   B. Many of the familiar names we give historical eras, such as "Roaring Twenties" and "Fabulous Fifties," were given because of the predominance of the automobile.

C. Americans' tastes in clothing have been determined primarily by the cars they drive.
D. Teenagers have had a fascination for automobiles ever since the motorcar was first invented.

19. Since the 1960s, an important issue for Canada has been the status of minority French-speaking Canadians, especially in the province of Quebec, whose inhabitants make up 30% of the Canadian population and trace their ancestry back to a Canada that preceded British influence. In response to pressure from Quebec nationalists, the government in 1982 added a Charter of Rights to the constitution, restoring important rights that dated back to the time of aboriginal treaties. Separatism is still a prominent issue, though successive referendums and constitutional inquiries have not resulted in any realistic progress toward Quebec's independence.

19.____

A. Despite the fact that Quebec's inhabitants have their roots in Canada's original settlers, they have been constantly oppressed by the descendants of those who came later, the British.
B. It seems unavoidable that Quebec's linguistic and cultural differences with the rest of Canada will some day lead to its secession.
C. French-speaking Quebec's activism over the last several decades has led to concessions by the Canadian government, but it seems that Quebec will remain a part of the country for some time.
D. The inhabitants of Quebec are an aboriginal culture that has been exploited by the Canadian government for years, but they are gradually winning back their rights.

20. For years, musicians and scientists have tried to discover what it is about an eighteenth-century Stradivarius violin-which may sell for more than $1 million on today's market-that gives it its unique sound. In 1977, American scientist Joseph Nagyvary discovered that the Stradivarius is made of a spruce wood that came from Venice, where timber was stored beneath the sea, and unlike the dry-seasoned wood from which other violins were made, this spruce contains microscopic holes which add resonance to the violin's sound. Nagyvary also found the varnish used on the Stradivarius to be equally unique, containing tiny mineral crystals that appear to have come from ground-up gemstones, which would filter out high-pitched tones and give the violin a smoother sound.

20.____

A. After carefully studying Stradivarius violins to discover the source of their unique sound, an American scientist discovered two qualities in the construction of them that set them apart from other instruments: the wood from which they were made, and the varnish used to coat the wood.
B. The two qualities that give the Stradivarius violin such a unique sound are the wood, which adds resonance, and the finish, which filters out high-pitched tones.
C. The Stradivarius violin, because of the unique wood and finish used in its construction, is widely regarded as the finest string instrument ever manufactured in the world.
D. A close study of the Stradivarius violin has revealed that the best wood for making violins is Venetian spruce, stored underwater.

21. People who watch the display of fireflies on a clear summer evening are actually witnessing a complex chemical reaction called "bioluminescence," which turns certain organisms into living light bulbs. Organisms that produce this light undergo a reaction in which oxygen combines with a chemical called lucerfin and an enzyme called luciferase. Depending on the organism, the light produced from this reaction can range from the light green of the firefly to the bright red spots of a railroad worm. 21.____

   A. Although the function of most displays of bioluminescence is to attract mates, as is the case with fireflies, other species rely on bioluminescence for different purposes.
   B. Bioluminescence, a phenomenon produced by several organisms, is the result of a chemical reaction that takes place within the body of the organism.
   C. Of all the organisms in the world, only insects are capable of displaying bioluminescence.
   D. Despite the fact that some organisms display bioluminescence, these reactions produce almost no heat, which is why the light they create is sometimes referred to as cold light.

22. The first of America's "log cabin" presidents, Andrew Jackson rose from humble backcountry origins to become a U.S. congressman and senator, a renowned military hero, and the seventh president of the United States. Among many Americans, especially those of the western frontier, he was acclaimed as a symbol of the "new" American: self-made, strong through closeness to nature, and endowed with a powerful moral courage. 22.____

   A. Andrew Jackson was the first American president to rise from modest origins.
   B. Because he was born poor, President Andrew Jackson was more popular among Americans of the western frontier.
   C. Andrew Jackson's humble background, along with his outstanding achievements, made him into a symbol of American strength and self-sufficiency.
   D. Andrew Jackson achieved success as a legislator, soldier, and president because he was born humbly and had to work for every honor he ever received.

23. In the past few decades, while much of the world's imagination has focused on the possibilities of outer space, some scientists have been exploring a different frontier-the ocean floor. Although ships have been sailing the oceans for centuries, only recently have scientists developed vehicles strong enough to sustain the pressure of deep-sea exploration and observation. These fiberglass vehicles, called submersibles, are usually just big enough to take two or three people to the deepest parts of the oceans' floors. 23.____

   A. Modern submersible vehicles, thanks to recent technological innovations, are now explore underwater cliffs, crevices and mountain ranges that were once unreachable.
   B. While most people tend to fantasize about exploring outer space, they should be turning toward a more accessible realmthe depths of the earth's oceans.
   C. Because of the necessarily small size of submersible vehicles, exploration of the deep ocean is not a widespread activity.
   D. Recent technological developments have helped scientists to turn their attention from deep space to the deep ocean.

24. The panda—a native of the remote mountainous regions of China—subsists almost entirely on the tender shoots of the bamboo plant. This restrictive diet has allowed the panda to evolve an anatomical structure that is completely different from that of other bears, whose paws are aligned for running, stabbing, and scratching. The panda's paw has an over-developed wrist bone that juts out below the other claws like a thumb, and the panda uses this "thumb" to grip bamboo shoots while it strips them of their leaves.

24.____

   A. The panda is the only bear-like animal that feeds on vegetation, and it has a kind of thumb to help it grip bamboo shoots.
   B. The panda's limited diet of bamboo has led it to evolve a thumb-like appendage for grasping bamboo shoots.
   C. The panda's thumb-like appendage is a factor that limits its diet to the shoots of the bamboo plant.
   D. Because bamboo shoots must be held tightly while eaten, the panda's thumb-like appendage ensure that it is the only bear-like animal that eats bamboo.

25. The stability and security of the Balkan region remains a primary concern for Greece in post-Cold War Europe, and Greece's active participation in peacekeeping and humanitarian operations in Georgia, Albania, and Bosnia are substantial examples of this commitment. Due to its geopolitical position, Greece believes it necessary to maintain, at least for now, a more nationalized defense force than other European nations. It is Greece's hope that the new spirit of integration and cooperation will help establish a common European foreign affairs and defense policy that might ease some of these regional tensions, and allow a greater level of Greek participation in NATO's integrated military structure.

25.____

   A. Greece's proximity to the unstable Balkan region has led it to keep a more nationalized military, though it hopes to become more involved in a common European defense force.
   B. The Balkan states present a greater threat to Greece than any other European nation, and Greece has adopted a highly nationalist military force as a result.
   C. Greece, the only Balkan state to belong to NATO, has an isolationist approach to defense, but hopes to achieve greater integration in the organization's combined forces.
   D. Greece's failure to become more militarily integrated with the rest of Europe can be attributed to the failure to establish a common European defense policy.

KEY (CORRECT ANSWERS)

1.	A	11.	A
2.	B	12.	D
3.	B	13.	C
4.	D	14.	B
5.	C	15.	D
6.	B	16.	D
7.	C	17.	B
8.	D	18.	A
9.	C	19.	C
10.	D	20.	A

21. B
22. C
23. D
24. B
25. A

PREPARING WRITTEN MATERIAL

PARAGRAPH REARRANGEMENT
COMMENTARY

The sentences which follow are in scrambled order. You are to rearrange them in proper order and indicate the letter choice containing the correct answer at the space at the right.

Each group of sentences in this section is actually a paragraph presented in scrambled order. Each sentence in the group has a place in that paragraph; no sentence is to be left out. You are to read each group of sentences and decide upon the best order in which to put the sentences so as to form as well-organized paragraph.

The questions in this section measure the ability to solve a problem when all the facts relevant to its solution are not given.

More specifically, certain positions of responsibility and authority require the employee to discover connections between events sometimes, apparently, unrelated. In order to do this, the employee will find it necessary to correctly infer that unspecified events have probably occurred or are likely to occur. This ability becomes especially important when action must be taken on incomplete information.

Accordingly, these questions require competitors to choose among several suggested alternatives, each of which presents a different sequential arrangement of the events. Competitors must choose the MOST logical of the suggested sequences.

In order to do so, they may be required to draw on general knowledge to infer missing concepts or events that are essential to sequencing the given events. Competitors should be careful to infer only what is essential to the sequence. The plausibility of the wrong alternatives will always require the inclusion of unlikely events or of additional chains of events which are NOT essential to sequencing the given events.

It's very important to remember that you are looking for the best of the four possible choices, and that the best choice of all may not even be one of the answers you're given to choose from.

There is no one right way to solve these problems. Many people have found it helpful to first write out the order of the sentences, as they would have arranged them, on their scrap paper before looking at the possible answers. If their optimum answer is there, this can save them some time. If it isn't, this method can still give insight into solving the problem. Others find it most helpful to just go through each of the possible choices, contrasting each as they go along. You should use whatever method feels comfortable, and works, for you.

While most of these types of questions are not that difficult, we've added a higher percentage of the difficult type, just to give you more practice. Usually there are only one or two questions on this section that contain such subtle distinctions that you're unable to answer confidently, and you then may find yourself stuck deciding between two possible choices, neither of which you're sure about.

Preparing Written Material

EXAMINATION SECTION
TEST 1

DIRECTIONS: The following groups of sentences need to be arranged in an order that makes sense. Select the letter preceding the sequence that represents the best sentence order. *PRINT THE LETTER OF THE CORRECT ANSWER IN THE SPACE AT THE RIGHT.*

Question 1   1._____

1. The ostrich egg shell's legendary toughness makes it an excellent substitute for certain types of dishes or dinnerware, and in parts of Africa ostrich shells are cut and decorated for use as containers for water.
2. Since prehistoric times, people have used the enormous egg of the ostrich as a part of their diet, a practice which has required much patience and hard work-to hard-boil an ostrich egg takes about four hours.
3. Opening the egg's shell, which is rock hard and nearly an inch thick, requires heavy tools, such as a saw or chisel; from inside, a baby ostrich must use a hornlike projection on its beak as a miniature pick-axe to escape from the egg.
4. The offspring of all higher-order animals originate from single egg cells that are carried by mothers, and most of these eggs are relatively small, often microscopic.
5. The egg of the African ostrich, however, weighs a massive thirty pounds, making it the largest single cell on earth, and a common object of human curiosity and wonder.

   The best order is

   A. 5 4 1 2 3
   B. 1 4 5 3 2
   C. 4 2 3 5 1
   D. 4 5 2 3 1

Question 2   2._____

1. Typically only a few feet high on the open sea, individual tsunami have been known to circle the entire globe two or three times if their progress is not interrupted, but are not usually dangerous until they approach the shallow water that surrounds land masses.
2. Some of the most terrifying and damaging hazards caused by earthquakes are tsunami, which were once called "tidal waves"— a poorly chosen name, since these waves have nothing to do with tides.
3. Then a wave, slowed by the sudden drag on the lower part of its moving water column, will pile upon itself, sometimes reaching a height of over 100 feet.
4. Tsunami (Japanese for "great harbor wave") are seismic waves that are caused by earthquakes near oceanic trenches, and once triggered, can travel up to 600 miles an hour on the open ocean.
5. A land-shoaling tsunami is capable of extraordinary destruction; some tsunami have deposited large boats miles inland, washed out two-foot-thick seawalls, and scattered locomotive trains over long distances.

   The best order is

   A. 4 1 3 2 5
   B. 1 3 4 2 5
   C. 5 1 3 2 4
   D. 2 4 1 3 5

Question 3

1. Soon, by the 1940's, jazz was the most popular type of music among American intellectuals and college students.
2. In the early days of jazz, it was considered "lowdown" music, or music that was played only in rough, disreputable bars and taverns.
3. However, jazz didn't take long to develop from early ragtime melodies into more complex, sophisticated forms, such as Charlie Parker's "bebop" style of jazz.
4. After charismatic band leaders such as Duke Ellington and Count Basic brought jazz to a larger audience, and jazz continued to evolve into more complicated forms, white audiences began to accept and even to enjoy the new American art form.
5. Many white Americans, who then dictated the tastes of society, were wary of music that was played almost exclusively in black clubs in the poorer sections of cities and towns.

The best order is

A. 5 4 3 2 1
B. 2 5 3 4 1
C. 4 5 3 1 2
D. 1 2 4 3 5

Question 4

1. Then, hanging in a windless place, the magnetized end of the needle would always point to the south.
2. The needle could then be balanced on the rim of a cup, or the edge of a fingernail, but this balancing act was hard to maintain, and the needle often fell off.
3. Other needles would point to the north, and it was important for any traveler finding his way with a compass to remember which kind of magnetized needle he was carrying.
4. To make some of the earliest compasses in recorded history, ancient Chinese "magicians" would rub a needle with a piece of magnetized iron called a lodestone.
5. A more effective method of keeping the needle free to swing with its magnetic pull was to attach a strand of silk to the center of the needle with a tiny piece of wax.

The best order is

A. 4 2 5 1 3
B. 4 3 5 2 1
C. 4 5 2 1 3
D. 4 1 3 5 2

Question 5

1. The now-famous first mate of the *HMS Bounty*, Fletcher Christian, founded one of the world's most peculiar civilizations in 1790.
2. The men knew they had just committed a crime for which they could be hanged, so they set sail for Pitcairn, a remote, abandoned island in the far eastern region of the Polynesian archipelago, accompanied by twelve Polynesian women and six men.
3. In a mutiny that has become legendary, Christian and the others forced Captain Bligh into a lifeboat and set him adrift off the coast of Tonga in April of 1789.
4. In early 1790, the *Bounty* landed at Pitcairn Island, where the men lived out the rest of their lives and founded an isolated community which to this day includes direct descendants of Christian and the other crewmen.
5. The *Bounty*, commanded by Captain William Bligh, was in the middle of a global voyage, and Christian and his shipmates had come to the conclusion that Bligh was a reckless madman who would lead them to their deaths unless they took the ship from him.

The best order is

A. 4 5 3 2 1
B. 1 3 5 2 4
C. 1 5 3 2 4
D. 3 1 5 4 2

Question 6

1. But once the vines had been led to make orchids, the flowers had to be carefully hand-pollinated, because unpollinated orchids usually lasted less than a day, wilting and dropping off the vine before it had even become dark.
2. The Totonac farmers discovered that looping a vine back around once it reached a five-foot height on its host tree would cause the vine to flower.
3. Though they knew how to process the fruit pods and extract vanilla's flavoring agent, the Totonacs also knew that a wild vanilla vine did not produce abundant flowers or fruit.
4. Wild vines climbed along the trunks and canopies of trees, and this constant upward growth diverted most of the vine's energy to making leaves instead of the orchid flowers that, once pollinated, would produce the flavorful pods.
5. Hundreds of years before vanilla became a prized food flavoring in Europe and the Western World, the Totonac Indians of the Mexican Gulf Coast were skilled cultivators of the vanilla vine, whose fruit they literally worshipped as a goddess.

The best order is

A. 2 3 4 1 5
B. 2 4 3 1 5
C. 5 3 4 2 1
D. 3 4 1 2 5

Question 7

1. Once airborne, the spider is at the mercy of the air currents—usually the spider takes a brief journey, traveling close to the ground, but some have been found in air samples collected as high as 10,000 feet, or been reported landing on ships far out at sea.
2. Once a young spider has hatched, it must leave the environment into which it was born as quickly as possible, in order to avoid competing with its hundreds of brothers and sisters for food.
3. The silk rises into warm air currents, and as soon as the pull feels adequate the spider lets go and drifts up into the air, suspended from the silk strand in the same way that a person might parasail.
4. To help young spiders do this, many species have adapted a practice known as "aerial dispersal," or, in common speech, "ballooning."
5. A spider that wants to leave its surroundings quickly will climb to the top of a grass stem or twig, face into the wind, and aim its back end into the air, releasing a long stream of silk from the glands near the tip of its abdomen.

The best order is

A. 5 4 2 3 1
B. 5 2 4 1 3
C. 2 5 4 3 1
D. 2 4 5 3 1

Question 8

1. For about a year, Tycho worked at a castle in Prague with a scientist named Johannes Kepler, but their association was cut short by another argument that drove Kepler out of the castle, to later develop, on his own, the theory of planetary orbits.
2. Tycho found life without a nose embarrassing, so he made a new nose for himself out of silver, which reportedly remained glued to his face for the rest of his life.
3. Tycho Brahe, the 17th-century Danish astronomer, is today more famous for his odd and arrogant personality than for any contribution he has made to our knowledge of the stars and planets.
4. Early in his career, as a student at Rostock University, Tycho got into an argument with the another student about who was the better mathematician, and the two became so angry that the argument turned into a sword fight, during which Tycho's nose was sliced off.
5. Later in his life, Tycho's arrogance may have kept him from playing a part in one of the greatest astronomical discoveries in history: the elliptical orbits of the solar system's planets.

The best order is

A. 1 4 2 3 5
B. 4 2 3 5 1
C. 4 2 1 3 5
D. 3 4 2 5 1

Question 9

1. The processionaries are so used to this routine that if a person picks up the end of a silk line and brings it back to the origin—creating a closed circle—the caterpillars may travel around and around for days, sometimes starving ar freezing, without changing course.
2. Rather than relying on sight or sound, the other caterpillars, who are lined up end-to-end behind the leader, travel to and from their nests by walking on this silk line, and each will reinforce it by laying down its own marking line as it passes over.
3. In order to insure the safety of individuals, the processionary caterpillar nests in a tree with dozens of other caterpillars, and at night, when it is safest, they all leave together in search of food.
4. The processionary caterpillar of the European continent is a perfect illustration of how much some insect species rely on instinct in their daily routines.
5. As they leave their nests, the processionaries form a single-file line behind a leader who spins and lays out a silk line to mark the chosen path.

The best order is

A. 4 3 5 2 1
B. 3 5 4 2 1
C. 3 5 2 1 4
D. 4 5 3 1 2

Question 10

1. Often, the child is also given a handcrafted walker or push cart, to provide support for its first upright explorations.
2. In traditional Indian families, a child's first steps are celebrated as a ceremonial event, rooted in ancient myth.
3. These carts are often intricately designed to resemble the chariot of Krishna, an important figure in Indian mythology.
4. The sound of these anklet bells is intended to mimic the footsteps of the legendary child Rama, who is celebrated in devotional songs throughout India.
5. When the child's parents see that the child is ready to begin walking, they will fit it with specially designed ankle bracelets, adorned with gently ringing bells.

The best order is

A. 2 3 4 1 5
B. 2 5 3 1 4
C. 5 4 1 3 2
D. 5 3 2 1 4

Question 11   11.___

1. The settlers planted Osage orange all across Middle America, and today long lines and rectangles of Osage orange trees can still be seen on the prairies, running along the former boundaries of farms that no longer exist.
2. After trying sod walls and water-filled ditches with no success, American farmers began to look for a plant that was adaptable to prairie weather, and that could be trimmed into a hedge that was "pig-tight, horse-high, and bull-strong."
3. The tree, so named because it bore a large (but inedible) fruit the size of an orange, was among the sturdiest and hardiest of American trees, and was prized among Native Americans for the strength and flexibility of bows which were made from its wood.
4. The first people to practice agriculture on the American flatlands were faced with an important problem: what would they use to fence their land in a place that was almost entirely without trees or rocks?
5. Finally, an Illinois farmer brought the settlers a tree that was native to the land between the Red and Arkansas rivers, a tree called the Osage orange.

The best order is

A. 2 1 5 3 4
B. 1 2 3 4 5
C. 4 2 5 3 1
D. 4 2 1 3 5

Question 12   12.___

1. After about ten minutes of such spirited and complicated activity, the head dancer is free to make up his or her own movements while maintaining the interest of the New Year's crowd.
2. The dancer will then perform a series of leg kicks, while at the same time operating the lion's mouth with his own hand and moving the ears and eyes by means of a string which is attached to the dancer's own mouth.
3. The most difficult role of this dance belongs to the one who controls the lion's head; this person must lead all the other "parts" of the lion through the choreographed segments of the dance.
4. The head dancer begins with a complex series of steps, alternately stepping forward with the head raised, and then retreating a few steps while lowering the head, a movement that is intended to create the impression that the lion is keeping a watchful eye for anything evil.
5. When performing a traditional Chinese New Year's lion dance, several performers must fit themselves inside a large lion costume and work together to enact different parts of the dance.

The best order is

A. 5 3 4 2 1
B. 3 4 2 5 1
C. 3 1 5 4 2
D. 4 2 3 5 1

Question 13

1. For many years the shell of the chambered nautilus was treasured in Europe for its beauty and intricacy, but collectors were unaware that they were in possession of the structure that marked a "missing link" in the evolution of marine mollusks.
2. The nautilus, however, evolved a series of enclosed chambers in its shell, and invented a new use for the structure: the shell began to serve as a buoyancy device.
3. Equipped with this new flotation device, the nautilus did not need the single, muscular foot of its predecessors, but instead developed flaps, tentacles, and a gentle form of jet propulsion that transformed it into the first mollusk able to take command of its own destiny and explore a three-dimensional world.
4. By pumping and adjusting air pressure into the chambers, the nautilus could spend the day resting on the bottom, and then rise toward the surface at night in search of food.
5. The nautilus shell looks like a large snail shell, similar to those of its ancestors, who used their shells as protective coverings while they were anchored to the sea floor.

The best order is

A. 5 2 4 1 3
B. 5 1 2 3 4
C. 1 2 5 3 4
D. 1 5 2 4 3

Question 14

1. While France and England battled for control of the region, the Acadiens prospered on the fertile farmland, which was finally secured by England in 1713.
2. Early in the 17th century, settlers from western France founded a colony called Acadie in what is now the Canadian province of Nova Scotia.
3. At this time, English officials feared the presence of spies among the Acadiens who might be loyal to their French homeland, and the Acadiens were deported to spots along the Atlantic and Caribbean shores of America.
4. The French settlers remained on this land, under English rule, for around forty years, until the beginning of the French and Indian War, another conflict between France and England.
5. As the Acadien refugees drifted toward a final home in southern Louisiana, neighbors shortened their name to "Cadien," and finally "Cajun," the name which the descendants of early Acadiens still call themselves.

The best order is

A. 1 4 2 3 5
B. 2 1 3 5 4
C. 2 1 4 3 5
D. 5 2 3 4 1

Question 15   15._____

1. Traditional households in the Eastern and Western regions of Africa serve two meals a day-one at around noon, and the other in the evening.
2. The starch is then used in the way that Americans might use a spoon, to scoop up a portion of the main dish on the person's plate.
3. The reason for the starch's inclusion in every meal has to do with taste as well as nutrition; African food can be very spicy, and the starch is known to cool the burning effect of the main dish.
4. When serving these meals, the main dish is usually served on individual plates, and the starch is served on a communal plate, from which diners break off a piece of bread or scoop rice or fufu in their fingers.
5. The typical meals usually consist of a thick stew or soup as the main course, and an accompanying starch—either bread, rice, or *fufu, a* starchy grain paste similar in consistency to mashed potatoes.

The best order is

A. 5 2 3 4 1
B. 5 1 4 3 2
C. 1 4 5 3 2
D. 1 5 4 2 3

Question 16   16._____

1. In the early days of the American Midwest, Indiana settlers sometimes came together to hold an event called an apple peeling, where neighboring settlers gathered at the homestead of a host family to help prepare the hosts' apple crop for cooking, canning, and making apple butter.
2. At the beginning of the event, each peeler sat down in front of a ten- or twenty-gallon stone jar and was given a crock of apples and a paring knife.
3. Once a peeler had finished with a crock, another was placed next to him; if the peeler was an unmarried man, he kept a strict count of the number of apples he had peeled, because the winner was allowed to kiss the girl of his choice.
4. The peeling usually ended by 9:30 in the evening, when the neighbors gathered in the host family's parlor for a dance social.
5. The apples were peeled, cored, and quartered, and then placed into the jar.

The best order is

A. 1 5 3 4 2
B. 2 5 3 4 1
C. 1 2 5 3 4
D. 2 1 5 4 3

Question 17

1. If your pet turtle is a land turtle and is native to temperate climates, it will stop eating some time in October, which should be your cue to prepare the turtle for hibernation.
2. The box should then be covered with a wire screen, which will protect the turtle from any rodents or predators that might want to take advantage of a motionless and helpless animal.
3. When your turtle hasn't eaten for a while and appears ready to hibernate, it should be moved to its winter quarters, most likely a cellar or garage, where the temperature should range between 40° and 45° F.
4. Instead of feeding the turtle, you should bathe it every day in warm water, to encourage the turtle to empty its intestines in preparation for its long winter sleep.
5. Here the turtle should be placed in a well-ventilated box whose bottom is covered with a moisture-absorbing layer of clay beads, and then filled three-fourths full with almost dry peat moss or wood chips, into which the turtle will burrow and sleep for several months.

The best order is

A. 1 4 3 5 2
B. 3 4 2 5 1
C. 3 2 4 1 5
D. 4 5 2 3 1

Question 18

1. Once he has reached the nest, the hunter uses two sturdy bamboo poles like huge chopsticks to pull the nest away from the mountainside, into a large basket that will be lowered to people waiting below.
2. The world's largest honeybees colonize the Nepalese mountainsides, building honeycombs as large as a person on sheer rock faces that are often hundreds of feet high.
3. In the remote mountain country of Nepal, a small band of "honey hunters" carry out a tradition so ancient that 10,000 year-old drawings of the practice have been found in the caves of Nepal.
4. To harvest the honey and beeswax from these combs, a honey hunter climbs above the nests, lowers a long bamboo-fiber ladder over the cliff, and then climbs down.
5. Throughout this dangerous practice, the hunter is stung repeatedly, and only the veterans, with skin that has been toughened over the years, are able to return from a hunt without the painful swelling caused by stings.

The best order is

A. 2 4 3 5 1
B. 2 4 1 5 3
C. 5 3 2 4 1
D. 3 2 4 1 5

Question 19

1. After the Romans left Britain, there were relentless attacks on the islands from the barbarian tribes of northern Germany—the Angles, Saxons, and Jutes.
2. As the empire weakened, Roman soldiers withdrew from Britain, leaving behind a country that continued to practice the Christian religion that had been introduced by the Romans.
3. Early Latin writings tell of a Christian warrior named Arturius (Arthur, in English) who led the British citizens to defeat these barbarian invaders, and brought an extended period of peace to the lands of Britain.
4. Long ago, the British Isles were part of the far-flung Roman Empire that extended across most of Europe and into Africa and Asia.
5. The romantic legend of King Arthur and his knights of the Round Table, one of the most popular and widespread stories of all time, appears to have some foundation in history.

The best order is

A. 5 4 3 2 1
B. 5 4 2 1 3
C. 4 5 2 3 1
D. 4 3 2 1 5

Question 20

1. The cylinder was allowed to cool until it sould stand on its own, and then it was cut from the tube and split down the side with a single straight cut.
2. Nineteenth-century glassmakers, who had not yet discovered the glazier's modern techniques for making panes of glass, had to create a method for converting their blown glass into flat sheets.
3. The bubble was then pierced at the end to make a hole that opened up while the glassmaker gently spun it, creating a cylinder of glass.
4. Turned on its side and laid on a conveyor belt, the cylinder was strengthened, or tempered, by being heated again and cooled very slowly, eventually flattening out into a single rectangular piece of glass.
5. To do this, the glassmaker dipped the end of a long tube into melted glass and blew into the other end of the tube, creating an expanding bubble of glass.

The best order is

A. 2 5 3 4 1
B. 2 4 5 3 1
C. 3 5 2 4 1
D. 3 1 4 5 2

Question 21

1. The splints are almost always hidden, but horses are occasionally born whose splinted toes project from the leg on either side, just above the hoof.
2. The second and fourth toes remained, but shrank to thin splints of bone that fused invisibly to the horse's leg bone.
3. Horses are unique among mammals, having evolved feet that each end in what is essentially a single toe, capped by a large, sturdy hoof.
4. Julius Caesar, an emperor of ancient Rome, was said to have owned one of these three-toed horses, and considered it so special that he would not permit anyone else to ride it.
5. Though the horse's earlier ancestors possessed the traditional mammalian set of five toes on each foot, the horse has retained only its third toe; its first and fifth toes disappeared completely as the horse evolved.

The best order is

A. 3 5 2 1 4
B. 5 3 2 4 1
C. 3 2 5 1 4
D. 5 2 3 1 4

21._____

Question 22

1. The new building materials—some of which are twenty feet long, and weigh nearly six tons—were transported to Pohnpei on rafts, and were brought into their present position by using hibiscus fiber ropes and leverage to move the stone columns upward along the inclined trunks of coconut palm trees.
2. The ancestors built great fires to heat the stone, and then poured cool seawater on the columns, which caused the stone to contract and split along natural fracture lines.
3. The now-abandoned enclave of Nan Madol, a group of 92 man-made islands off the shore of the Micronesian island of Pohnpei, is estimated to have been built around the year 500 A.D.
4. The islanders say their ancestors quarried stone columns from a nearby island, where large basalt columns were formed by the cooling of molten lava.
5. The structures of Nan Madol are remarkable for the sheer size of some of the stone "logs" or columns that were used to create the walls of the offshore community, and today anthropologists can only rely on the information of existing local people for clues about how Nan Madol was built.

The best order is

A. 5 4 3 2 1
B. 5 3 1 4 2
C. 3 5 4 2 1
D. 3 1 4 2 5

22._____

Question 23

1. One of the most easily manipulated substances on earth, glass can be made into ceramic tiles that are composed of over 90% air.
2. NASA's space shuttles are the first spacecraft ever designed to leave and re-enter the earth's atmosphere while remaining intact.
3. These ceramic tiles are such effective insulators that when a tile emerges from the oven in which it was fired, it can be held safely in a person's hand by the edges while its interior still glows at a temperature well over 2000° F.
4. Eventually, the engineers were led to a material that is as old as our most ancient civilizations—glass.
5. Because the temperature during atmospheric re-entry is so incredibly hot, it took NASA's engineers some time to find a substance capable of protecting the shuttles.

The best order is

A. 5 2 1 3 4
B. 2 5 4 1 3
C. 2 3 1 2 5
D. 5 4 3 1 2

Question 24

1. The secret to teaching any parakeet to talk is patience, and the understanding that when a bird "talks," it is simply imitating what it hears, rather than putting ideas into words.
2. You should stay just out of sight of the bird and repeat the phrase you want it to learn, for at least fifteen minutes every morning and evening.
3. It is important to leave the bird without any words of encouragement or farewell; otherwise it might combine stray remarks or phrases, such as "Good night," with the phrase you are trying to teach it.
4. For this reason, to train your bird to imitate your words you should keep it free of any distractions, especially other noises, while you are giving it "lessons."
5. After your repetition, you should quietly leave the bird alone for a while, to think over what it has just heard.

The best order is

A. 1 4 2 5 3
B. 1 2 4 3 5
C. 3 2 1 5 4
D. 3 1 5 4 2

Question 25   25._____

1. As a school approaches, fishermen from neighboring communities join their fishing boats together as a fleet, and string their gill nets together to make a huge fence that is held up by cork floats.
2. At a signal from the party leaders, or *nakura,* the family members pound the sides of the boats or beat the water with long poles, creating a sudden and deafening noise.
3. The fishermen work together to drag the trap into a half-circle that may reach 300 yards in diameter, and then the families move their boats to form the other half of the circle around the school of fish.
4. The school of fish flee from the commotion into the awaiting trap, where a final wall of net is thrown over the open end of the half-circle, securing the day's haul.
5. Indonesian people from the area around the Sulu islands live on the sea, in floating villages made of lashed-together or stilted homes, and make much of their living by fishing their home waters for migrating schools of snapper, scad, and other fish.

The best order is

A. 1 5 3 4 2
B. 1 2 4 3 5
C. 5 1 2 3 4
D. 5 1 3 2 4

KEY (CORRECT ANSWERS)

1.	D	11.	C
2.	D	12.	A
3.	B	13.	D
4.	A	14.	C
5.	C	15.	D
6.	C	16.	C
7.	D	17.	A
8.	D	18.	D
9.	A	19.	B
10.	B	20.	A

21. A
22. C
23. B
24. A
25. D

REPORT WRITING

EXAMINATION SECTION
TEST 1

DIRECTIONS: Each question or incomplete statement is followed by several suggested answers or completions. Select the one that *BEST* answers the question or completes the statement. *PRINT THE LETTER OF THE CORRECT ANSWER IN THE SPACE AT THE RIGHT.*

1. Following are six steps that should be taken in the course of report preparation:
   I. Outlining the material for presentation in the report
   II. Analyzing and interpreting the facts
   III. Analyzing the problem
   IV. Reaching conclusions
   V. Writing, revising, and rewriting the final copy
   VI. Collecting data

   According to the principles of good report writing, the CORRECT order in which these steps should be taken is:

   A. VI, III, II, I, IV, V B. III, VI, II, IV, I, V
   C. III, VI, II, I, IV, V D. VI, II, III, IV, I, V

2. Following are three statements concerning written reports:
   I. Clarity is generally more essential in oral reports than in written reports.
   II. Short sentences composed of simple words are generally preferred to complex sentences and difficult words.
   III. Abbreviations may be used whenever they are customary and will not distract the attention of the reader

   Which of the following choices correctly classifies the above statements in to whose which are valid and those which are not valid?

   A. I and II are valid, but III is not valid.
   B. I is valid, but II and III are not valid.
   C. II and III are valid, but I is not valid.
   D. III is valid, but I and II are not valid.

3. In order to produce a report written in a style that is both understandable and effective, an investigator should apply the principles of unit, coherence, and emphasis. The one of the following which is the BEST example of the principle of coherence is

   A. interlinking sentences so that thoughts flow smoothly
   B. having each sentence express a single idea to facilitate comprehension
   C. arranging important points in prominent positions so they are not overlooked
   D. developing the main idea fully to insure complete consideration

4. Assume that a supervisor is preparing a report recommending that a standard work procedure be changed. Of the following, the MOST important information that he should include in this report is

   A. a complete description of the present procedure
   B. the details and advantages of the recommended procedure

A. the type and amount of retraining needed
B. the percentage of men who favor the change

5. When you include in your report on an inspection some information which you have obtained from other individuals, it is MOST important that

   A. this information have no bearing on the work these other people are performing
   B. you do not report as fact the opinions of other individuals
   C. you keep the source of the information confidential
   D. you do not tell the other individuals that their statements will be included in your report.

6. Before turning in a report of an investigation of an accident, you discover some additional information you did not know about when you wrote the report.
   Whether or not you re-write your report to include this additional information should depend MAINLY on the

   A. source of this additional information
   B. established policy covering the subject matter of the report
   C. length of the report and the time it would take you to re-write it
   D. bearing this additional information will have on the conclusions in the report

7. The *most desirable FIRST* step in the planning of a written report is to

   A. ascertain what necessary information is readily available in the files
   B. outline the methods you will employ to get the necessary information
   C. determine the objectives and uses of the report
   D. estimate the time and cost required to complete the report

8. In writing a report, the practice of taking up the *least* important points *first* and the *most* important points *last* is a

   A. *good* technique since the final points made in a report will make the greatest impression on the reader
   B. *good* technique since the material is presented in a more logical manner and will lead directly to the conclusions
   C. *poor* technique since the reader's time is wasted by having to review irrelevant information before finishing the report
   D. *poor* technique since it may cause the reader to lose interest in the report and arrive at incorrect conclusions about the report

9. Which one of the following serves as the BEST guideline for you to follow for effective written reports? Keep sentences

   A. *short* and limit sentences to *one* thought
   B. *short* and use *as many* thoughts as possible
   C. *long* and limit sentences to *one* thought
   D. *long* and use *as many* thoughts as possible

10. One method by which a supervisor might prepare written reports to management is to begin with the conclusions, results, or summary, and to follow this with the supporting data.
    The BEST reason why management may *prefer* this form of report is that

A. management lacks the specific training to understand the data
B. the data completely supports the conclusions
C. time is saved by getting to the conclusions of the report first
D. the data contains all the information that is required for making the conclusions

11. When making written reports, it is MOST important that they be

    A. well-worded
    B. brief
    B. accurate as to the facts
    D. submitted immediately

12. Of the following, the MOST important reason for a supervisor to prepare good written reports is that

    A. a supervisor is rated on the quality of his reports
    B. decisions are often made on the basis of the reports
    C. such reports take less time for superiors to review
    D. such reports demonstrate efficiency of department operations

13. Of the following, the BEST test of a good report is whether it

    A. provides the information needed
    B. shows the good sense of the writer
    C. is prepared according to a proper format
    D. is grammatical and neat

14. When a supervisor writes a report, he can BEST show that he has an understanding of the subject of the report by

    A. including necessary facts and omitting nonessential details
    B. using statistical data
    C. giving his conclusions but not the data on which they are based
    D. using a technical vocabulary

15. Suppose you and another supervisor on the same level are assigned to work together on a report. You disagree strongly with one of the recommendations the other supervisor wants to include in the report but you cannot change his views.
Of the following, it would be BEST that

    A. you refuse to accept responsibility for the report
    B. you ask that someone else be assigned to this project to replace you
    C. each of you state his own ideas about this recommendation in the report
    D. you give in to the other supervisor's opinion for the sake of harmony

16. Standardized forms are often provided for submitting reports.
Of the following, the MOST important advantage of using standardized forms for reports is that

    A. they take less time to prepare than individually written reports
    B. the person making the report can omit information he considers unimportant
    C. the responsibility for preparing these reports can be turned over to subordinates
    D. necessary information is less likely to be omitted

17. A report which may *BEST* be classed as a *periodic* report is one which   17. ___

    A. requires the same type of information at regular intervals
    B. contains detailed information which is to be retained in permanent records
    C. is prepared whenever a special situation occurs
    D. lists information in graphic form

18. In the writing of reports or letters, the ideas presented in a paragraph are usually of   18. ___
    unequal importance and require varying degrees of emphasis.
    All of the following are methods of placing extra stress on an idea EXCEPT

    A. repeating it in a number of forms
    B. placing it in the middle of the paragraph
    C. placing it either at the beginning or at the end of the paragraph
    D. underlining it

Questions 19-25.

DIRECTIONS: Questions 19 to 25 concern the subject of report writing and are based on the information and incidents described in the paragraph below. (In answering these questions, assume that the facts and incidents in the paragraph are true.)

On December 15, at 8 a.m., seven Laborers reported to Foreman Joseph Meehan in the Greenbranch Yard in Queens. Meehan instructed the men to load some 50-pound boxes of books on a truck for delivery to an agency building in Brooklyn. Meehan told the men that, because the boxes were rather heavy, two men should work together, helping each other lift and load each box. Since Michael Harper, one of the Laborers, was without a partner, Meehan helped him with the boxes for a while. When Meehan was called to the telephone in a nearby building, however, Harper decided to lift a box himself. He appeared able to lift the box, but, as he got the box halfway up, he cried out that he had a sharp pain in his back. Another Laborer, Jorge Ortiz, who was passing by, ran over to help Harper put the box down. Harper suddenly dropped the box, which fell on Ortiz' right foot. By this time Meehan had come out of the building. He immediately helped get the box off Ortiz' foot and had both men lie down. Meehan covered the men with blankets and called an ambulance, which arrived a half hour later. At the hospital, the doctor said that the X-ray results showed that Ortiz' right foot was broken in three places.

19. What would be the *BEST* term to use in a report describing the injury of Jorge Ortiz?   19. ___

    A. Strain   B. Fracture   C. Hernia   D. Hemorrhage

20. Which of the following would be the MOST accurate summary for the Foreman to put in   20. ___
    his report of the incident?

    A. Ortiz attempted to help Harper carry a box which was too heavy for one person, but Harper dropped it before Ortiz got there.
    B. Ortiz tried to help Harper carry a box but Harper got a pain in his back and accidentally dropped the box on Ortiz' foot.
    C. Harper refused to follow Meehan's orders and lifted a box too heavy for him; he deliberately dropped it when Ortiz tried to help him carry it.
    D. Harper lifted a box and felt a pain in his back; Ortiz tried to help Harper put the box down but Harper accidentally dropped it on Ortiz' foot.

21. One of the Laborers at the scene of the accident was asked his version of the incident. Which information obtained from this witness would be LEAST important for including in the accident report?

    A. His opinion as to the cause of the accident
    B. How much of the accident he saw
    C. His personal opinion of the victims
    D. His name and address

21.___

22. What should be the MAIN objective of writing a report about the incident described in the above paragraph? To

    A. describe the important elements in the accident situation
    B. recommend that such Laborers as Ortiz be advised not to interfere in another's work unless given specific instructions
    C. analyze the problems occurring when there are not enough workers to perform a certain task
    D. illustrate the hazards involved in performing routine everyday tasks

22.___

23. Which of the following is information *missing* from the passage above but which *should be included* in a report of the incident? The

    A. name of the Laborer's immediate supervisor
    B. contents of the boxes
    C. time at which the accident occurred
    D. object or action that caused the injury to Ortiz' foot

23.___

24. According to the description of the incident, the accident occurred *because*

    A. Ortiz attempted to help Harper who resisted his help
    B. Harper failed to follow instructions given him by Meehan
    C. Meehan was not supervising his men as closely as he should have
    D. Harper was not strong enough to carry the box once he lifted it

24.___

25. Which of the following is MOST important for a foreman to *avoid* when writing up an official accident report?

    A. Using technical language to describe equipment involved in the accident
    B. Putting in details which might later be judged unnecessary
    C. Giving an opinion as to conditions that contributed to the accident
    D. Recommending discipline for employees who, in his opinion, caused the accident

25.___

KEY (CORRECT ANSWERS)

1. B
2. C
3. A
4. B
5. B

6. D
7. C
8. D
9. A
10. C

11. B
12. B
13. A
14. A
15. C

16. D
17. A
18. B
19. B
20. D

21. C
22. A
23. C
24. B
25. D

TEST 2

DIRECTIONS: Each question or incomplete statement is followed by several suggested answers or completions. Select the one that BEST answers the question or completes the statement. *PRINT THE LETTER OF THE CORRECT ANSWER IN THE SPACE AT THE RIGHT.*

1. Lieutenant X is preparing a report to submit to his commanding officer in order to get approval of a plan of operation he has developed.
The report starts off with the statement of the problem and continues with the details of the problem. It contains factual information gathered with the help of field and operational personnel. It contains a final conclusion and recommendation for action. The recommendation is supplemented by comments from other precinct staff members on how the recommendations will affect their areas of responsibility. The report also includes directives and general orders ready for the commanding officer's signature. In addition, it has two statements of objections presented by two precinct staff members.
Which one of the following, if any, is *either* an item that Lieutenant X should have included in his report and which is not mentioned above, *or* is an item which Lieutenant X improperly did include in his report?

   A. Considerations of alternative courses of action and their consequences should have been covered in the report.
   B. The additions containing documented objections to the recommended course of action should not have been included as part of the report.
   C. A statement on the qualifications of Lieutenant X, which would support his expertness in the field under consideration, should have been included in the report.
   D. The directives and general orders should not have been prepared and included in the report until the commanding officer had approved the recommendations.
   E. None of the above, since Lieutenant X's report was both proper and complete.

   1. ___

2. During a visit to a section, the district supervisor criticizes the method being used by the assistant foreman to prepare a certain report and orders him to modify the method. This change ordered by the district supervisor is in direct conflict with the specific orders of the foreman. In this situation, it would be BEST for the assistant foreman to

   A. change the method and tell the foreman about the change at the first opportunity
   B. change the method and rely on the district supervisor to notify the foreman
   C. report the matter to the foreman and delay the preparation of the report
   D. ask the district supervisor to discuss the matter with the foreman but use the old method for the time being

   2. ___

3. A department officer should realize that the *most usual* reason for writing a report is to

   A. give orders and follow up their execution
   B. establish a permanent record
   C. raise questions
   D. supply information

   3. ___

4. A very important report which is being prepared by a department officer will soon be due on the desk of the district supervisor. No typing help is available at this time for the officer. For the officer to write out this report in longhand in such a situation would be

   4. ___

A. *bad;* such a report would not make the impression a typed report would
   B. *good;* it is important to get the report in on time
   C. *bad;* the district supervisor should not be required to read longhand reports
   D. *good;* it would call attention to the difficult conditions under which this section must work

5. In a well-written report, the length of each paragraph in the report should be

   A. varied according to the content
   B. not over 300 words
   C. pretty nearly the same
   D. gradually longer as the report is developed and written

6. A clerk in the headquarters office complains to you about the way in which you are filling out a certain report. It would be *BEST* for you to

   A. tell the clerk that you are following official procedures in filling out the report
   B. ask to be referred to the clerk's superior
   C. ask the clerk exactly what is wrong with the way in which you are filling out the report
   D. tell the clerk that you are following the directions of the district supervisor

7. The use of an outline to help in writing a report is

   A. *desirable* in order to insure good organization and coverage
   B. *necessary* so it can be used as an introduction to the report itself
   C. *undesirable* since it acts as a straight jacket and may result in an unbalanced report
   D. *desirable* if you know your immediate supervisor reads reports with extreme care and attention

8. It is advisable that a department officer do his paper work and report writing as soon as he has completed an inspection *MAINLY* because

   A. there are usually deadlines to be met
   B. it insures a steady work-flow
   C. he may not have time for this later
   D. the facts are then freshest in his mind

9. Before you turn in a report you have written of an investigation that you have made, you discover some additional information you didn't know about before. Whether or not you re-write your report to include this additional information should depend *MAINLY* on the

   A. amount of time remaining before the report is due
   B. established policy of the department covering the subject matter of the report
   C. bearing this information will have on the conclusions of the report
   D. number of people who will eventually review the report

10. When a supervisory officer submits a periodic report to the district supervisor, he should realize that the *CHIEF* importance of such a report is that it

    A. is the principal method of checking on the efficiency of the supervisor and his subordinates
    B. is something to which frequent reference will be made

C. eliminates the need for any personal follow-up or inspection by higher echelons
D. permits the district supervisor to exercise his functions of direction, supervision, and control better

11. Conclusions and recommendations are usually better placed at the *end* rather than at the *beginning* of a report because 11.____

   A. the person preparing the report may decide to change some of the conclusions and recommendations before he reaches the end of the report
   B. they are the most important part of the report
   C. they can be judged better by the person to whom the report is sent after he reads the facts and investigations which come earlier in the report
   D. they can be referred to quickly when needed without reading the rest of the report

12. The use of the same method of record-keeping and reporting by *all* agency sections is 12.____

   A. desirable, MAINLY because it saves time in section operations
   B. undesirable, MAINLY because it kills the initiative of the individual section foreman
   C. desirable, MAINLY because it will be easier for the administrator to evaluate and compare section operations
   D. undesirable, MAINLY because operations vary from section to section and uniform record-keeping and reporting is not appropriate

13. The *GREATEST* benefit the section officer will have from keeping complete and accurate records and reports of section operations is that

   A. he will find it easier to run his section efficiently
   B. he will need less equipment
   C. he will need less manpower
   D. the section will run smoothly when he is out

14. You have prepared a report to your superior and are ready to send it forward. But on re-reading it, you think some parts are not clearly expressed and your superior may have difficulty getting your point. 14.____
Of the following, it would be *BEST* for you to

   A. give the report to one of your men to read, and if he has no trouble understanding it send it through
   B. forward the report and call your superior the next day to ask whether it was all right
   C. forward the report as is; higher echelons should be able to understand any report prepared by a section officer
   D. do the report over, re-writing the sections you are in doubt about

15. The *BEST* of the following statements concerning reports is that 15.____

   A. a carelessly written report may give the reader an impression of inaccuracy
   B. correct grammar and English are unimportant if the main facts are given
   C. every man should be required to submit a daily work report
   D. the longer and more wordy a report is, the better it will read

16. In writing a report, the question of whether or not to include certain material could be determined BEST by considering the

    A. amount of space the material will occupy in the report
    B. amount of time to be spent in gathering the material
    C. date of the material
    D. value of the material to the superior who will read the report

17. Suppose you are submitting a fairly long report to your superior. The one of the following sections that should come FIRST in this report is a

    A. description of how you gathered material
    B. discussion of possible objections to your recommendations
    C. plan of how your recommendations can be put into practice
    D. statement of the problem dealt with

Questions 18-20.

DIRECTIONS: A foreman is asked to write a report on the incident described in the following passage. Answer Questions 18 through 20 based on the following information.

On March 10, Henry Moore, a laborer, was in the process of transferring some equipment from the machine shop to the third floor. He was using a dolly to perform this task and, as he was wheeling the material through the machine shop, laborer Bob Greene called to him. As Henry turned to respond to Bob, he jammed the dolly into Larry Mantell's leg, knocking Larry down in the process and causing the heavy drill that Larry was holding to fall on Larry's foot. Larry started rubbing his foot and then, infuriated, jumped up and punched Henry in the jaw. The force of the blow drove Henry's head back against the wall. Henry did not fight back; he appeared to be dazed. An ambulance was called to take Henry to the hospital, and the ambulance attendant told the foreman that it appeared likely that Henry had suffered a concussion. Larry's injuries consisted of some bruises, but he refused medical attention.

18. An adequate report of the above incident should give as minimum information the names of the persons involved, the names of the witnesses, the date and the time that each event took place, and the

    A. names of the ambulance attendants
    B. names of all the employees working in the machine shop
    C. location where the accident occurred
    D. nature of the previous safety training each employee had been given

19. The only one of the following which is NOT a fact is

    A. Bob called to Henry
    B. Larry suffered a concussion
    C. Larry rubbed his foot
    D. the incident took place in the machine shop

20. Which of the following would be, the MOST accurate summary of the incident for the foreman to put in his report of the accident? 20.___

    A. Larry Mantell punched Henry Moore because a drill fell on his foot and he was angry. Then Henry fell and suffered a concussion.
    B. Henry Moore accidentally jammed a dolly into Larry Mantell's foot, knocking Larry down. Larry punched Henry, pushing him into the wall and causing him to bang his head against the wall.
    C. Bob Greene called Henry Moore. A dolly then jammed into Larry Mantell and knocked him down. Larry punched Henry who tripped and suffered some bruises. An ambulance was called.
    D. A drill fell on Larry Mantell's foot. Larry jumped up suddenly and punched Henry Moore and pushed him into the wall. Henry may have suffered a concussion as a result of falling.

Questions 21-25.

DIRECTIONS: Answer Questions 21 through 25 *only* on the basis of the information provided in the following passage.

A written report is a communication of information from one person to another. It is an account of some matter especially investigated, however routine that matter may be. The ultimate basis of any good written report is facts, which become known through observation and verification. Good written reports may seem to be no more than general ideas and opinions. However, in such cases, the facts leading to these opinions were gathered, verified, and reported earlier, and the opinions are dependent upon these facts. Good style, proper form and emphasis cannot make a good written report out of unreliable information and bad judgment; but, on the other hand, solid investigation and brilliant thinking are not likely to become very useful until they are effectively communicated to others. If a person's work calls for written reports, then his work is often no better than his written reports.

21. Based on the information in the passage, it can be concluded that opinions expressed in a report should be 21.___

    A. based on facts which are gathered and reported
    B. emphasized repeatedly when they result from a special investigation
    C. kept to a minimum
    D. separated from the body of the report

22. In the above passage, the one of the following which is mentioned as a way of establishing facts is 22.___

    A. authority   B. communication
    C. reporting   D. verification

23. According to the passage, the characteristic shared by *all* written reports is that they are 23.___

    A. accounts of routine matters
    B. transmissions of information
    C. reliable and logical
    D. written in proper form

24. Which of the following conclusions can *logically* be drawn from the information given in the passage?

    A. Brilliant thinking can make up for unreliable information in a report.
    B. One method of judging an individual's work is the quality of the written reports he is required to submit.
    C. Proper form and emphasis can make a good report out of unreliable information.
    D. Good written reports that seem to be no more than general ideas should be rewritten.

25. Which of the following suggested titles would be MOST appropriate for this passage?

    A. Gathering and Organizing Facts
    B. Techniques of Observation
    C. Nature and Purpose of Reports
    D. Reports and Opinions: Differences and Similarities

KEY (CORRECT ANSWERS)

1.	A	11.	C
2.	A	12.	C
3.	D	13.	A
4.	B	14.	D
5.	A	15.	A
6.	C	16.	D
7.	A	17.	D
8.	D	18.	C
9.	C	19.	B
10.	D	20.	B

21. A
22. D
23. B
24. B
25. C

TEST 3

Questions 1-5.

DIRECTIONS: The following is an accident report similar to those used in departments for reporting accidents. Answer Questions 1 to 5 using *only* the information given in this report.

ACCIDENT REPORT

FROM *John Doe*	DATE OF REPORT *June 23*
TITLE *Sanitation Man*	
DATE OF ACCIDENT *June 22* time *3* AM ~~PM~~	CITY *Metropolitan*
PLACE *1489 Third Avenue*	
VEHICLE NO. *1*	VEHICLE NO. *2*
OPERATOR *John Doe, Sanitation Man* TITLE	OPERATOR *Richard Roe*
VEHICLE CODE NO. *14-238*	ADDRESS *498 High Street*
LICENSE NO. *0123456*	OWNER *Henry Roe* LIC NUMBER *5N1492* ADDRESS *786 E. 83 St*
DESCRIPTION OF ACCIDENT *Light green Chevrolet sedan while trying to pass drove in to rear side of Sanitation truck which had stopped to collect garbage. No one was injured but there was property damage.*	
NATURE OF DAMAGE TO PRIVATE VEHICLE *Right front fender crushed, bumper bent.*	
DAMAGE TO CITY VEHICLE *Front of left rear fender pushed in. Paint scraped.*	
NAME OF WITNESS *Frank Brown*	ADRESS *48 Kingsway*
John Doe Signature of person making this report	BADGE NO. *428*

1. Of the following, the one which has been omitted from this accident report is the

    A. location of the accident
    B. drivers of the vehicles involved
    C. traffic situation at the time of the accident
    D. owners of the vehicles involved

1. ___

2. The address of the driver of Vehicle No. 1 is not required because he

    A. is employed by the department
    B. is not the owner of the vehicle
    C. reported the accident
    D. was injured in the accident

2. ___

3. The report indicates that the driver of Vehicle No. 2 was *probably*

- A. passing on the wrong side of the truck
- B. not wearing his glasses
- C. not injured in the accident
- D. driving while intoxicated

4. The number of people *specifically* referred to in this report is

   A. 3   B. 4   C. 5   D. 6

5. The license number of Vehicle No. 1 is

   A. 428   B. 5N1492   C. 14-238   D. 0123456

6. In a report of unlawful entry into department premises, it is *LEAST* important to include the

- A. estimated value of the property missing
- B. general description of the premises
- C. means used to get into the premises
- D. time and date of entry

7. In a report of an accident, it is *LEAST* important to include the

- A. name of the insurance company of the person injured in the accident
- B. probable cause of the accident
- C. time and place of the accident
- D. names and addresses of all witnesses of the accident

8. Of the following, the one which is_____ *NOT* required in the preparation of a weekly functional expense report is the

- A. hourly distribution of the time by proper heading in accordance with the actual work performed
- B. signatures of officers not involved in the preparation of the report
- C. time records of the men who appear on the payroll of the respective locations
- D. time records of men working in other districts assigned to this location

KEY (CORRECT ANSWERS)

1. C
2. A
3. C
4. B

5. D
6. B
7. A
8. B

Food Preparation-Handling and Storage

1. FOOD PREPARATION

    Begin with clean, fresh food. Handle food only when necessary.

    Don't dip fingers into food or use a stirring spoon to taste.

    Use oysters, clams and other frozen foods, fluid milk products and frozen milk desserts from approved sources.

    Never lean or sit on work surfaces.

    Foods should never be prepared in yards, alleys, stairs or hallways.

    Keep food that is on display covered so it can't be touched or coughed on by customers or contaminated by flies and other bugs.

    Always follow the recipe. Cook custards and cream sauces well. Chill them at once.

    Wash thoroughly with brush and clean water all vegetables and fruits which are to be served raw.

    As a food safeguard, boil leftover vegetables, gravies, soups, and other liquid foods before serving.

    Make sure that all mixing, grinding and chopping machines are thoroughly cleaned after each use. In order to properly clean one of these machines, one should know how to take it apart and assemble it.

    Work only in a well-lighted area that is well-ventilated.

2. FOOD STORAGE AND HANDLING

    Food should be stored well off the floor, away from walls or dripping pipes.

    Keep all food, bulk or otherwise, covered and safe from contamination.

    Check food daily and throw away any spoiled or dirty food.

    Store cleaning, disinfection, insect and rodent-killing powders and liquids away from foods, PLAINLY MARKED.

    Keep foods in refrigerator at temperature of $45°$ F or below.

    Check the temperature regularly with a good thermometer.

    Keep all cooling compartments closed except when you're using them.

    Store food in a refrigerator in such a way that inside air can circulate freely.

    Always refrigerate meats, creamed foods and custard desserts.

    Keep all refrigerated foods covered, and use up stored leftovers quickly.

    When dishes and utensils are sparkling clean, keep them that way by proper storage. Keep all cups and glasses inverted.

    Cakes, doughnuts and fruit pies may be kept inside a covered display area.

    The only goods that should be left on the counter uncovered are those which are wrapped and do not contain anything which could spoil at room temperature.

    Don't set dirty dishes, pots, cartons or boxes on food tables.

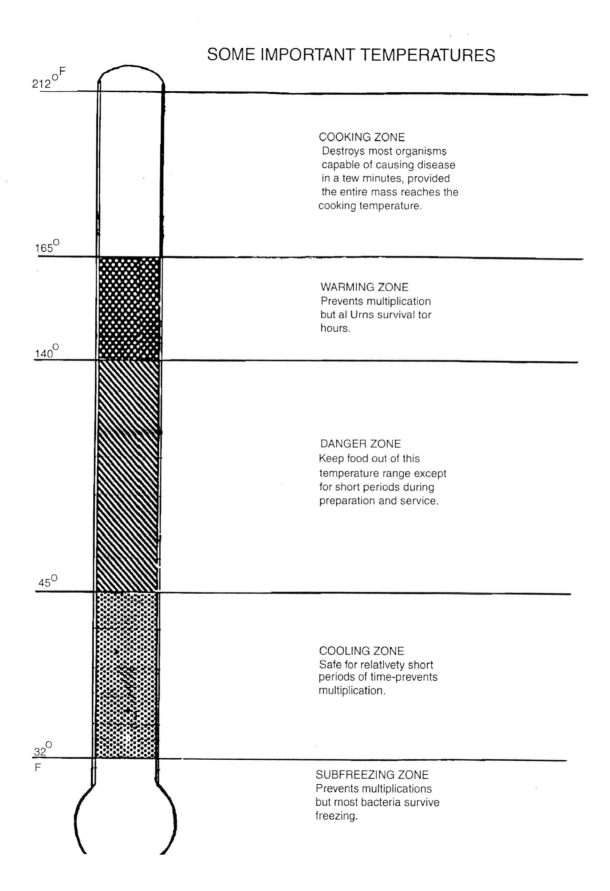

TEMPERATURE RANGE FOR SAFE STORAGE OF FOODS

Zone I   Sub-freezing temperatures 0° F to -15° F (-18° to -9.4° C)

   A. Frozen meat, fish, and vegetables
   B. Frozen fruits
   C. Ice Cream
   D. Homemade frozen deserts

Zone II   High Humidity (85%) and Moderate Air Circulation 34° to 37° F (1.1° to 2.7 °C)

   A. Fresh meat, chicken, and fish
   B. Sliced smoked ham and bacon
   C. Sliced cold cuts of meat
   D. Leftover canned and cooked meat

Zone III   38° to 40° F (3.3° to 4.4° C)

   A. Fresh milk, cream, and buttermilk
   B. Cottage cheese and butter (both covered)
   C. Fresh orange and tomato juice (covered)
   D. Bottled beverage (for chilling)

Zone IV   40° to 43° F (4.4° to 6.1° C) Moderate Humidity

   A. Berries, pears, and peaches
   B. Ripe grapefruit and oranges
   C. Ripe tomatoes (short time only)
   D. Fresh eggs
   E. Margarine
   F. Custards and puddings (day or two only)
   G. Prepared salads (for chilling)

Zone V   40° to 45° F (4.4° to 7.2° C) High Humidity

   A. Cherries and cranberries
   B. Lettuce and celery
   C. Spinach, kale, and other greens
   D. Beets, carrots, parsnips, and turnips
   E. Peas and lima beans
   F. Cucumbers and eggplant (short time only)

Zone VI   55° to 60° F (12.7° to 15.1° C) Fairly High Humidity and Moderate Circulation. (Good Fruit Cellar or Storage Cellar Well Ventilated).

   A. Apples, cabbage, potatoes, pumpkin, squash, unripened tomatoes, and maple syrup (in tight container)

Zone VII   Normal Room Temperature. Dry Storage
- A. Ready prepared cereals
- B. Crackers
- C. Bottled beverages

Zone VIII   Normal Room Temperature Storage

- A. Peanut Butter and honey
- B. Salad oils and vegetable shortenings
- C. Catsup and pickles
- D. Jelly and preserves
- E. Dried fruits and bananas (short time)
- F. Flour
- G. Dried peas and beans
- H. Sugar and salt

MICROBIOLOGY OF FOODS: BACTERIA

In order to understand the reasons behind food sanitation practices, it is necessary to know a few facts about the microorganisms which cause food spoilage and foodborne disease.

Bacteria, commonly called germs, are extremely small, plant-like organisms which must be viewed through a microscope in order to be seen. If 25,000,000 bacteria were placed in a line, that line would be only one inch long; one million could fit on the head of a pin. Like any living thing, bacteria require food, moisture, and the proper temperature for growth. Most of them need air, but some can thrive only in the absence of air (these are called anaerobic) and some can grow with or without air (facultative). Bacteria are found everywhere on the earth, in the air, and in the water. Soil abounds with bacteria which grow on dead organic matter.

SHAPES OF BACTERIA

One method of classifying bacteria is by their shape. All bacteria can be assigned to one of the following categories.

    A. Cocci (plural of coccus) are round or spherical in shape. While they are able to live alone, they often exist in groups. Single chains are called streptococci. Those which form a grape-like cluster are called staphylococci, while those that form pairs are called diplococci. Some bacteria are named after the portion of the human anatomy they infect; for example, pneumococci infect the lungs, enterococci infect the intestines, and meningococci infect the meninges (protective sheath around the brain). Some of the common diseases caused by the cocci group are pneumonia, septic sore throat, scarlet fever, and meningitis.

    B. Bacilli (plural of bacillus) are rod-shaped. Some of these also congregate in the single chain form, and are called streptobacilli. Some common diseases caused by bacilli are typhoid fever, tuberculosis, and anthrax.

    C. Spirilla (plural of spirillum) are spiral or comma-shaped. Diseases caused by spirilla include cholera and syphilis.

SPORES

Some bacilli are able to protect themselves under adverse conditions by forming a protective shell or wall around themselves; in this form they are in the non-vegetative stage and are called spores. These bacterial spores can be likened to the seeds of a plant which are also resistant to adverse conditions. During the spore stage, bacteria do not reproduce or multiply. As soon as these spores find themselves under proper conditions of warmth, moisture, food and possibly air requirements. they resume their normal (vegetative) stage, and resume their growth. Since spores are designed to withstand rigorous conditions, they are difficult to destroy by the normal methods. Much higher killing temperatures and longer time periods are required. Fortunately, there are only a relatively few pathogenic or disease-causing bacilli which are spore formers. Tetanus, anthrax, and botulism are diseases caused by spore formers.

BACTERIAL REPRODUCTION

Bacteria reproduce by splitting in two, this is called binary fission. For this reason, their numbers are always doubling: one bacterium generates two; each of these generates two, resulting in a new total of four: etc. The time it takes for bacteria to double (generation time) is roughly fifteen to thirty minutes under good conditions.

TYPES OF BACTERIA ACCORDING TO THEIR EFFECT ON MAN

Types of bacteria, classified according to their effect on us, are:

    A. Harmful or disease-producing
    B. Undesirable
    C. Beneficial
    D. Benign

A. Harmful or disease-producing bacteria are known as pathogenic bacteria or pathogens. They cause various diseases of man, animals, and plants.

B. Undesirable bacteria, which cause decomposition of foods, are often referred to as putrefying bacteria. Bacteria that act on sugars in food, resulting in souring, are called saccharolytic bacteria.

C. Beneficial bacteria are used in the production of various foods, including cultured milk, yogurt, cheese, and sauerkraut.

The large intestine, or colon, contains millions of bacteria which are normal inhabitants of the intestinal tract, and we call this type *"coliform"* bacteria. It can be seen, therefore, that where coliform bacteria are found in food or water, they are an indication of fecal contamination. The coliforms themselves are not pathogenic, but where fecal contamination occurs, it is probable that other pathogenic organisms from the intestine may be present. The presence of coliform bacteria is often used as an index of good or bad sanitary practices.

Bacteria are essential in the operation of certain sewage disposal plants, known as *"activated sludge plants"*. In these plants the bacteria digest the organic sewage and either liquefy the solid matter which is in colloid form, or change it so that it settles out.

The greatest number of bacteria are found in the soil where they thrive on dead organic matter. They are constantly decomposing it, so that eventually it is changed into an inorganic form. This essential process of nature makes it possible for plants to absorb inorganic nutriment. Other types of bacteria *"fix"* nitrogen from the air, forming nitrates in the soil, generally on the roots of legumes.

D. Benign bacteria, as far as we know at the present time, are neither helpful nor harmful to man. Of the hundreds of thousands of strains of bacteria, most fall into this category.

It must be realized that may bacteria are essential in the balance of nature, and the destruction of all bacteria in the world would be catastrophic. Our main objective in public health protection, in which food handling plays a vital role, is the control and destruction of the pathogenic bacteria and those that cause food spoilage.

CONDITIONS FOR GROWTH

A. Food - Bacterial require food for growth. Food must be absorbed in liquid form through the cell wall of the organism. Generally bacteria prefer neutral foods (ph 6-8) but some can thrive on highly acid or alkaline media.

B. Moisture - Moisture (water) is an essential requirement. If moisture is not present, bacteria will not multiply and eventually may die. Processes which depend on removing available water, i.e., water in liquid form, from bacteria are used to preserve foods. Such methods include dehydration, freezing, and preserving in salt or sugar.

C. Temperature - In general, bacteria prefer a warm temperature and grow best between 90-100° F. (Optimum temperature) The temperature of the body, 98.6° F, is excellent for bacterial growth; when bacteria are cultured in the laboratory, they are kept at this temperature. However, different types of bacteria prefer different temperatures, and are as follows:

    <u>Mesophilic</u>: Grow best at temperatures between
    50-110° F. Most bacteria are in this group.

Thermophilic: Love heat. These grow best at temperatures between 110-150° F. or mo.re

Psychrophilic: Love cold. These grow best at temperatures below 50° F.

Where heat is employed to destroy pathogenic bacteria, the food processor often must contend with thermophilic or thermoduric bacteria, which may withstand the pasteurizing or sterilizing processes. These bacteria are not pathogenic, but may be putrefactive.

D. Air - With respect to air atmospheric oxygen, we find that some bacteria can grow only where air is present; these are called aerobes. Some bacteria can grow only in a medium where air is absent, and these are called anaerobes. They can thrive in a sealed can, jar, or bottle of food. Those bacteria which prefer to live where air is present but may grow without air are termed facultative aerobes, and those which prefer to grow in the absence of air but may grow where air is present are called facultative anaerobes.

LOCOMOTION

Bacteria cannot crawl, fly, or move about. A few types do have thread-like appendages called flagella, with which they can propel themselves to a very limited extent. Therefore, they must be carried from place to place by some vehicle or through some channel. The channels of transmission include: air, water, food, hands, coughing, sneezing, insects, rodents, dirty equipment, unsafe plumbing connections, and unclean utensils. Hands are one of the most dangerous vehicles. There is no doubt that better care of food handlers' hands would aid greatly in cutting down the transmission of disease.

DESTRUCTION BY HEAT

The most reliable and time-tested method of destroying bacteria is heat. This method is effective only when both time and temperature factors are applied. In other words, not only do we have to reach the desired temperature to kill bacteria, but we must allow sufficient time to permit the heat to kill the more sturdy members. The lower the temperature (to certain limits, of course) the longer the time required to kill bacteria. Conversely, the higher the temperature, the less time is necessary. An example of this principle involves the two accepted methods for pasteurizing milk. In the *"holding"* method, milk is held at a temperature of 145° F for thirty minutes. In the more recently developed *"flash"* or *"high temperature-short time"* method, milk is held at 161° F for fifteen seconds.

In sterilizing foods for canning, the type of food and size of the containers must be taken into consideration in determining the proper time and temperature. The smaller the container, the faster the heat will be conducted through the food.

It is important to note once more that in order to destroy spore-forming bacilli completely, very high temperatures, often higher than 212° F are required for long time periods.

DESTRUCTION BY CHEMICALS

Bacteria can be destroyed by chemical agents. Those which kill all bacteria are called germicides or bactericides. Examples are phenol (carbolic acid), formaldehyde, iodine, chlorine, and others, such as the group of chemicals known as quarternary compounds. The effectiveness of the chemical bactericide depends on the concentration and the method with which it is used. If it is used to kill pathogenic organisms only, it is called a disinfectant. If a mild concentration is used on wounds to inhibit the growth of disease organisms, it is called an antiseptic. Some chemicals have been used in foods to inhibit the growth of spoilage bacteria, and these are called preservatives. Examples of these are sulphur dioxide, benzoate of soda, salt, sugar, and vinegar.

OTHER METHODS OF DESTRUCTION

When exposed to air and sunlight, bacteria are destroyed due to the combined effects of lack of moisture and food and exposure to the natural ultraviolet rays of the sun. Ultraviolet lamps are used for bactericidal purposes but their field is limited. Aeration is not used commercially as the sole means of sterilizing a product.

REFRIGERATION

Refrigeration of foods in refrigerators (32-45° F) does not kill bacteria. However, these temperatures do inhibit the growth of bacteria, both putrefactive and pathogenic, so that foods under proper refrigeration remain wholesome and free from disease for some time.

MICROBIOLOGY OF FOODS: BACTERIA AND OTHER MICROORGANISMS

Extremely low freezing temperatures for prolonged periods may result in the death of some bacteria, while others may survive. However, refrigeration or freezing should never be considered as a means of destroying bacteria; these methods merely retard bacterial growth.

VIRUSES

Viruses are minute organic forms which seem to be intermediate between living cells and organic compounds. They are smaller than bacteria, and are sometimes called filterable viruses because they are so small that they can pass through the tiny pores of a porcelain filter which retain bacteria. They cannot be seen through a microscope (magnification of 1500 x) but can be seen through an electron microscope (magnification of 1,000,000 x). Viruses cause poliomyelitis, smallpox, measles, mumps, encephalitis, influenza, and the common cold. Viruses, like bacteria are presumed to exist everywhere.

YEASTS

Yeasts are one-celled organisms which are larger than bacteria. They, too, are found everywhere, and require food, moisture, warmth, and air for proper growth. Unlike some bacteria which live without air, yeasts must have air in order to grow. They need sugar, but have the ability to change starch into sugar. When yeasts act on sugar, the formation of alcohol and carbon dioxide results. In the baking industry, yeast is used to *"raise dough"* through the production of carbon dioxide. The alcohol is driven off by the heat of the oven. In wine production, the carbon dioxide gas bubbles off, leaving the alcohol. The amount of alcohol produced by yeasts is limited to 18%, because yeasts are killed at this concentration of alcohol.

Yeasts reproduce by budding, which is similar to binary fission. Generally, the methods described for the destruction of bacteria will kill yeasts as well.

Yeasts are not generally considered to be pathogenic or harmful although a few of them do cause skin infections. Wild yeasts or those that get into a food by accident rather than by design of the food processor cause food spoilage and decomposition of starch and sugar, and therefore are undesirable.

MOLDS

Molds are multicellular (many-celled) microscopic plants which become visible to the naked eye when growing in sufficient quantity. Mold colonies have definite colors (white, black, green, etc.) They are larger than bacteria or yeasts. Some molds are pathogenic, causing such diseases as athletes' foot, ringworm, and other skin diseases. However, moldy foods usually do not cause illness. In fact, molds are encouraged to grow in certain cheeses to produce a characteristic flavor.

The structure of the mold consists of a root-like structure called the mycelium, a stem (ariel filament) called the hypha, and the spore sac, called the sporangium. All molds reproduce by means of spores. Molds are the lowest form of life that have these specialized reproductive cells.

Molds require moisture and air for growth and can grow on almost any organic matter, which does not necessarily have to be food. Molds do not require warmth, and grow very well in refrigerators. Neither do molds require much moisture, although the more moisture present, the better they multiply.

Methods of destruction for molds are similar to those required for bacteria. Heat, chemicals, and ultraviolet rays destroy mold spores as well as the molds. Refrigeration does not necessarily retard their growth.

Certain chemicals act as mold inhibitors. Calcium propionate (Mycoban) is one used in making bread. This chemical when used in the dough, retards the germination of mold spores, and bread so treated will remain mold-free for about five days.

One of the most beneficial molds is the Penicillium mold from which penicillin, an antibiotic, is extracted. The discovery, by Dr. Alexander Fleming, of the mold's antibiotic properties open up a whold field of research, and other antibiotic products from molds have been discovered.

CLASSIFICATION OF FOODBORNE DISEASE

Several terms are used to describe illness in which the causative agent is obtained by ingestion of food; the expression *"food poisoning"* is commonly employed to describe any of these. However, such usage is inaccurate and confusing.

Foodborne diseases caused by bacteria are divided into two classes. The first is called food intoxication (this is the real food poisoning) and designates illnesses due to toxins (poisons) secreted by bacteria growing in large numbers on the food prior to ingestion. In the second type of bacterial disease, called food infection, the symptoms are caused by the activity of large numbers of bacterial cells, having grown to some extent in the contaminated food, within the gastrointestinal system of the victim.

Other microbial contaminants of food, such as viruses, rickettsiae, and protozoa, can cause disease, as can other parasites. Chemical poisonings are characterized by a relatively sudden onset of symptoms, often in minutes. In addition, certain plants and animals contain chemical poisons, some of which produce illness within a short period after ingestion.

I. Food Intoxications
    A. Botulism
        1. Toxins are produced by growth of Clostridium botulinum in foods under anaerobic conditions. There are six major types of toxins: A, B, C, D, E and F. Types A, B, and E affect man. Antitoxins exist, although few hospitals routinely stock them.
        2. Symptoms: Toxin affects the central nervous system, producing difficulty in swallowing, double vision, and difficulty in speech and respiration, followed by death from paralysis of muscles of respiration.
        3. Onset of symtoms: 2 hours to 8 days, average 1 to 2 days.
        4. Inactivation of toxins: 15 minutes at 212° F.
        5. Foods usually involved: home-canned, low-acid vegetables. On rare occasions, commercially packed tuna, smoked fish, mushrooms, and vichysoisse.
    B. Staphylococcus Food Poisoning
        1. Toxin produced by coagulase positive Staphylococcus aureus.
        2. Symptoms: Nausea, vomiting, diarrhea, acute prostration, and abdominal cramps.
        3. Onset of symptoms: 1 to 6 hours, average 2-3 hours.
        4. Inactivation of toxin: Not inactivated by normal cooking times and temperatures.
        5. Foods usually involved: Ham, poultry, cream-filled bakery goods, protein salads.

II. Bacterial Food Infections
    A. Salmonellosis
        1. Salmonella typhimurium, Salmonella enteritidis, and others.
        2. Symptoms: Abdominal pain, diarrhea, chills, fever, frequent vomiting, and prostration.
        3. Onset of symptoms: 7 to 12 hours; average 12 to 24 hours.
        4. Inactivation: 165° F for period of cooking or heating.
        5. Foods usually involved: poultry, poultry products, inadequately cooked egg products, meats, and other foods.

B. Bacillary dysentery (Shigellosis)
 1. Various species of Shigella (Shigella dysenteriae, Shigella sonnei, and others.)
 2. Symptoms: Diarrhea, bloody stools, fever.
 3. Onset of symptoms: 1 to 7 days; average 2-3 days.
 4. Inactivation: 165° for period of cooking.
 5. Foods usually involved: Moist prepared foods and dairy products contaminated with excreta from carrier.

C. Streptococcal Infections (Scarlet fever or septic sore throat)
 1. Certain strains of beta-hemolytic streptococci
 2. Symptoms: Fever, sore throat.
 3. Onset of symptoms: 1 to 7 days; average 3 days.
 4. Inactivation: 165° F for period of cooking.
 5. Foods usually involved: Food contaminated with nasal or oral discharges from a case or carrier; raw milk from infected cows.

D. Enterococci (Fecal Streptococci)
 1. Various strains of Streptococcus fecalis.
 2. Symptoms: Nausea, sometimes vomiting and diarrhea.
 3. Onset of symptoms: 2 to 18 hours
 4. Inactivation: 165° F for period of cooking.
 5. Foods usually involved: Prepared food products contaminated with excreta.

E. Clostridium Perfringens
 1. Growth of Clostridium perfringens in food under anaerobic conditions.
 2. Symptoms: Acute abdominal pain and diarrhea, nausea, and rarely, vomiting.
 3. Onset of symptoms: 8 to 22 hours; average 8-12 hours.
 4. Inactivation: Variable, usually not inactivated by cooking temperatures.
 5. Foods usually involved: Poultry and meat products.

III. Viral Infections
 A. Infectious Hepatitis
  1. Virus of infectious hepatitis
  2. Symptoms: Fever, lack of appetite, malaise, fatigue, headache, nausea, chills, vomiting, jaundice may be present.
  3. Onset of symptoms: 14 to 35 days, average 25 days.
  4. Inactivation: not known.
  5. Foods usually involved: Shellfish (oyster, clams, mussels) taken from polluted waters and eaten raw; foods contaminated with excreta from an infected person.

IV. Parasitic Infections
 A. Trichinosis
  1. Trichinella spiralis.
  2. Symptoms: Nausea, vomiting, diarrhea (during digestion of trichinae); muscular pains, fever labored breathing, swelling of eyelids. Occassionally fatal.

3. Onset of symptoms: 2 to 28 days; average 9 days.
4. Inactivation: All parts of meat must reach 150° F to destroy cysts.
5. Foods usually involved: Raw or insufficiently cooked pork and pork products. Whale, seal, bear, and walrus meat have also been implicated.

B. Tapeworm (Taeniasis)
1. Taenia saginata (beef tapeworm); Taenia solium (pork tapeworm).
2. Symptoms: Beef tapeworm: abdominal pain, hungry feeling, vague discomfort. Pork tapeworm: varies from mild chronic digestive disorder to severe malaise.
3. Onset of symptoms: Several weeks.
4. Inactivation: All parts of the meat must reach 150° F.
5. Foods usually involved: Raw or insufficiently cooked beef or pork containing live larvae.

C. Fish Tapeworm Disease (Diphyllobothriasis)
1. Diphyllobothrium latum.
2. Symptoms: Anemia in heavy infections.
3. Onset of symptoms: 3 to 6 weeks.
4. Inactivation: All parts of fish meat must reach 150° F.
5. Foods usually involved: Raw or insufficiently cooked fish containing live larvae.

D. Amebic Dysentery
1. Entamoeba histolytica
2. Symptoms: Chronic diarrhea of varying severity or diarrhea alternating with constipation; occasionally fatal.
3. Onset of symptoms: 5 days to several months; average 3 to 4 weeks.
4. Inactivation: Cysts on vegetables destroyed by heating 30 minutes in water at 122° F.
5. Foods usually involved: Moist food contaminated with excreta from a carrier; contaminated water.

V. Poisonous Plants
A. Mushroom poisoning
1. Symptoms caused by phalloidine and other alkaloids of certain species of mushrooms.
2. Symptoms: Salivation: abdominal pain, intense thirst, nausea, vomiting, water stools, excessive perspiration, flow of tears; often fatal.
3. Onset of symptoms: 15 minutes to 15 hours.
4. Inactivation: Not inactivated by cooking.
5. Foods usually involved: Wild mushrooms, such as Amanita phalloides and Amanita muscaria, which are mistaken for edible mushrooms.

VI. Dangerous Chemicals
A. Antimony

1. Occurrence: Chipped grey enamelware in contact with acid foods and beverages.
2. Symptoms: Nausea, violent vomiting.
3. Onset of symptoms: 15 to 30 minutes.
4. Duration: Several hours.

B. Cadmium
1. Occurence: Cadmium used as plating, e.g., ice cube trays, dissolved in food or beverages.
2. Symptoms: Propulsive vomiting, nausea.
3. Onset of symptoms: 15 to 30 minutes.
4. Duration: Several hours.

C. Cyanide
1. Occurrence: Foods contaminated with silver polish containing cyanide.
2. Symptoms: Cyanosis (bluish discoloration of skin) mental confusion, glassy eyes, blue lips, often fatal.
3. Onset of symptoms: Almost instantaneous.

D. Lead
1. Occurrence: Food containers, solder containing more that 5% lead used on food equipment.
2. Symptoms: Blue line on gums, cramps in stomach, bowels, and legs, constipation, loss of appetite, headache, irritability.

E. Copper
1. Occurrence: Foods contaminated by copper salts (verdigris) on unclean copper utensils; beverages containing copper salts due to action of carbonation (carbon dioxide and water) on copper tubing.
2. Symptoms: Vomiting, abdominal pain, diarrhea.
3. Onset of symptoms: Usually immediate.

F. Zinc
1. Occurrence (rare): Acid foods cooked in galvanized (zinc-plated) utensils.
2. Symptoms: Dizziness, nausea, vomiting, tightness of throat.
3. Onset of symptoms: a few minutes to two hours.

G. Nitrites
1. Occurrence: Contamination of foods by nitrates, or nitrites used as a preservative in excess of 200 parts per million.
2. Symptoms: Cyanosis, shock, lowered blood pressure, methemoglobinemia (hemoglobin in blood combines with nitrites instead of oxygen producing internal asphyxiation.)
3. Onset of symptoms: 15 to 30 minutes.

H. Pesticides
1. Occurence: Foods accidentally contaminated with pesticides.

VII. Dangerous Animals
A. Shellfish
1. Occurrence: Shellfish grown in polluted waters, if eaten raw, can cause typhoid fever, cholera, and infectious hepatitis.

DISEASE PREVENTION IN RESTAURANTS

WHAT ARE THE MOST FAVORABLE CONDITIONS FOR THE GROWTH OF DISEASE GERMS?

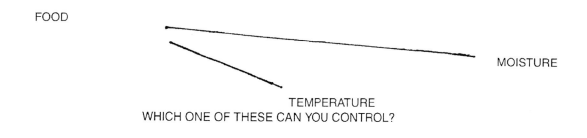

WHICH ONE OF THESE CAN YOU CONTROL?

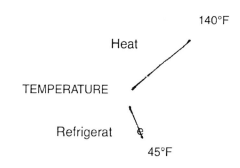

YOU CAN SPREAD DISEASE BY:

Carelessness
　　Not washing hands before touching food, dishes, or utensils. Leaving food unprotected from dust, sneezes, rodents and insects. Using dirty equipment.
　　Leaving food stand at room temperature.

Working when sick or with open sores
　　Through food you infect.
　　By direct contact with customers and fellow workers.
　　By contaminating dishes and utensils.

YOU CAN GET DISEASE BY:
　　Infection from a sick customer or fellow worker.
　　Careless handling of soiled dishes.
　　Eating infected food.
　　Infection from rats, mice and insects.

FOOD PROTECTION

To Prevent Bacterial Food Poisoning and Infection
　　Keep harmful bacteria out if possible.
　　Keep them from growing if they do get in.
　　How? By watching time and temperature, as well as cleanliness.

TIME
　　Don't let food ready to serve stand longer than one hour at room temperature.

TEMPERATURE

Keep cold foods refrigerated at 45° F or lower until they are served.

Keep hot foods hot, above 140° F, until they are served.
WATCH THESE FOODS ESPECIALLY-BACTERIA LOVE THEM!
Cream filled or custard filled pastries, cakes and puddings.
Any dish made with cream sauce.
Meats, poultry and fish.
Dressing for poultry or meat.
Sandwiches, sandwich filling.

To Prevent Chemical Food Poisoning

Be sure all poisons are clearly labeled.
Never store poisons in food preparation areas.
Don't use insect sprays over or near food.
Don't keep any acid food or drink in a galvanized container.

SAFE STORAGE METHODS

Clean storage rooms, used for no other purpose.
All food stored at least six inches above floor.
Clean, neat refrigerator.
Food refrigerated in shallow containers, always covered.
Refrigerator shelves free of shelf-coverings.

SEVEN EASY RULES FOR SAFE FOOD
1. KEEP COLD FOODS COLD-HOT FOODS HOT. Don't let foods stand at room temperature.
2. KEEP HANDS CLEAN and touch food with hands as little as possible.
3. Don't let anyone with a skin infection or a cold handle food.
4. Keep kitchen, dining rooms and storage rooms free from rats, mice and insects.
5. Protect food from sneezes, customer handling, and dust.
6. Be sure poisons are well labeled and kept away from food preparation areas.
7. Wash dishes, glasses, silver and utensils by methods recommended by your health department.

BIOLOGY-BACTERIOLOGY

The science of biology is concerned with the study of living organisms, their habits, food requirements, and general functions. Among the myriad types of living organisms which inhabit this planet, the bacteria form a very important part. The study of biology and of bacteriology is of basic importance since these sciences are the foundations upon which sanitation and sewage treatment are based. Without knowledge of the fundamental factors concerning these living organisms and their relation to one another and to human beings it would be difficult to understand the principles upon which all treatment processes are based.

BACTERIOLOGY

Bacteria are minute living organisms, each consisting of a single cell. These organisms are so small that they can be seen only when magnified under a microscope. Thus they are included in the term microorganisms. Food assimilation, waste excretion, respiration, growth and all other activities are carried on through the action of the one single cell. Many bacteria have characteristics ordinarily associated with the animal kingdom and others generally applied to the plant kingdom. In some respects, they form a link between these two types of living organisms. There are many different kinds of bacteria, varying widely in size, shape and function.

The cells of the bacteria consist of an outer shell or membrane, an inner jelly-like material called protoplasm, and a nucleus within the protoplasm of the cell. As with all other living organisms, bacteria can reproduce, but they do this by a process known as fission. The adult cell constricts in the middle, the constriction increases until finally the cell divides into two smaller cells, each a complete living organism. These two daughter cells grow and in turn divide to continue the process. It is estimated that the average bacterium will divide at intervals of 20-30 minutes. Thus, the increase in the number of bacteria under favorable conditions is tremendous in a short period of time, such as 12 hours, if all the daughter cells were to survive. (Figure 29).

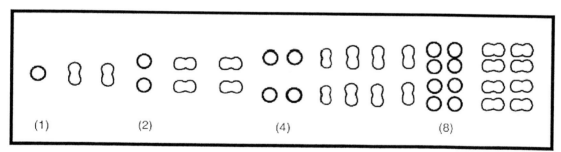

FIGURE 1 - REPRODUCTION OF BACTERIA

Bacteria are found everywhere in our environment. They are present in the soil, and thru the agency of dust they are suspended in the air. They are found in water as the result of passage of rain through the air and the various water sources flowing through and over the ground. Bacteria are present in the bodies of all living organisms and many of them carry on very useful and necessary functions related to the life of the larger organism.

Bacilli are rod-shaped cells, some longer or shorter than others with the different kinds also varying in width. A single rod-shaped cell is called a bacillus.

Cocci appear as round or spherial cells. Some occur as pairs and are called diplococci, others as chain and are designated as *streptococci,* still others are arranged in irregular shaped groups and are called *staphylococci.*

Other bacteria have different shapes, such as a comma or crescent, others are spiral. Each is designated by a special name but the bacilli and cocci are the most common.

Flagella are hair-like projections from the shell of a microorganism. Movement of these flagella provide a means of locomotion for the cell which can then move in its environment, a process generally ascribed to an animal. Not all bacteria have this property and as such, are more nearly like plants.

Saprophytes are bacteria that can carry on an independent existence finding their own food supply adapting themselves to the conditions of their environment and carrying on their work without stimulus from other organisms.

The saprophytic bacteria, in general, obtain their food from dead organic matter which they attack and decompose or break down into simpler substances. Thus, they can obtain the food supply that is necessary for their continued growth, while at the same time carrying on the very useful function of destroying the dead matter. Without the action of the saprophytic bacteria, it would be impossible for other organisms to live on this planet since there would be no way to dispose of the dead organisms which would eventually cover the earth preventing growth of plants and the carrying on of natural functions essential for living organisms. Saprophytic bacteria break down the complex organic components of matter through the process known as decay or decomposition into simpler substances. These, in turn, serve as a food supply for plants, which become a food supply for animals, and the cycle of life is continued without the loss of matter. As an illustration of the changes in dead organic matter that are brought about by the activity of the bacteria, we might consider the natural process of decay and decomposition of organic compounds containing nitrogen, as shown by the nitrogen cycle. (Figure 30)

All living matter contains nitrogen bound with carbon, oxygen, hydrogen and other elements to form organic molecules. When these organisms die, the dead material is immediately a source of food for the saprophytic bacteria, which change these complex organic

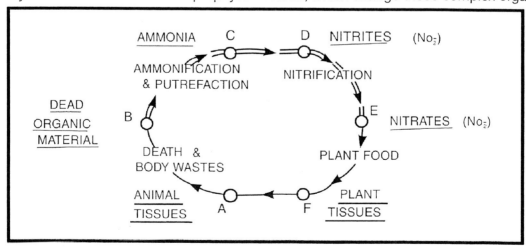

FIGURE 2 - THE NITROGEN CYCLE

molecules to simpler forms of nitrogenous matter, thence to ammonia, then to nitrites, and then to nitrates. The nitrates are the end product and the simplest and most useful form in which nitrogen exists. The nitrates are the basis of fertilizers and serve as a food for plants, which grow and become the food for living animals, which in turn grow until finally they die, and the cycle is completed and continues on and on. Thus, there is no loss of matter and complete usage is made of all of the elements composing living matter. In a similar manner, organic compounds containing sulfur, phosphorous, carbon and other chemical elements are decomposed through serving as a food supply for saprophytic bacteria.

Parasites, as contrasted to the saprophytic organisms, are bacteria that cannot live an independent existence, cannot find their own food supply, but must remain in close association with some other living organisms, from which they can obtain food already prepared. Parasites are dependent on the body of the host organisms to secure the environmental conditions upon which their existence and growth depend. They, however, carry on a similar type of decay and decomposition of this food supply, producing as a result end products which are necessary for the nourishment of the host. Most of these parasitic bacteria are beneficient and are necessary for the proper functioning of the living organism with which they are associated.

Pathogens. Among the parasitic bacteria are some which produce end products of their growth that are poisonous to the host organism and which produce a condition that is called disease. Some of them are pathogenic only to human beings in that they produce disease only in the body of human beings. Others are pathogenic to certain types of warm-blooded animals and some are pathogenic only to plants. There are a few types of saprophytic bacteria which have all of the characteristics of that class but which can, if they find entry into the body of an animal, produce end products which cause disease, such as anthrax or tetanus, in the body of the invaded animal. These particular saprophytic bacteria are also termed pathogenic.

Bacterial Growth. All bacteria require food for their continued life and growth and all are affected by the conditions of their environment. Like human beings, they consume food, they respire, they need moisture, they require heat, and they give off waste products. Their food requirements are very definite and have been, in general, already outlined. Without an adequate food supply of the type the specific organism requires, bacteria will not grow and multiply at their maximum rate and they will, therefore, not perform their full and complete functions.

Aerobic Bacteria. All bacteria require oxygen for their growth processes. Some require oxygen in its elementary gaseous form, which they obtain from the air. Such bacteria are designated as aerobic.

Anaerobic Bacteria. Some bacteria cannot live in the presence of free gaseous oxygen, but must obtain the oxygen needed for their respiration by decomposing or breaking down complex substances. These bacteria are designated as anaerobic.

Facultative Bacteria. There is a third type of bacteria which, though normally aerobic, can accustom itself to living in the absence of free gaseous oxygen or which, though normally anaerobic, can accustom itself to living in the presence of free gaseous oxygen. These are termed facultative bacteria.

Temperature Requirements. Bacteria are very sensitive to heat. Some live best at ordinary outdoor temperatures, varying from 60° to 68° F. Some, particularly the parasitic forms, require higher temperatures, approximately that of the body of living animals, 98° F. Some can live only at very cold temperatures, just above the freezing point of water. Any marked change from the optimum temperature requirements of specific bacteria causes a reduction in the activities of the bacteria, and if severe enough, may cause their death. If the temperature of the environment is raised to the boiling point of water, nearly all types of bacteria are destroyed.

Moisture Requirements. Bacteria require a moist environment for their most effective activities. If removed from such an environment for any length of time and drying takes place, most bacterial cells are destroyed. Under the most optimum environmental conditions of temperature, moisture, food supply and oxygen, the bacteria will multiply and grow at their maximum rate, producing their maximum amount of work. Any changes in the environmental conditions will cause an immediate decrease in the rate of growth, and possibly the death and destruction of the living forms.

Spore Formation. Some bacteria particularly those of the saprophytic type, when obliged to live in a very unfavorable environment with an inadequate food supply for any length of time, develop into a resistant form called a spore or seed. These spores are not affected by the environment, no food is required for their existence, and no growth results. A nucleus of life, however, is maintained and when the spore is again placed in a favorable environment it will sprout or develop into an active cell again. Parasitic bacteria, in general, do not form spores while saprophytes frequently do.

NORMAL CHARACTERISTICS OF SAPROPHYTIC AND PARASITIC BACTERIA

	Saprophytes	*Parasites*
Optimum temperature	Atmospheric	Body
Normal food material	Dead organic	Living
Oxygen requirements	Aerobic and anaerobic	Most anaerobic
Spore formation	Usually	Seldom
Effect on animals	Mostly non-pathogenic	Pathogenic and non-pathogenic

Mutual Activities. In the process of growth all bacteria produce waste products just as all other organisms do, and if these waste products were allowed to accumulate, they would destroy the particular form which produced them. However, other types of bacteria may find these waste products a satisfactory food supply, grow in their presence, and carry decomposition of the organic matter a step further until in turn their food supply is exhausted or their waste products accumulate to a sufficient degree to cause their destruction. Thus, the decay of organic matter is continuously carried on by many different types of bacteria, each of which carries the process of chemical decomposition forward. This is essentially what occurs in familiar process of sewage solids digestion. When the food supply is plentiful it is possible for two or more varieties of bacteria to exist side by side provided that the waste production of one strain is not toxic for the other. If the food supply lessens, or if waste products produced by one strain are toxic to other strains, the phenomena known as overgrowth may appear. This is a condition where one strain of organism may predominate to the exclusion of all others. Eventually however, waste products of the metabolism of the organism, unless they are removed, will become deleterious to the organism itself and the number of cells in a culture will decrease.

Toxic Agents. Living bacteria are sensitive not only to changes in the environment but can readily be poisoned or destroyed by many chemical substances. Such things as large concentrations of salt will destroy certain types of bacteria and this process has been used for many centuries to preserve such dead organic matter as meat or fish. Others are destroyed by strong acids or strong alkalis and by the addition to the environment of such chemical substances as chlorine, iodine or bromine. The destructive action of chemicals is a time-concentration effect. Thus, a low concentration will kill when present in the environment for a long period of time and a large concentration will kill in a short time.

WATER BIOLOGY

Bacteria. Bacteria are so widely distributed in nature that it is not surprising that all natural waters contain a fairly large variety. Some of these are saprophytic bacteria leached from the soil, others may be parasitic. Even pathogenic bacteria may be present in the water through contamination by waste matter of human or animal origin. Any water supply contaminated by sewage is certain to contain a bacterial group called "coliform." This is a group comprising more than 20 individual strains and termed coliform because of the fact that they have their natural habitat in the large intestine of human beings and animals. These bacteria are not usually pathogenic. The presence of pathogenic bacteria in water, as a result of contamination by sewage, is dependent upon an individual contributing to that sewage being ill of an intestinal disease and upon the survival of the pathogen in an environment which is not favorable to it. Coliform bacteria, on the other hand, are always present if sewage is present and are, generally much more hardy than pathogens. It is for this reason that the bacteriologic evaluation of water is always based upon a bacteriologic analysis to determine if coliform bacteria are present and in what concentration.

PLANKTON

In addition to bacteria other living organisms are commonly found in water and sewage. These are plankton. They are higher in the life scale than bacteria. They range in size from minute one-cell organisms only slightly larger than bacteria to much larger forms easily visible to the unaided eye. Some are plants, other are animals; some are capable of independent motion while others are not. Some idea of the complexity of size, shape, and metabolism of plankton may be gained by consideration of some characteristics of the most important groups of organisms included under that designation.

Algae. This is a very large group of plant forms distinguished by the fact that they contain chlorophyl—the green coloring matter of plants. Under favorable conditions they grow prolifically in water and sewage and heavy growths are easily detected by the presence of green-colored scum or "bloom." Under the influence of sunlight, chlorophyl-bearing plants absorb carbon dioxide and evolve oxygen. Pond waters which have heavy growths of algae frequently are saturated with oxygen during the daylight hours although the oxygen level decreases as darkness advances. Using water, carbon dioxide, and mineral matter secured from the environment, algae synthesize the complex proteins, fats, and cellulose constituents which made up their cell structure. The growth of algae is stimulated by the presence of nitrogen and phosphorous salts and also to some extent by calcium and magnesium salts. Growths in hard water are therefore usually heavier than in soft waters. Some algae are very tiny and have a single cell structure, other are multicellular and grow in a variety of forms, including branching plant-like structures hundreds of feet long. Many have pigments other than chlorophyl so that the actual color may be green, blue-green, or even red or brown. They are found most often in relatively pure water although not exclusively so. Some of the blue-green varieties are capable of growing quite well in heavily polluted water and even in sewage.

Fungi. Fungi are also plants, but in contract to the algae they do not contain chlorophyl. They are filamentous type organisms. For the purposes of simplicity, when we speak of sewage fungi we include filamentous bacteria and filamentous algae although, strictly speaking, these latter are not fungi. Fungi are commonly found in water and sewage and in the latter they are often observed growing in gray-colored cottony masses which attach themselves to the walls and structures in sewage treatment units. A common organism of this type is known as sphaerotilus. Fungi masses frequently clog the pipes and screens in the sewage plant and reduce the flow in channels. Their metabolism is dependent upon the availability of oxygen and a plentiful supply of organic matter.

Protozoa. Animals coming under the heading of plankton include, among other forms, protozoa. These are generally considered to be higher forms of life than the algae. They are frequently motile and are usually associated with sewage pollution. There are very many varieties and most of them feed on other microscopic organisms, primarily bacteria. They are frequently found growing in large masses as well as individual cells suspended in the water. There are thousands of varieties ranging in size from submicroscopic to macroscopic.

Crustaceae. These are small animals ranging in size from 0.2 to 0.3 millimeter long which move very rapidly through the water in search of food. They have recognizable head and posterior sections. They form a principal source of food for small fish and are found largely in relatively fresh natural water.

Rotifera. These are tiny animal forms which are characterized by the presence of cilia- short hair-like appendages which serve the double purpose of providing locomotion and creating a current in the water so that food will be drawn to the organism. Rotifera feed on decomposing organic matter and are found in bodies of water where such matter is present.

Worms. Flat worms or nematodes are varieties of worms which may be found in water and in sewage. Flat worms feed principally on algae and are found in the lower depths of ponds because they dislike and avoid light. They range in size from the fraction of a millimeter to several centimeters. Nematodes are parasitic worms living on other organisms, including man. It is believed that those which are parasitic in man are usually associated with contaminated food rather than contaminated water. Nematodes are very hardy and will survive over wide variations in temperature and humidity. They even survive under prolonged drying. They are very abundant in sewage sludge and are believed to play an important part in the stabilization of sludge.

Water Borne Disease. Pathogenic bacteria, which cause certain diseases, when discharged into water, can survive and be transferred through the agency of the water from one person to another. Among these so-called water-borne diseases are typhoid fever, dysentery, cholera, and various types of diarrheal ailments designated as gastro enteritis. Thus, the presence of these organisms in water causes a contamination of the water and renders it both unfit and unsafe for consumption. People who drink the water containing these particular pathogenic bacteria can readily acquire the corresponding disease in this way.

Safe Water. Obviously, then, the removal of bacteria is a necessary step in making water suitable for human consumption. Another necessary step is to prevent these pathogenic bacteria from getting into a water supply. Only water free from pathogenic bacteria can be considered of safe and satisfactory quality.

Laboratory Control. To determine if water is safe or if our precautionary methods are eliminating waste, and thus pathogenic bacteria from water, it is necessary that some means be devised for detecting the number of bacteria in water. To actually detect such pathogenic bacteria as those causing typhoid fever, dysentery, or other water-borne diseases is a very laborious, time-consuming process. Contrary to the opinion of most people, such examinations of water are not made. Rather, it is desirable to determine whether polluting material in the form of waste products from living animals has entered the water and to prevent further contamination from this means, or to remove the bacteria from water which has already received this type of polluting material. The procedure used is to determine the presence of an organism indicative of contamination of a water supply by the waste products from the intestinal discharges of warm-blooded animals.

Coliform organism. All warm-blooded animals harbor in their intestinal tract parasitic bacteria of various types. All members of this one specific group are designated as the coliform group of bacteria. These microorganisms are not normally pathogenic and function in the digestive processes of the host organism. They are discharged from the intestinal tract in tremendous numbers. They will always be present in large numbers in sewage, which usually contains at least 4,000,000 to 5,000,000 coliform bacteria per ml. If sewage enters a water, the bacteria are carried with it and will survive there for long periods of time. Thus, their presence provides positive evidence of pollution and the possible presence of the pathogenic bacteria from the discharges of the animal bodies. Their detection by laboratory examination is relatively simple.

Index of Pollution. The number of these bacteria that are present in any definite volume of water is a measure of the amount of sewage or waste which has been discharged into that water, and can be interpreted as a measure of the safety of the water for human consumption. If large numbers of these bacteria are present, there will be a large amount of pollution and the water is unsatisfactory and potentially unsafe. A smaller number of these microorganisms, of course, shows a lesser concentration of pollution. A very few coliform bacteria, less than one per 100 ml of water, indicates that the amount of pollution is too small to present a definite hazard and that it can be considered of safe quality.

GLOSSARY OF BACTERIOLOGICAL TERMS

Contents

		Page
ACID-FAST BACTERIA	AMYLASE	1
ANAEROBES	ATTENUATED	2
AUTOCLAVE	BY-PRODUCTS	3
CAPSULE.............................	COLUMELLA	4
COMMENSALISM...................	DIFFUSE NUCLEI	5
DIPLOID NUCLEUS................	EXTRACELLULAR ENZYMES	6
FACULTATIVELY ANAEROBIC	HAPLOID NUCLEUS	7
HUMUS	INTRACELLULAR ENZYMES	8
INTRAMOLECULAR RESPIRATION........................	METABIOSIS	9
METABOLISM	MYCELIUM	10
NATURAL IMMUNITY	PARASITES	11
PASSIVE IMMUNITY...............	PLASMOLYSIS	12
PLEOMORPHISM...................	REFLECTED LIGHT	13
RENNIN	SEWERAGE	14
SLIME LAYER	STRICK PARASITES	15
STRINGY MILK	TOXOID	16
TRANSMITTED LIGHT	WINOGRADSKY TEST	17
YEAST..................................	ZYGOTE	18

GLOSSARY OF BACTERIOLOGICAL TERMS

A

ACID-FAST BACTERIA
Bacteria that strongly resist decoloration with acid-alcohol after being stained with a hot dye such as carbol fuchsin. *Mycobacterium tuberculosis* is a typical example.

ACQUIRED IMMUNITY
Immunity that an individual obtains after a period of natural susceptibility.

ACTIVATED SLUDGE PROCESS
A method of sewage purification in which a little "ripe" sewage is added to the fresh sewage to be treated, which is then submitted to extensive aeration.

ACTIVE IMMUNITY
Immunity in which the immunizing agent is produced by the metabolism of the immunized individual.

AEROBES
Organisms that can grow in the presence of air.

AGAR
1. A polysaccharide material extracted from sea weeds.
2. A common term applied to a culture medium solidified with this material, such as nutrient agar.

AGGLUTINATION
The clumping together of bacteria through the action of agglu-tinins homologous with them.

AGGLUTININS
A kind of antibody that causes the clumping together of the corresponding antigen particles, such as bacterial bodies.

ALGAE
Thallophytic plants that carry on photosynthesis with the aid of chlorophyll or other pigment.

ALLERGY
A state of hypersentivity to a foreign substance such as protein.

AMMONIFICATION
The formation of ammonia from organic compounds.

AMPHITRICHIC
With a tuft of flagella at each end of the cell. Resulting from cell division but not separation of two sister cells each carrying flagella at one end. Terminal flagellation.

AMYLASE
The enzyme that hydrolyzes starch to maltose. Diastase. Ptyalin.

ANAEROBES
Organisms that cannot grow in the presence of air.

ANAPHYLACTIC SHOCK
The response of the body to the injection of a substance to which the body is abnormally sensitive.

ANAPHYLAXIS
A state of hypersensitiveness to a foreign protein or other substance, brought about by an initial injection of the substance.

ANOREXIA
Loss of appetite.

ANTAGONISM
A relationship between species of microorganisms in which one kills or injures the other. Antibiosis.

ANTIBIOTIC
A substance produced by a living organism which will inhibit or destroy other forms of life, expecially pathogenic microorganisms. Examples are penicillin, streptomycin, bacitracin, etc.

ANTIBODY
A substance produced by the body under the stimulus of an antigen and capable of reacting with it *in vitro*.

ANTIGEN
A substance, usually a foreign protein, that, if injected into the body, stimulates the production of an antibody such as antitoxin.

ANTISEPTIC
A chemical substance that, in the strength used, will inhibit the activities of microorganisms without killing them.

ANTITOXIN
An antibody that has the power of neutralizing the effects of the homologous toxin that served as an antigen for its production.

ASCOSPORES
Spores produced in definite numbers, usually eight, by free cell formation within a sac or ascus.

ASCUS
The spore-bearing sac of the *Ascomycetes*.

ATTENUATED
Made weaker than normal, or less pathogenic.

AUTOCLAVE
An apparatus used for heating materials under steam pressure. Similar in principle to a pressure cooker.

AUTOLYSIS
Self-digestion due to the action of enzymes upon the tissues that produced them, as the over-ripening of bananas and other kinds of fruit, or the breakdown of dead bacterial cells.

AUTOTROPHIC BACTERIA
Bacteria that can live without a supply of organic matter, and can obtain energy from inorganic materials, or in some instances from sunlight.

<u>B</u>

BACTEREMIA
The presence of bacteria in the blood stream. Septicemia.

BACTERIOLYSIS
The disintegration of bacterial cells.

BACTERIOPHAGE
A specific virus capable of destroying living bacteria.

BALLISTOSPORES
Asexual spores formed by yeasts of the family *Sporobolo-mycetaceae.* They arise on sterigmata and are shot off by a drop excretion mechanism.

BARRIERS OF INFECTION
Mechanical obstructions, such as skin and mucous membranes, that prevent pathogenic organisms from reaching a vulnerable region.

BROWNIAN MOVEMENT
The movement of visible particles by the bombardment of molecules of the suspending fluid.

BUDDING
A method of cell division in which a small area of the cell wall softens and protoplasm including a nucleus is forced out and is later cut off by constriction, thus forming a new cell.

BUTTER CULTURE
A pure culture or a definite mixture of bacterial species added to cream after pasteurization to give desired flavor and consistency to the butter made from it.

BY-PRODUCTS
Substances that remain after certain elements have been removed for use by the organism, e.g., nitrites, after oxygen has been removed from nitrates.

C

CAPSULE
A thickened slime layer of carbohydrate material surrounding the cell wall of many species of bacteria.

CARBOHYDRASES
The group of enzymes that hydrolyze complex carbohydrates to simpler ones. The amylolytic group.

CARRIER OF DISEASE
A person or animal that harbors the organisms of disease without showing symptoms.

CATEGORIES
The several group names order, families, genera, etc., used for classifying living things.

CELLULASE
The enzyme that hydrolyzes cellulose into cellobiose.

CHEMOSYNTHESIS
The obtaining of energy by the oxidation of inorganic substances, followed by its use for the building of organic compounds.

CHEMOTAXIS
The ability of organisms to respond to chemical stimuli by moving toward or away from the region of greatest concentration.

CHLAMYDOSPORES
Thick-walled spores formed by a rounding up of cells of a mycelium.

CHROMOGENESIS
The production of pigment.

COCCI
Bacterial that are spherical or nearly so.

COLIFORM GROUP
All aerobic and facultatively anerobic gram negative non-spore forming rods which ferment lactose with gas formation.

COLIPHAGE
A specific bacteriophage that is capable of destroying Escherichia coli.

COLONY
A visible collection of bacteria resulting from the multiplication and growth of a single individual.

COLUMELLA
A dome-shaped, non-sporeforming structure extending upward from the sporangiophore into the base of a sporangium, as in Rhizopus.

COMMENSALISM
A relationship between species of organisms in which one receives benefit and the other neither benefit nor harm. Metabiosis.

COMPLEMENT
A thermolabel, non-specific constituent of the normal blood of man aiding in the destruction of all kinds of bacteria.

CONDENSER
A large lens beneath the stage of a microscope, for concentrating light on the object from below.

CONIDIA
Fungus spores cut off from the tips of hyphae by construction.

CONIDIOPHORE
A stalk arising from the vegetative mycelium and supporting sterigmata that produce one or more conidia.

CONJUGATION
The union of two gamete cells in sexual reproduction.

CONSTRICTION
A method of cell division in which the cell is cut in two by a circular furrow surrounding it.

<u>D</u>

DARK-FIELD ILLUMINATION
A method of illuminating objects for microscopic examination whereby the object is made to appear luminous against a dark background.

DECAY
The destruction of organic materials through the action of enzymes produced by microorganisms.

DEHYDROGENASES
A group of enzymes that remove hydrogen from compounds and thus produce the effect of oxidation.

DENITRIFICATION
The formation of free nitrogen of nitrous oxide from nitrates.

DICK TEST
A skin test to determine whether a person is susceptible to scarlet fever.

DIFFUSE NUCLEI
Nuclei composed of chromatin material scattered throughout the cytoplasm rather than enclosed within a nuclear membrane.

DIPLOID NUCLEUS
A neucleus having a complete number of paired chromosomes for the species. See HAPLOID.

DISINFECTANTS
Chemical substances capable of killing pathogenic microorganisms.

E

EFFLUENT
Partially or completely treated sewage flowing out of any sewage treatment device.

ELECTRON MICROSCOPE
A microscope similar in principle to the compound light microscope but which uses electrons instead of light as a source of radiation.

ENDOENZYMES
Same as intracellular enzymes.

ENDOTOXINS
Toxins that remain within the cells that produce them and do not stimulate the production of corresponding antitoxins.

ENVIRONMENT
The composite of all conditions surrounding an organism.

ENZYME
A biological catalyst.

EPIDEMIOLOGY
The science of tracing the sources from which diseases spread.

ETIOLOGY
The science of causes, e.g., causes of disease.

EXCRETIONS
Substances that have become so changed in composition through metabolism that they are no longer useful to the organism that produced them and are cast off, e.g., carbon dioxide.

EXOENZYMES
Same as EXTRACELLULAR ENZYMES.

EXOTOXINS
Toxins that diffuse from the cells that produce them into the surrounding medium. They are antigenic and stimulate the formation of antitoxins.

EXTRACELLULAR ENZYMES
Enzymes that diffuse out of the cells that formed them.

F

FACULTATIVELY ANAEROBIC
Organisms that can grow in either the presence or absence of air.

FACULTATIVELY PARASITIC
Organisms that can live either as parasites or as saprophytes.

FALSE BRANCHING
A kind of branching of filaments in which the cells do not branch, but the branch of the filament is held to the main filament by a common sheath surrounding both.

FERMENTATION
A process carried on by microorganisms whereby organic materials, usually carbohydrates, are decomposed with the formation of acids and sometimes carbon dioxide and alcohol.

FISSION
A method of cell division by constriction in which two daughter cells of equal size are formed.

FLAGELLA
Slender protoplasmic strands that extend from the cell and serve as organs of locomotion.

FUNGI IMPERFECTI
A heterogeneous group of fungi that have no sexual stage. Apparently most of them are degenerate *Asoomycetes.*

FUNGUS
A thallophytic plant that lacks chlorophyll and is of filmentous structure.

G

GAMETES
Two haploid cells that unite in sexual reproduction.

GENOTYPE
The sum total of the determinants controlling the reaction range of an individual or a cell.

GROWTH
1. Increase in size of an individual.
2. Increase in numbers of microorganisms.
3. A visible mass of microorganisms formed by reproduction and enlargement.

H

HANGING DROP
A drop of liquid suspended for study from the under side of a cover glass mounted on a slide with a depression in the surface.

HAPLOID NUCLEUS
A nucleus having a complete number of single chromosomes for the species. See DIPLOID.

HUMUS
  Organic matter decomposed to such an extent that its original structure is no longer recognizable.

HYDROLASES
  Enzymes that bring about chemical change by the addition of water that goes into chemical union with the substance acted upon.

HYPERSENSITIVITY
  An abnormally high degree of sensitiveness to foreign substances such as proteins.

HYPERTROPHY
  An abnormal multiplication of cells resulting in the formation of nodules, tumors, etc.

HYPHAE
  Branches of a fungus mycelium.

I

IMHOFF TANK
  A specially constructed septic tank having a flow chamber above and a sludge chamber below.

IMMUNITY
  The ability of an animal or plant to resist disease even when the pathogenic organisms or their products reach a vulnerable region.

IMPRESSED VARIATION
  A kind of variation brought about by some recognizably unfavorable condition.

INFLAMMATION
  A morbid condition characterized by swelling, redness, and pain, usually in a localized region.

INFLUENT
  Sewage, treated or partially treated, flowing into any sewage treatment device.

INOCULUM
  Material containing microorganisms and used for the inoculation of media or hosts.

INTERMITTENT STERILIZATION
  A sterilization process involving the heating of the material to a temperature of 80-100 C. for a time up to an hour on each of three successive days. Fractional sterilization. Tyndal-lization.

INTERMOLECULAR RESPIRATION
  A form of respiration in which oxygen is taken from one kind of molecule and used to oxidize another.

INTRACELLULAR ENZYMES
  Enzymes that remain within the cells that produced them. Endoenzymes.

INTRAMOLECULAR RESPIRATION
A form of respiration in which there is a rearrangement of atoms within the molecule resulting in a release of energy.

INVOLUTION FORMS
Cells of microorganisms large in size and of unusual form. Generally considered abnormal.

IRON BACTERIA
Bacteria that contain ferric hydroxide in the stalk or the sheath.

IRRITABILITY
The capacity of an organism for response to change in the environment.

L

LENS
A piece of glass or other transparent substance used for magnifying or reducing the apparent size of objects.

LIPOLYTIC ENZYMES
Enzymes that hydrolyze fats into fatty acids and glycerol.

LOPHOTRICHIC
With flagella in a tuft at one end of the cell. Terminal flagellation.

LYOPHILIZE
To dry a protein, usually from the frozen state, in such a way so it is still soluble. As applied to microorganisms it involves the freezing and drying of the organisms so that many of the cells will remain viable for long periods of time.

LYSIN
An enzyme or other substance that breaks down or dissolves organic substances.

M

MANTOUX TEST
A tuberculin test in which the tuberculin is injected in-tradermally.

MASS MORPHOLOGY
The morphology of bacterial groups, colonies, etc., as contrasted with individual cells.

MECHANISM OF INFECTION
The means by which microorganisms produce disease.

MESOPHILES
Bacteria that grow best at moderate temperatures, having an optimum of $25°$ C. to $45°$ C.

METABIOSIS
Same as COMMENSALISM.

METABOLISM
Any chemical change brought about by a living thing in its use of food.

MICROAEROPHILIC
Organisms that require free oxygen of less concentration than that found in the atmosphere.

MICROMANIPULATOR
A complicated piece of apparatus used for fine dissection under the microscope, or for single cell isolation.

MICRON
A unit of measurement having a value of 0.001 of a millimeter.

MICROORGANISMS
Forms of life that are microscopic in size, or nearly so.

MICROPHILES
Bacteria having a narrow temperature range for growth.

MILLIMICRON
0.001 micron or 0.000001 mm. A unit of measurement often used in designating the size of virus particles.

MITOSIS
Division of a cell with a diploid nucleus in which all of the chromosomes divide, resulting in two diploid daughter cells.

MOLD
A saprophytic fungus that is of simple filamentous structure.

MONOTRICHIC
With a flagellum occurring at one end of the cell. Terminal flagellation.

MORBIDITY
The frequency of occurrence of cases of a disease.

MORPHOLOGY
That branch of biological science that deals with qualities that appear to the eye size, form, color, etc.

MORTALITY
The percentage of deaths among those afflicted with a disease.

MUTATION
A change from some parental character occurring in the offspring. More permanent than variation.

MYCELIUM
The branching, thread-like structure that makes up the vegetative body of a fungus.

N

NATURAL IMMUNITY
Immunity that an individual possesses by virtue of its race or species. Immunity present from the beginning of life of the individual.

NECROSIS
The death of tissues.

NITRATE REDUCTION
The formation of nitrites or ammonia from nitrates.

NITRIFICATION
The formation of nitric acid or nitrates from ammonia.

NITROGEN FIXATION
The formation of nitrogen compounds from free nitrogen.

NON-SYMBIOTIC NITROGEN FIXATION
Fixation of nitrogen by organisms living independently, as *Azotobacter* and *Clostridium*.

NOSEPIECE
The portion of a microscope into which the objectives are screwed.

O

OBJECTIVE
The system of lenses in a compound microscope that is used next to the object to be studied.

OCULAR
The combination of lenses at the top of a compound microscope. Also called an eyepiece.

OIDIA
Thin walled spores formed by the separation of undifferentiated cells of a mycelium.

OPSONINS
Antibodies which make bacteria more readily ingested by phagocytes.

OSMOSIS
The tendency of fluids to pass through a membrane that separates two portions of different concentration.

P

PARASITES
Organisms that obtain their food from the living substance of other organisms.

PASSIVE IMMUNITY
Immunity in which the immunized individual does not produce its own immunizing agent but receives it from one with active immunity.

PASTEURIZATION
Heating at a temperature that will kill most objectionable microorganisms, excepting spore-forming bacteria and ther-mophiles.

PATHOGENICITY
The ability to produce disease.

PATHOGENS
Organisms that cause disease in other forms of life.

PATHOLOGY
A study of the abnormal conditions that occur in the tissues as a result of disease.

PERITRICHIC
With flagella distributed all over the cell body. Lateral flagellation.

PHAGOCYTES
Leucocytes or other living cells that have the power of ingesting bacteria.

PHENOL COEFFICIENT
The killing strength of a disinfectant, relative to that of phenol.

PHOTOGENESIS
The production of light. Phosphorescence.

PHOTOSYNTHESIS
The formation of carbohydrates from simpler food materials, using light as the source of energy.

PHYSIOLOGY
That branch of biological science which deals with the functions and activities of living things nutrition, growth, reproduction, irritiability, etc.

PLAQUES
Clear zones in streaks of bacterial growth resulting from the lysis of bacteria by bacteriophage.

PLANE OF DIVISION
The direction in which a cleavage furrow divides a cell.

PLASMODESMID
A protoplasmic strand extending from one bacterial cell to another.

PLASMOLYSIS
The shrinkage of cell contents through the withdrawal of water by osmotic action.

PLEOMORPHISM
Exhibiting several forms or shapes. Polymorphism.

PLEUROPNEUMONIA GROUP
Microorganisms that grow in cell-free culture media with the development of polymorphic structures as rings, globules, filaments, and minute reproductive bodies.

POLYMORPHISM
Exhibiting several forms or shapes. Pleomorphism.

PORTALS OF INFECTION
Openings through which pathogenic organisms pass into the body of the host.

POST-FISSION MOVEMENTS
Movements of cells following fission, whereby the two adjacent cells are finally separated.

PRECIPITINS
A kind of antibody that forms a precipitate with an antigen that was previously in solution.

PROCESSING
Preliminary treatment, canning, and sterilization of foods. The term is often used for a single one of these operations such as sterilization.

PROTEOLYSIS
The destruction of proteins by enzymes.

PROTEOLYTIC ENZYMES
Enzymes that hydrolze proteins and related compounds.

PROTOZOA
Unicellular members of the animal kingdom.

PSYCHROPHILES
Bacteria that grow best at relatively low temperatures, having an optimum of 15 C to 20 C.

PUTREFACTION
The chemical decomposition of proteins and related compounds, usually with the production of disagreeable odors.

<u>R</u>

R-COLONIES
Colonies that have a rough surface, although belonging to a species that usually produces smooth colonies.

REFLECTED LIGHT
Light that strikes the surface of an object being studied with a microscope and is reflected back into the lens.

RENNIN
  The enzyme that changes the soluble casein of milk into the solid paracasein in the presence of calcium.

RESOLVING POWER
  The ability of a lens to reveal fine detail. It is measured in terms of the least distance between two points at which they can be identified as two rather than as a single blurred object.

RESPIRATION
  Any chemical reaction whereby energy is released for life processes.

RICKETTSIAE
  Microorganisms that are obligate intracellular parasites or that are dependent directly on living cells. They are not ultramicroscopic but are adapted to intracellular life in arthropod tissue.

ROPY MILK
  Milk that is viscid because of the presence of capsule-forming bacteria such as *Alcaligenes viscosus*.

<u>S</u>

SAPROPHYTES
  Organisms that use non-living organic matter for food.

SCHICK TEST
  A skin test to determine whether a person is susceptible to diphtheria. Similar to the Dick test for scarlet fever.

S-COLONIES
  Colonies that have a smooth surface, although belong to a species that may produce rough-surfaced colonies.

SECONDARY INVADERS
  Saprophytic organisms that invade the body of a host in the wake of a pathogenic species.

SECRETIONS
  Substances that serve a useful purpose to the organisms that produce them, e.g., enzymes.

SEPTATE MYCELIUM
  A mycelium subdivided into cells by cross-walls or septa.

SEPTIC TANK
  A deep vat or chamber used for the anaerobic treatment of sewage.

SEPTICEMIA
  The presence of bacteria in the blood stream. Bacteremia.

SEWERAGE
  The system employed for the handling of sewage.

SLIME LAYER
A carbohydrate layer surrounding all bacterial cells which, if it becomes extensive, is called a capsule.

SLUDGE
The mass of solids remaining after a sewage treating process is completed or wet sewage solids which have been deposited by sedimentation.

SOURCES OF INFECTION
Places from which disease-producing organisms were acquired by the host.

SPECIFICITY
The limitation of a species of microorganisms to one species of host, or to at least a small number.

SPONTANEOUS COMBUSTION
Ignition of material by heat generated through its oxidation.

SPONTANEOUS GENERATION
The origin of living things from non-living materials.

SPORANGIA
Sacs in which fungus spores are formed.

SPORANGIOPHORE
A stalk that produces a sporangium.

SPORANGIUM
A sac that contains spores, usually numerous and indefinite in number.

SPORE
1. A simple reproductive body of a lower plant, capable of growing directly into a new plant.
2. Among bacteria, a thick-walled resistant cell.

STERIGMATA
Tiny stalks that produce spores at their tips, as in *Asper-gillus, Penicillium,* and mushrooms.

STERILIZATION
Killing microorganisms, usually by means of heat.

STOCK CULTURE
Cultures of microorganisms kept as a reserve for future use.

STREAK CULTURES
Cultures made by applying the organisms with a loop or other instrument to the surface of a medium, usually agar slanted in a test tube.

STRICK PARASITES
Organisms that require a living host.

STRINGY MILK
 Milk that contains tough stringy clots as it is drawn from an inflamed udder.

SULFUR BACTERIA
 Bacteria that use sulfur or hydrogen sulfide for food and oxidize it. Some forms store granules of sulfur in their cells.

SUPPURATION
 The formation of pus.

SYMBIOSIS
 A relationship between species of organisms whereby each receives some form of benefit.

SYMBIOTIC NITROGEN FIXATION
 Nitrogen fixation by bacteria living symbiotically with higher plants.

SYMPTOMS
 Functional disturbances brought about by diseased conditions.

SYNERGISM
 The ability of two or more species of organisms to bring about chemical changes that neither can bring about alone.

T

THERMODURIC BACTERIA
 Organisms capable of withstanding high temperatures.

THERMOGENESIS
 Heat production by microorganisms.

THERMOLABILE
 Destroyed by a temperature below the boiling point of water.

THERMOPHILES
 Bacteria that grow best at relatively high temperatures, having an optimum of 55 C or higher.

THERMOSTABLE
 Resistant to heat at the boiling point of water or thereabout.

TOXEMIA
 A condition characterized by toxins in the blood.

TOXINS
 Poisonous substances of complex nitrogenous composition produced by bacteria and some higher organisms.

TOXOID
 A detoxified toxin that remains antigenic and can be used to confer active immunity.

TRANSMITTED LIGHT
Light that passes through the object that is being studied with a microscope.

TRICKLING FILTER
A sewage purification plant in which the sewage is sprayed onto a layer of crushed rock or similar material to provide an extensive surface for aeration.

TUBERCULIN TEST
A test to determine whether a person or animal has been infected with *Mycobacterium tuberculosis*.

U

ULTRAMICROSCOPE
A microscope that reveals very minute objects by the use of light that strikes them obliquely and is reflected into the objective.

UREASE
The enzyme that hydrolyzes urea into ammonium carbonate.

V

VACCINE
Anything which, if injected into the body, causes it to develop active immunity.

VARIATION
The departure of the offspring from the parent with respect to some character. Usually more temporary than mutation.

VECTORS OF DISEASE
Insects or other forms of animal life that transfer pathogenic organisms from host to host.

VEHICLE OF INFECTION
Food or water containing pathogenic microorganisms.

VIRULENCE
In bacteriology, the ability to produce disease.

VIRUSES
Etiological agents of disease, typically of small size, most being capable of passing filters that retain bacteria, increasing only in the presence of living cells, and giving rise to new strains by mutation, not arising spontaneously.

W

WIDAL TEST
The agglutination test for typhoid fever.

WINOGRADSKY TEST
A soil test for fertility by determining its suitability for growing *Asotobacter*.

Y

YEAST
A kind of fungus which has been reduced to a more or less unicellular state by loss of mycelium.

Z

ZYGOSPORE
The zygote of certain kinds of fungi and algae, e.g., *Rhizopus, Mucor* and *Spirogyra*.

ZYGOTE
A diploid cell formed by the union of two haploid gamete cells in sexual reproduction.

ANSWER SHEET

TEST NO. ______________ PART ______ TITLE OF POSITION ______________________________
(AS GIVEN IN EXAMINATION ANNOUNCEMENT - INCLUDE OPTION, IF ANY)

PLACE OF EXAMINATION ______________________ (CITY OR TOWN) ______________________ (STATE) DATE ______________

RATING

USE THE SPECIAL PENCIL. MAKE GLOSSY BLACK MARKS.

1 A B C D E	26 A B C D E	51 A B C D E	76 A B C D E	101 A B C D E
2 A B C D E	27 A B C D E	52 A B C D E	77 A B C D E	102 A B C D E
3 A B C D E	28 A B C D E	53 A B C D E	78 A B C D E	103 A B C D E
4 A B C D E	29 A B C D E	54 A B C D E	79 A B C D E	104 A B C D E
5 A B C D E	30 A B C D E	55 A B C D E	80 A B C D E	105 A B C D E
6 A B C D E	31 A B C D E	56 A B C D E	81 A B C D E	106 A B C D E
7 A B C D E	32 A B C D E	57 A B C D E	82 A B C D E	107 A B C D E
8 A B C D E	33 A B C D E	58 A B C D E	83 A B C D E	108 A B C D E
9 A B C D E	34 A B C D E	59 A B C D E	84 A B C D E	109 A B C D E
10 A B C D E	35 A B C D E	60 A B C D E	85 A B C D E	110 A B C D E

Make only ONE mark for each answer. Additional and stray marks may be counted as mistakes. In making corrections, erase errors COMPLETELY.

11 A B C D E	36 A B C D E	61 A B C D E	86 A B C D E	111 A B C D E
12 A B C D E	37 A B C D E	62 A B C D E	87 A B C D E	112 A B C D E
13 A B C D E	38 A B C D E	63 A B C D E	88 A B C D E	113 A B C D E
14 A B C D E	39 A B C D E	64 A B C D E	89 A B C D E	114 A B C D E
15 A B C D E	40 A B C D E	65 A B C D E	90 A B C D E	115 A B C D E
16 A B C D E	41 A B C D E	66 A B C D E	91 A B C D E	116 A B C D E
17 A B C D E	42 A B C D E	67 A B C D E	92 A B C D E	117 A B C D E
18 A B C D E	43 A B C D E	68 A B C D E	93 A B C D E	118 A B C D E
19 A B C D E	44 A B C D E	69 A B C D E	94 A B C D E	119 A B C D E
20 A B C D E	45 A B C D E	70 A B C D E	95 A B C D E	120 A B C D E
21 A B C D E	46 A B C D E	71 A B C D E	96 A B C D E	121 A B C D E
22 A B C D E	47 A B C D E	72 A B C D E	97 A B C D E	122 A B C D E
23 A B C D E	48 A B C D E	73 A B C D E	98 A B C D E	123 A B C D E
24 A B C D E	49 A B C D E	74 A B C D E	99 A B C D E	124 A B C D E
25 A B C D E	50 A B C D E	75 A B C D E	100 A B C D E	125 A B C D E

ANSWER SHEET

TEST NO. _____ PART _____ TITLE OF POSITION _____
(AS GIVEN IN EXAMINATION ANNOUNCEMENT - INCLUDE OPTION, IF ANY)

PLACE OF EXAMINATION _____ DATE _____
(CITY OR TOWN)   (STATE)

RATING

USE THE SPECIAL PENCIL.   MAKE GLOSSY BLACK MARKS.

	A B C D E		A B C D E		A B C D E		A B C D E		A B C D E
1	⁞ ⁞ ⁞ ⁞ ⁞	26	⁞ ⁞ ⁞ ⁞ ⁞	51	⁞ ⁞ ⁞ ⁞ ⁞	76	⁞ ⁞ ⁞ ⁞ ⁞	101	⁞ ⁞ ⁞ ⁞ ⁞
2	⁞ ⁞ ⁞ ⁞ ⁞	27	⁞ ⁞ ⁞ ⁞ ⁞	52	⁞ ⁞ ⁞ ⁞ ⁞	77	⁞ ⁞ ⁞ ⁞ ⁞	102	⁞ ⁞ ⁞ ⁞ ⁞
3	⁞ ⁞ ⁞ ⁞ ⁞	28	⁞ ⁞ ⁞ ⁞ ⁞	53	⁞ ⁞ ⁞ ⁞ ⁞	78	⁞ ⁞ ⁞ ⁞ ⁞	103	⁞ ⁞ ⁞ ⁞ ⁞
4	⁞ ⁞ ⁞ ⁞ ⁞	29	⁞ ⁞ ⁞ ⁞ ⁞	54	⁞ ⁞ ⁞ ⁞ ⁞	79	⁞ ⁞ ⁞ ⁞ ⁞	104	⁞ ⁞ ⁞ ⁞ ⁞
5	⁞ ⁞ ⁞ ⁞ ⁞	30	⁞ ⁞ ⁞ ⁞ ⁞	55	⁞ ⁞ ⁞ ⁞ ⁞	80	⁞ ⁞ ⁞ ⁞ ⁞	105	⁞ ⁞ ⁞ ⁞ ⁞
6	⁞ ⁞ ⁞ ⁞ ⁞	31	⁞ ⁞ ⁞ ⁞ ⁞	56	⁞ ⁞ ⁞ ⁞ ⁞	81	⁞ ⁞ ⁞ ⁞ ⁞	106	⁞ ⁞ ⁞ ⁞ ⁞
7	⁞ ⁞ ⁞ ⁞ ⁞	32	⁞ ⁞ ⁞ ⁞ ⁞	57	⁞ ⁞ ⁞ ⁞ ⁞	82	⁞ ⁞ ⁞ ⁞ ⁞	107	⁞ ⁞ ⁞ ⁞ ⁞
8	⁞ ⁞ ⁞ ⁞ ⁞	33	⁞ ⁞ ⁞ ⁞ ⁞	58	⁞ ⁞ ⁞ ⁞ ⁞	83	⁞ ⁞ ⁞ ⁞ ⁞	108	⁞ ⁞ ⁞ ⁞ ⁞
9	⁞ ⁞ ⁞ ⁞ ⁞	34	⁞ ⁞ ⁞ ⁞ ⁞	59	⁞ ⁞ ⁞ ⁞ ⁞	84	⁞ ⁞ ⁞ ⁞ ⁞	109	⁞ ⁞ ⁞ ⁞ ⁞
10	⁞ ⁞ ⁞ ⁞ ⁞	35	⁞ ⁞ ⁞ ⁞ ⁞	60	⁞ ⁞ ⁞ ⁞ ⁞	85	⁞ ⁞ ⁞ ⁞ ⁞	110	⁞ ⁞ ⁞ ⁞ ⁞

Make only ONE mark for each answer.   Additional and stray marks may be counted as mistakes.   In making corrections, erase errors COMPLETELY.

	A B C D E		A B C D E		A B C D E		A B C D E		A B C D E
11	⁞ ⁞ ⁞ ⁞ ⁞	36	⁞ ⁞ ⁞ ⁞ ⁞	61	⁞ ⁞ ⁞ ⁞ ⁞	86	⁞ ⁞ ⁞ ⁞ ⁞	111	⁞ ⁞ ⁞ ⁞ ⁞
12	⁞ ⁞ ⁞ ⁞ ⁞	37	⁞ ⁞ ⁞ ⁞ ⁞	62	⁞ ⁞ ⁞ ⁞ ⁞	87	⁞ ⁞ ⁞ ⁞ ⁞	112	⁞ ⁞ ⁞ ⁞ ⁞
13	⁞ ⁞ ⁞ ⁞ ⁞	38	⁞ ⁞ ⁞ ⁞ ⁞	63	⁞ ⁞ ⁞ ⁞ ⁞	88	⁞ ⁞ ⁞ ⁞ ⁞	113	⁞ ⁞ ⁞ ⁞ ⁞
14	⁞ ⁞ ⁞ ⁞ ⁞	39	⁞ ⁞ ⁞ ⁞ ⁞	64	⁞ ⁞ ⁞ ⁞ ⁞	89	⁞ ⁞ ⁞ ⁞ ⁞	114	⁞ ⁞ ⁞ ⁞ ⁞
15	⁞ ⁞ ⁞ ⁞ ⁞	40	⁞ ⁞ ⁞ ⁞ ⁞	65	⁞ ⁞ ⁞ ⁞ ⁞	90	⁞ ⁞ ⁞ ⁞ ⁞	115	⁞ ⁞ ⁞ ⁞ ⁞
16	⁞ ⁞ ⁞ ⁞ ⁞	41	⁞ ⁞ ⁞ ⁞ ⁞	66	⁞ ⁞ ⁞ ⁞ ⁞	91	⁞ ⁞ ⁞ ⁞ ⁞	116	⁞ ⁞ ⁞ ⁞ ⁞
17	⁞ ⁞ ⁞ ⁞ ⁞	42	⁞ ⁞ ⁞ ⁞ ⁞	67	⁞ ⁞ ⁞ ⁞ ⁞	92	⁞ ⁞ ⁞ ⁞ ⁞	117	⁞ ⁞ ⁞ ⁞ ⁞
18	⁞ ⁞ ⁞ ⁞ ⁞	43	⁞ ⁞ ⁞ ⁞ ⁞	68	⁞ ⁞ ⁞ ⁞ ⁞	93	⁞ ⁞ ⁞ ⁞ ⁞	118	⁞ ⁞ ⁞ ⁞ ⁞
19	⁞ ⁞ ⁞ ⁞ ⁞	44	⁞ ⁞ ⁞ ⁞ ⁞	69	⁞ ⁞ ⁞ ⁞ ⁞	94	⁞ ⁞ ⁞ ⁞ ⁞	119	⁞ ⁞ ⁞ ⁞ ⁞
20	⁞ ⁞ ⁞ ⁞ ⁞	45	⁞ ⁞ ⁞ ⁞ ⁞	70	⁞ ⁞ ⁞ ⁞ ⁞	95	⁞ ⁞ ⁞ ⁞ ⁞	120	⁞ ⁞ ⁞ ⁞ ⁞
21	⁞ ⁞ ⁞ ⁞ ⁞	46	⁞ ⁞ ⁞ ⁞ ⁞	71	⁞ ⁞ ⁞ ⁞ ⁞	96	⁞ ⁞ ⁞ ⁞ ⁞	121	⁞ ⁞ ⁞ ⁞ ⁞
22	⁞ ⁞ ⁞ ⁞ ⁞	47	⁞ ⁞ ⁞ ⁞ ⁞	72	⁞ ⁞ ⁞ ⁞ ⁞	97	⁞ ⁞ ⁞ ⁞ ⁞	122	⁞ ⁞ ⁞ ⁞ ⁞
23	⁞ ⁞ ⁞ ⁞ ⁞	48	⁞ ⁞ ⁞ ⁞ ⁞	73	⁞ ⁞ ⁞ ⁞ ⁞	98	⁞ ⁞ ⁞ ⁞ ⁞	123	⁞ ⁞ ⁞ ⁞ ⁞
24	⁞ ⁞ ⁞ ⁞ ⁞	49	⁞ ⁞ ⁞ ⁞ ⁞	74	⁞ ⁞ ⁞ ⁞ ⁞	99	⁞ ⁞ ⁞ ⁞ ⁞	124	⁞ ⁞ ⁞ ⁞ ⁞
25	⁞ ⁞ ⁞ ⁞ ⁞	50	⁞ ⁞ ⁞ ⁞ ⁞	75	⁞ ⁞ ⁞ ⁞ ⁞	100	⁞ ⁞ ⁞ ⁞ ⁞	125	⁞ ⁞ ⁞ ⁞ ⁞